Where the Mountains Meet the Prairies

Parks and Heritage Series

Where the Mountains Meet the Prairies
A History of Waterton Country
by Graham A. MacDonald

Guardians of the Wild
A History of the Warden Service of Canada's National Parks
by Robert J. Burns with Mike Schintz

The Road to the Rapids
Church and Society at St. Andrew's Parish, Red River, 1829-1929
by Robert J. Coutts

Where the Mountains Meet the Prairies

A History of Waterton Country

Graham A. MacDonald

UNIVERSITY OF
CALGARY
PRESS

University of Calgary Press. Parks and Heritage Series, no. 1

University of Calgary Press
2500 University Drive NW
Calgary, Alberta
Canada T2N 1N4

Canadian Cataloguing in Publication

MacDonald, Graham, 1944-
Where the mountains meet the prairies

    (Parks and heritage series, ISSN 1494-0426; 1)
    Includes bibliographical references and index.
    ISBN 1-55238-014-9

    1. Waterton Lakes National Park (Alta.)—History. 2. Waterton-Glacier
International Peace Park (Alta. and Mont.)—History. I. Title. II. Series.
FC3664.W38M32 2000   971.23'4   C00-910455-0
F1079.W3M32 2000

Canada We acknowledge the financial support of the Government of Canada through the Book Publishing Industry Development Program (BPIDP) for our publishing activities.

The Canada Council for the Arts
Le Conseil des Arts du Canada

The publisher would like to acknowledge the support of the Waterton Natural History Association and Parks Canada in publishing this book.

Printed and bound in Canada by Hignell Book Printing.
∞ This book is printed on acid-free paper.

Cover and page design by Kristina Schuring.
Cover imagery reproduced courtesy of the Glenbow Museum, Calgary. Painting, "Windblown Tree at Lee's Lake," Annora Brown, no date, watercolour and casein on paper.

We divided our holidays evenly between riding and boating. One day we would ride to a lake high in the mountains – to Upper Carthew, Lower Carthew, Bertha Alderson, or Crypt. Next day we would row to the end of Cameron Lake. Almost always we had these lakes to ourselves. These were days when that part of me that revelled in solitude, the nearness of growing things, and the earth itself, was fed to repletion.

– Annora Brown, *Sketches from Life* (1981)

Contents

Maps

Acknowledgements

In the preparation of this book, thanks are extended by the author to many colleagues in and outside of Parks Canada with whom I have had the pleasure of working over the last ten years. C. J.Taylor and Bill Yeo facilitated preparation of an historical report on Waterton in 1991, supported at Waterton by Janice Smith, Interpretive Officer, and Park Warden, Rob Watt. From that modest beginning, the current book has evolved. Thanks to Kurt Seel, former Chief Naturalist at Waterton, and to Duane Barrus, former Chief of Interpretation, for conversations. Gwyn Langemann gave advice on the archaeology of Waterton. Rob Storeshaw worked on the maps. Thanks to Mike Schintz, retired Warden, for his continuing interest in all phases of Parks Canada history and many conversations; to the always helpful staff of the Glenbow Alberta Archives, Library, and Museum for their assistance, particularly to Lindsay Moir and Jennifer Churchill. In Ottawa, Jeff Murray, Pat Burden, and Greg Eamon of the National Archives for their cheerful assistance. Thanks to Frank Goble of Cardston, Alberta for sharing the results of his own research into the history of the relief camps at Waterton during the 1930s, camps of which he had direct experience; to Victoria Williams at the Hastings Museum and Art Gallery, Hastings England and Mr. Jonathan Frewen, Brede Place, England, for assistance with respect to Clare Sheridan. Thanks to Marty Magne, Chief of Cultural Resource Management, Calgary, for his support of the project and to Joyce Sasse and the members of the Waterton Natural History Association for their involvement as joint-sponsors with the University of Calgary Press. Thanks finally to Walter Hildebrandt, John King, Kristina Schuring, and their editorial associates at the University of Calgary Press for their ethusiasm and support of the project. Max Foran and Ian Clarke undertook a much needed editorial mauling of the initial manuscript.

    The author and the University of Calgary Press acknowledge and thank the following individuals and institutions for the use of photographs and images in their possession: British Columbia Provincial Archives; Bruno Engler, Canmore, Alberta; Jonathan Frewen, Hastings, U.K.; Alexander Galt Museum and Archives, Lethbridge; Geological Survey of Canada; Glacier Park Archives, West Glacier, Montana; Glenbow Alberta Archives, Calgary; Frank Goble, Cardston, Alberta; Hastings Museum and Art Gallery, U.K.; Ernie Haug Family; Sophi Hicken, Lethbridge Alberta; J. C. Holroyd Family; Manitoba Department of Culture, Heritage and Tourism; Montana Historical Society; Montana State University Library; State of Montana Archives; National Archives of Canada; Parks Canada; Saskatchewan Archives Board; Whyte Museum of the Canadian Rockies. The individual works have been cited as to provenance in the text.

A Note on Spellings and Terms

In the interest of consistency and familiarity, many traditional names for Indian tribes have been retained in the text, although at the initial mention of these tribes, the assumed preferred contemporary spelling used by tribal organizations is noted in brackets. Spellings and usages for several of the tribes have been many and various over the years. For the Ktunaxa, for example, the traditional Canadian spelling – Kootenay – has been used, which conforms also to the place names in southern British Columbia (Kootenay Lake, etc.). The preferred American spelling for this tribe is usually Kutenai. For John George "Kootenai" Brown, who appears regularly in this study, and whose name is spelled variously in the literature, the spelling used by his biographer has been retained. Points of confusion may arise over the three groups making up the Blackfoot Nation: the Peigan, the Blood, and the Blackfoot. In Alberta, the North Peigans (Aputoksi-pikuni) occupy a reserve west of Fort MacLeod. The South Peigans (Amiskapi pikuni) are located in Montana. The southern group is also incorporated as the Blackfeet Tribe of Montana. In Canada, the Siksika living in the Gleichen area are known as the Blackfoot. The Blood Tribe (Kainaiwa) has land north of Cardston. The Athapascan-speaking, Tsuu T'ina (Sarcee), now living to the west of Calgary, are mentioned less frequently in this study, but were, as a group, part of the Blackfoot Confederacy. Where quotations are involved, the spelling of the source has naturally been retained. On the use of tribal terms, the author has been guided by Turner, *Plant Technology of First Peoples* (1998), and Dempsey, *Indian Tribes of Alberta* (1997) and *Indians of the Rocky Mountain Parks* (1998).

On the
Waterton Country

The Waterton Lakes National Park in Southern Alberta, along with its larger and contiguous counterpart in Montana, Glacier National park, has taken on a revived identity in recent years as a component of what George Bird Grinnell, many years ago, described as "The Crown of the Continent."[1] In the late years of the nineteenth century, the veteran naturalist and long-time editor of *Forest and Stream*, became a strong advocate of park development in the United States His descriptive phrase related to the way in which the Waterton-Glacier country defined part of a hub of land hosting the headwaters of rivers that flowed in three directions: on group to the Arctic, another to the Pacific and the third to the Gulf of Mexico. (Map 1) In the 1890s, the American and Canadian frontiers were closing and Grinnell was just one voice among several, on both sides of the border, raised in favour of the setting aside of wildland areas as public reserves.

The idea was not new with this generation of advocates. The ubiquitous American frontier artist, George Catlin, had promoted such an idea as early as 1832.[2] The Yellowstone National Park in Wyoming was legislated into existence in 1872 and Canadian officials set aside a small park at Banff in 1885, the first of a series of Canadian park reserves placed on the books over the next thirty years.[3] A forest reserve was first declared in 1895 around the Waterton Lakes on the Canadian side, but Grinnell's hopes for a national park in Montana did not become a reality until 1910. Since that date the development of the two park areas has been somewhat parallel, and the unity of purpose that they represent was recognized in 1932 when Waterton and Glacier were linked as an international peace park (Map 2).

1

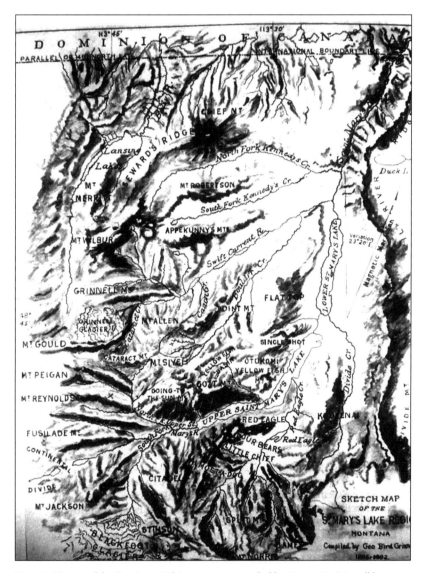

Map. 1. "Crown of the Continent." This map was compiled by George B. Grinnell between 1885 and 1892, during the course of his regular trips to the little-known region which now constitutes Glacier National Park. Chief Mountain is identified towards the top centre, with the Belly River and Waterton Lakes to the west. It first appeared in the *Century Magazine* in 1892.

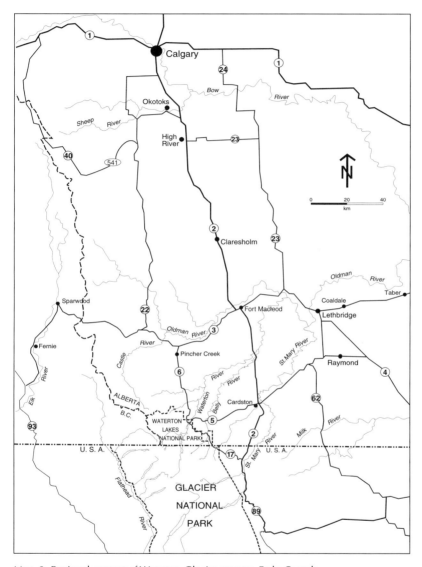

Map. 2. Regional context of Waterton-Glacier country. Parks Canada.

The following history attempts to provide a context for the Waterton country. As historical imagination recedes back in time, the 49th parallel becomes less relevant. For centuries, human actions in this mountainous terrain were guided by other kinds of boundary considerations: those imposed by season and climate, vegetation, wildlife movements, and by the acknowledged, or hotly defended, traditional zones of occupation exercised by generations of Native peoples. European-inspired imperial ambitions in the Waterton country were foreshadowed by the enterprise of fur-traders long anxious to tie together the eastern supply houses with opportunities in the unknown Columbia River Valley. Russia, France, Spain, England and America all vied for this new territory. The Spaniards, the French, and the Russians gradually withdrew as contenders, leaving a residual competition between Washington and London. Jay's Treaty of 1797 brought legal cartography to the fore in the West with implications for all residents. The 49th parallel took on significance as an international boundary in 1846. This boundary ran artificially across the Waterton-Glacier country, splitting, in political and economic terms, that which had never before been separated.

Much has been learned about the ancient setting and use of the lands in the "Crown of the Continent" since Grinnell coined the term. Post-1960 archaeology has been particularly productive in this regard, supplemented by the gathering of oral history and traditions from Native peoples. Contact with people still on the land has been instructive in restoring a knowledge of old place and group names, which preceded many of the current names bestowed by fur traders, explorers and others of more recent tenure.[4] The peoples speaking what has commonly been called the Blackfoot tongue were traditionally known as the *Nitsitapi*, and subdivided into three main groups: the Piikani (Peigan or Piegan), the Kainaiwa (the Blood) and the Siksika (Blackfoot). The Piikani are further recognized in two divisions: north and south, the former being resident in Alberta and the latter in Montana (the Blackfeet). The neighbours of the Blackfoot to the west included the Kootenay (Ktunaxa) who speak a language the associations of which are still not clearly understood, and also Salish-speaking peoples in the vicinity of Flathead Lake and to the northwest.

A striking landmark in the Crown of the Continent is Chief Mountain, a short distance south of the Canadian border. In the Blackfoot language Chief

Mountain is known as *Ninastakis*, and because of its dominance it has taken on origin-myth significance. "Nitsitapi traditions say that it was here that the three tribes were created in the long ago."[5]

The bestowing of place names on landmarks and territories in newly "discovered" lands has long been a favoured pastime of explorers and settlers of European background. Often the choices have reflected sentimental, patriotic, geological, or even ribald associations in the perception of the landscape. All of these motives may be noticed in the many place names in Waterton Lakes National Park. For example, the "Dardanelles and "Bosporus" channels separating Upper, Middle, and Lower Waterton Lakes, can logically be defended owing to the geographic similarity of the lake and river formations with their larger name-sakes in the Sea of Marmara near Istanbul in Turkey. But the granting of these names during World War I, at precisely the time the British Navy was attempting to wrest those strategic waters away from the Ottoman Empire, suggests more patriotic motives. Similarly, Vimy Ridge, the name attached to the prominent series of highland peaks in the south-central portion of the park, is derived from an important event in Canada's military history and honours local Alberta soldiers killed or returned from the front.[6]

As with the names of many national parks in Canada, the significance of the designation "Waterton" is not immediately apparent. The name "Waterton" has been associated with the park ever since Lieutenant Thomas Blakiston, then a member of John Palliser's British North American exploring expedition, emerged from the South Kootenay Pass in 1858 and so named the chain of lakes he found straddling the Canadian-United States border (Fig. 1).[7] A man of great curiosity and a naturalist of the first order, Blakiston had a penchant for bestowing place names in honour of those he considered to be his masters, or those to whom the scientific patronage of the day suggested an appropriate response.[8] He named a range in southeastern British Columbia in honour of Francis Galton (1822-1911), an outstanding scientist and a member of the Executive of the Royal Geographical Society, the body that approved and funded Palliser's expedition.[9] In naming the large glacial lake that today straddles the Canadian-American boundary, Blakiston gave recognition to one of England's most productive and unusual field naturalists, Charles Waterton

Fig. 1. Thomas Blakiston (1832-1891). The tallest peak in Waterton Lakes National Park is named after Lieutenant Blakiston, a member of the Royal Artillery. He was asked to join the Palliser Expedition of 1857-60 in the capacity of recorder of temperatures and magnetic inclinations. He was the only member of the expedition to travel across Waterton country and his map provides an important early reference. Saskatchewan Archives Board. R-A4983.

(1782-1865).[10] The place name has persisted, not only for the chain of lakes, but for the park that now surrounds them (Fig. 2).

Not all were in agreement with the use of this name. John George "Kootenai" Brown, whose later career is almost synonymous with the early administration of Waterton Park, favoured retaining the competing name "Kootenai," the better to reflect the local significance of the water bodies that constituted part of the home territory of the tribe of that name.[11] An Anglican clergyman at Cardston, Canon S. H. Middleton, long a promoter of the park, displayed a certain hostility toward the name "Waterton" as well:[12]

The name 'Waterton Lake Park' has no affinity with the glorious beauties of nature it represents. It is the most anemic title of all Canadian National Parks. 'Banff,' 'Jasper,' 'Yoho,' 'Kootenay,' 'Glacier' are all terms of euphony and description. There is something in the name. But the word 'Waterton' is weak, insipid, and lacks the appeal of romance. The mystic background of the Indian is ignored and tradition is not sustained.

Canon Middleton was not alone in holding such views about the abandonment of traditional place names in the Waterton Country and in the large American Glacier Park to the south. He credited the writer James W. Schultz, with much time spent in trying to resurrect the "obliterated Indian names of valleys and peaks throughout the Park areas."[13] Writer Mary Roberts Rinehart, an enthusiastic early visitor to Glacier in 1915, vented her spleen upon this trend

Fig. 2. Charles Waterton (1782-1865). The naming of the lakes at Waterton after this distinguished English naturalist is attributed to Thomas Blakiston. Waterton's main contributions to science are associated with his travels in South America, and while he did visit North America he never journeyed to the Rocky Mountains. A pioneer in conservation work, he transformed his family estate near Wakefield, England into a bird and wildlife sanctuary. National Portrait Gallery: London.

with some force. "What has happened? Look over the map of Glacier Park. The Indian names have been done away with." She took aim at the short-time visitor and explorer. "Any Government official, if he so desires, any white man seeking perpetuation on the map of his country, may fasten his name to a mountain, and go down in the school geographies." She pointed out some of the survivals. "What names in the world are more beautiful than Going-to-the-Sun and Rising Wolf?" She could thankfully still find "Almost-a-Dog Mountain, Two Medicine Lake," and "Red Eagle."[14] If having one's name added to the map was not quite as easily done as Rinehart contended, there was still something to the accusation of willful place-name elimination on both sides of the border.[15]

Fig. 3. George M. Dawson (1849-1901). Son of the noted Principal of McGill University, Sir J. W. Dawson, he left an imprint on Canadian place names through his work undertaken for the American-Canadian Boundary Survey and for the Geological Survey of Canada. From his maps, reports and photographs prepared during the 1870s and 1880s, come some of the earliest landscape impressions of Waterton country. Courtesy of the Geological Survey of Canada (photo number GSC KGS2375).

In the context of the times, place names were nevertheless often bestowed with a view to recognizing a genuine achievement. This might be said of scenic Lake McDonald in Glacier National Park. Here is a good case of a lake named not only for a local tradition connected to the Great Northern Railway survey of 1878, but also for a son of the fur trade. Of Native and European ancestry, Duncan McDonald had gone over to the cause of the Nez Perce Indians in their time of troubles. The aged Duncan McDonald was an honoured guest at the ceremonies opening Glacier's Going-to-the-Sun Road in 1932, and his biography seems to embrace and touch all aspects of regional history (Fig. 4).[16]

When Thomas Blakiston named the lakes after Charles Waterton, he was not only honouring an important fellow-ornithologist, but also a fellow-explorer. In the biographical details of that "strange career" are to be found the very stuff of scientific courage and romance.[17] Born in 1782 and into the relatively well-to-do circumstances of the English rural gentry, Charles Waterton was brought up in the bucolic surroundings of Walton Hall, Yorkshire, an ancestral home that he eventually turned into a bird sanctuary, perhaps the first on record.[18] The "squire" was possessed of an exaggerated sense of humour, which he occasionally mixed with his science. He was labelled as the "eccentric Waterton" – an "epithet" that he found "anything but congenial to my feelings" – and posterity has not always been as kind to him as might be warranted.[19] Typical of his love for an athletic prank was his climb to the top of St. Peter's in Rome, where he left

Fig. 4. Duncan McDonald (1849 - c.1939) A son of Scottish-born fur trader Angus McDonald, he followed in his father's footsteps and continued to run the Hudson's Bay Company's Fort Connah (Flathead Post) until 1871, when it was closed. He is shown here with his wife Louisa. McDonald fought with his Nez Perce kinsmen against the U.S. Army during the troubles of 1877. Lake McDonald in Glacier National Park was named in his honour by the people of Apgar. Glenbow Archives, Calgary. NA 1461-35.

his gloves on the lightening conductor as proof of his visit. His fervent Roman Catholicism probably contributed towards keeping him out of respectable English scientific circles. He was, to be sure, something of an outsider and a self-made naturalist, recalled now largely because of his contributions to ornithological studies and to general knowledge about the natural history of South America. The great Alexander von Humboldt had started to publish material on South America in English by 1814, but Waterton, with the publication of his *Wanderings* in 1825, was not that far behind. His biographer states that he was "certainly the pioneer among travelling English naturalists, preceding Darwin, Wallace, Huxley, Bates, Belt, and how many others."[20] In recent years, Calgary physician J. R. Maltby has outlined the important contributions made by Waterton to the practice of anesthesia through his studies of "curare," the resinous and bitter substance derived from certain South American plants and used by Native tribesmen on poisonous arrows (Fig.5).[21]

Complaints concerning the appropriateness of the name "Waterton" would probably not have gained the approval of one of the closest students of the western

Canadian landscape, George M. Dawson. During his geological surveys of the Rocky Mountains, carried out in the early 1880s, he made special reference to what he took to be a break with, rather than a denial of, tradition, in the names recently being employed in the Waterton area:[22]

> *Waterton Lake (Or Chief Mountain Lake, sometimes erroneously called Kootanie Lake) is nine and a half miles in total length.... The Waterton River has appeared under this on the map for about twenty-five years, but of late some confusion has arisen owing to the circumstance that settlers recently entering the country have re-named it the Kootanie, and that this name has never appeared on maps. There is nothing to be said in favour of this change, and the fact that another and much larger river on the west side of the range has long been known by the latter name, renders its introduction here particularly inconvenient and misleading.*

In the passage above, Dawson raises another name that was often attached to the Waterton Lakes – that of Chief Mountain. It appears as an alternative name on the official map included with the Palliser Expedition *Report* of 1860, and on a number of other maps. The previously mentioned late nineteenth century trader and writer, J. W. Schultz, then married to Natahki, a Blackfoot woman, recalled some of the names familiar in his time:[23]

> *Since arriving in the country, I had heard much about two large beautiful lakes, called by the Whites Chief Mountain Lakes; by the Blackfoot tribes, Puhktomuksi Kimiks, "Lakes Inside." We did not know then that in 1846, Father Lacombe, S.J., assisted by his faithful guide Hugh Monroe, had set up a cross at the foot of the lower one of the lakes with prayer and christened them St. Mary's lakes.*

The references here are to the Upper and Lower St. Mary's Lakes in Glacier National Park, south-east of Chief Mountain. Schultz left several contradictory accounts of this christening event and it is unlikely that Father Albert Lacombe was involved in this ceremony. It is more likely that the Belgian priest of the Oregon

Country, Pierre De Smet, had some connection, although exactly what is not clear.[24]

There remained some confusion over the proper identification of Chief Mountain Lake well into the 1870s. In 1854, surveyor James Doty was attempting to establish the limits of United States territory on the eastern slope of the Rockies, and he identified a Chief Mountain Lake well within American territory.[25] After the first Riel disturbance in Red River in 1870, William Francis Butler was sent west to assess the small pox situation. On the map that accompanied his book, *The Great Lone Land*, Waterton Lake is still clearly identified as Chief Mountain Lake.

The preferred name for the Waterton Lakes also remained somewhat ambiguous in the decades between 1880 and 1910. Two years after Dawson's 1886 report, William Pearce, the federal Superintendent of Mines, suggested that the Waterton Lakes area would be worthy of consideration, among others, as a park reserve for the public. Pearce used the name "Waterton" in his proposal.[26] F. W. Godsal and J. G. Brown in their early advocacy for park establishment, were just as likely to use the name "Kootenai" as "Waterton." Brown, for reasons which are perhaps obvious, was a strong proponent of retaining the name "Kootenai," being of the opinion that "modern officialism" was misguided having "ignored the wisdom of the ancients" by renaming the park "Waterton."[27] Long-time park employee and local historian, E. K. Goble, born on the Waterton River in the Glenwood area, recalled the use of the name "Kootenay Lakes" during his youth around 1910 and was of the opinion that Brown was the main influence behind the local use of the place name "Kootenai."[28] The idea that the name "Waterton" was somehow inappropriate for the park had not completely disappeared even in the 1950s.[29]

The history of the Waterton Lakes area is, at one level, the history of a gradual refinement of public park management philosophies towards an ethic favourable to the conservation of species, and there is something abidingly appropriate about the early choice of the name "Waterton" to honour this special landscape. Charles Waterton had stumbled upon certain principles well ahead of his time. With respect to his experiment in converting the family estate, Walton Hall, into a bird sanctuary, he explained that the "chief way to encourage birds is to forbid the use of firearms in the place of their resort. I have done so here, and to this precaution I chiefly owe my unparalleled success" (Fig. 5).[30] Charles Waterton did not fail to understand the need to alter attitudes towards wildlife in England among those

Fig. 5. Walton Hall. The traditional home of the Watertons in Yorkshire, England. When the estate fell to Charles Waterton, he set about converting the grounds into what some consider to be the first nature conservation area in England. Drawing by Captain Edward Jones, 1831.

ancient forerunners of the North American park warden service, the traditional English gamekeeper. His view of the matter was, once again, advanced. His head gamekeeper "did not take kindly to the eccentric order that not even birds of prey should be killed." He was only persuaded otherwise when the Squire caught him in the act of shooting at some Tawny owls: "I threatened to strangle him if ever, after this, he molested either the old birds or their young ones."[31] It was only in the mid-1920s that staff of Canada's National Parks Branch started to seriously question past policies with respect to predator control in the lands under their administration, thus finally falling in step with Charles Waterton.

Whatever the merits may have been of naming the park after Waterton, the recognition of place names more reflective of Native cultural history, local traditions, and significant global achievements is also evident throughout the park. The history of a park can never be a history merely of the park. Boundaries are often at their most artificial when imposed on a map for park establishment purposes. The extensive Glacier National Park adjoining the Waterton country cannot be ignored, nor the influences of land use and practices on adjacent lands. The present study does not treat of Glacier in any comprehensive way, but there are thematic areas of contact that have been pointed out where the story seems to warrant. The main themes in this book deal with the transformation of lands cut

12

out from the old aboriginal "commons" and into a system of formal land tenure; of changes in traditional ways of life and wildlife regimes; of social change brought on by the eclipse of the bison at about the same time in both countries, between 1872 and 1885; of how special land reserves that first served in a "multiple-use" natural resource context, then gradually freed themselves from that philosophy, and achieved identities as purer forms of recreational landscape; of how the coherence of the Waterton-Glacier country was given recognition in 1932 as an International Peace Park; of how early twentieth century notions of the "balance of nature" were gradually modified under the rising insights of the new science of ecology; of how mounting demand for access to parks, not by industry this time, but by visitors, has brought about more intense scientific scrutiny of such lands; of how insights have developed that parks are not isolated pockets of undisturbed "nature" but human constructs in which humankind has long been an aspect of that same "nature"; and finally of how the biosphere-reserve concept has been instituted in Waterton country, with a view to tempering such insights by means of extending stewardship ideas into the surrounding communities.

Chapter One

Beginnings

During the first half of the twentieth century, North American archaeologists tended to downplay the general prospects for discovering ancient site locations in areas of dramatic relief. Nevertheless, with much of the Rocky Mountains of Canada defined as national and provincial park or forest lands, opportunities to investigate high country for prehistoric remains became more frequent after World War II when universities, museums, and park agencies started to encourage archaeological surveys on these lands. During the early 1960s, the possibilities at Waterton were sensed by one student who had the great advantage of having been raised in the local area. In 1968, an eminent professor of archaeology was led to comment that Brian Reeves "is well on his way to giving the lie to the old notion that the mountainous regions (even pretty ones) are virtually devoid of prehistoric cultural remains."[1] The reference was to the body of knowledge that Brian Reeves and his associates had been developing since 1964 based on surveys undertaken in the park. In the years since that statement was made, survey work has continued and has been extended into the greater Glacier region to the south. Today, it is fair to say that a much more comprehensive view has been attained of the prehistoric setting of this portion of the Rockies.[2] Commenting on the import of these studies, Reeves observed that a "considerable number and variety of sites exist that relate to past Native peoples' seasonal presence in, and utilization of, the lower valley and Alpine areas for hunting, camping, stone tool quarrying, and religious purposes" (Plate 2 and Fig. 6).[3]

Fig. 6a. Brian Reeves of the University of Calgary, and his crews, commenced archaeological surveys of Waterton country in the mid-1960s. With family roots in the townsite, Reeves was well acquainted with the landscape of the area and the results of his work helped redirect much of the Alberta archaeological agenda towards mountain landscapes.

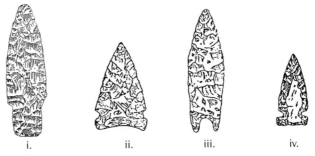

i.   ii.   iii.   iv.

Fig. 6b. Projectile Points.
i. A stemmed spear point from about 8500 to 8000 years BP was found on the beach of Lake Linnet. Stemmed and fluted spear points are well known from surface finds in Southern Alberta, but few are from excavated sites, and very few from within Waterton Lakes National Park itself.

ii. Bitterroot atlatl points from the Mummy Cave Complex (7750 – 5000 years BP) are common in the Southern Alberta foothills and plains. This complex marks the rapid replacement of spears by atlatl technology, but otherwise there is continuity in the cultural record between the bison hunting cultures of the Bitterroot and the preceding stemmed point period.

iii. McKean Complex atlatl points belong to an intrusive culture, with its origins in the great Basin. In the foothills (4500 – 3500 years BP), McKean sites are marked by the presence of stone boiling and roasting pits, and large amounts of fire-broken rock in the living floors, which suggests a change in bison processing techniques.

iv. Plains Side-notched arrow points belong to the Old Women's phase of the Late Prehistoric period (1400 – 200 years BP). This phase is generally thought to be the archaeological representative of the modern Blackfoot people. Parks Canada.

The Waterton-Glacier country, with its moderate, if periodically severe, climate, has been home to humans for at least 10,000 years. According to Reeves, the regular interplay of cold arctic air in winter with warm chinook winds coming through the mountain passes from the Pacific, provides a favourable, if somewhat erratic, climate in which many groups of Native peoples have been able to survive over the centuries. The high amounts of precipitation and strong winds have, on the other hand, set "definite limits on site location" for settlement purposes, with the result that "sheltered locales" have been "a requisite" owing to high winds and snow buildups in certain areas of the valleys.[4]

For the earliest known period in Waterton, the evidence is very scant, but the South Kootenay Pass, running east to west through Waterton Park, the so-called "Buffalo Trail," has undoubtedly been used from very early times for purposes of travel and trade. Later sites tend to reflect cultural values associated with peoples who had accommodated themselves to various environments: that is, peoples living in the great plateau of British Columbia and Washington, other groups with a greater affinity for living in both the mountains and on the plains, and finally those who were more firmly adapted to prairie conditions.[5]

The park theme statement – "Where the Mountains Meet the Prairies" – imparts a good deal of meaning for both the contemporary and ancient worlds of Waterton. The associated vegetation pattern was well established shortly after the retreat of the last glacial sheets about 10,000 years ago, facilitating penetration of the mountains. Projectile points reflecting a very early presence of hunters in Waterton have been recovered. Recently, a well-preserved ancient hearth of Clovis and other early hunters has been located near the St. Mary's Reservoir, east of Waterton, indicating rich use of a range of very ancient fauna types.[6] The opportunities in Waterton country were sufficient to foster an early form of "multiple-use." Some ancient sites in the park are located along Blakiston Valley and indicate a long history of bison slaughter and butchering. Other early artifacts have been found at sites around Lake Linnet and along Red Rock Canyon. Excavations at the "Narrows Site" between Upper and Middle Waterton Lakes suggest fishing camps were established there by 8,000 B.P. (Before the Present). The Narrows was an ideal spot "to intercept the spawning runs of Lake Trout and Whitefish."[7] Waterton Park's reputation as an excellent fishery is centuries old (Plate 3).

The archaeological record also suggests great continuity in what has been called the "seasonal round" of activities by which early peoples shifted their camps several times a year in order to make the best use of the resources available to them. Those who used the resources of both prairie and upland have been identified by some archaeologists as members of the "Plains/Mountain Complex." The practitioners of this way of life succeeded in fusing certain earlier traditions of the interior plateau and the plains into a viable mountain-based way of life.[8] According to this model, it is argued that, over time, resident groups did not necessarily become over-specialized, but instead adjusted to the opportunities of the moment. Thus, the large wintering site identified near the park entrance may have been one keyed to the movement of bison herds. The herds often moved into the Blakiston Valley in spring, followed by a summer shift to the alpine grasslands, a fall movement back to the lower pastures, and finally a move in winter to the relative shelter of the Waterton Lakes valley. Seasonal camps established for pursuit of the bison would not preclude others members of the band from prosecuting seasonal fisheries at the Narrows or from pursuing various gathering activities. Roasting pits in the Narrows area suggest that this site may have been an excellent one for intercepting big game as well as fishing. These pits may also have been used for cooking a much more diverse menu, for they are similar to the pits used to cook *camas* on the western slopes of the mountains.[9] Other plants widely used by early Native peoples include the prairie turnip, chokecherry, buffaloberry, and saskatoonberry.[10]

Modification of this "seasonal round" proceeded for several thousands of years and was probably affected by climatic changes, which brought on a prolonged period of warmer and drier conditions on the prairies. While opinions vary, this drought or *altithermal* period lasted roughly from about 7,500 B.P. to around 4,500 B.P. There has been much lively debate concerning the extent of this period and its significance for ancient Native populations and ways of life. Current thinking does not favour a view of uniform effects.[11] There is evidence to suggest that localized depopulation of the plains took place, and that the modern bison (*bison bison*) may have become dominant over the larger and now extinct form, *bison occidentalis* (Fig. 7).[12] This shift would foster increased Native use of bison through improvement in the relative ease of their capture. According to Anthony Buchner, there was a long-term trend throughout the Holocene period (i.e., that period identified with post-glacial geological history) towards size reduction in the bison population. The desiccation of the open prairie lands severely reduced the habitat of *bison occidentalis*. This, accompanied by the effects of human hunting, gradually led to the extinction of that great animal and a subsequent flourishing of smaller, more energy-efficient models, the ancestors of the modern bison. These smaller animals reproduced in greater numbers and in the period of the *altithermal* tended to crowd towards the foothills of the Rocky Mountains where more reliable

Fig. 7. Artist Larry Jamieson's conception of pre-historic bison *(bison bison occidentalis)* being hunted by means of an atlatl. Atlatl weight components have been found in the archaeological record at Waterton. Historic Resources Branch. Manitoba Department of Culture, Heritage and Tourism.

water and grazing areas were to be found. Under these conditions, few locations were more ideal than the Waterton area "where the mountains meet the prairies" in a very direct way.[13] The most interesting response to this general shift in animal ecology was the rise of the buffalo jump sometime in the last stages of the *altithermal* period of which the "Head-Smashed-In" site, west of Fort Macleod, is an outstanding and well-documented example.[14]

With the return of cooler condition and increased rainfall, sometime after 4,500 B.P., long-term trends were set in motion that consolidated various ways of life on the prairies, on the great plateau, and along the great river valleys that flow westward from the mountains towards the Pacific Ocean. It may be that the dry conditions of the *altithermal* helped to formulate these various Native traditions, as peoples accustomed to seeking their living on the prairies and in the dry desert areas of the southwest sought more hospitable environments by means of migration.[15] Archaeologists continue to refine knowledge about a number of specific cultures throughout the greater northwest, all adapted to specific local environments, the long-term outcome, perhaps, of previous migrations away from locales that had become too homogeneous in terms of economic opportunity.[16]

For centuries, Waterton Native traditions drew more or less continually upon the available resources of both mountain and prairie.[17] If there was one occasion when the relative merits of prairie resources may have prevailed, it would have been in the aftermath of the rise of what archaeologists call the "Avonlea" tradition, sometime after 200 A.D. This tradition was marked (perhaps for the first time) by the use of the bow and arrow.[18] The relative decline of the use of the Narrow's fishery at Waterton in Avonlea times may indicate a developing preference for the pursuit of the bison and greater seasonal use of the nearby prairie.[19]

The long period leading up to the time of European contact was marked by widespread exploitation of the bison by many groups on the plains. The precise ways in which these successions of people are connected is not well understood. If the bow and arrow was the hallmark of the Avonlea peoples, its modification and gradual diffusion was a central feature of the centuries between 200 A.D. and 1700 A.D. One noticeable social trend during these many centuries was the adaptation of several cultural groups to a way of life largely supported by the prairie environment. Other groups west of the great divide pursued a more diverse economy based on the fish resources of the interior plateau river valleys and flora and fauna of the mountain ranges. Establishing the ethnic makeup of these many groups, and how they relate to historic Native peoples, is a complex undertaking. Interpretations of this process draw upon several kinds of evidence taken from archaeology, the legacy of Native oral tradition, the distribution of Native language speakers, and the late written record left by Europeans.[20]

When European fur traders made an actual appearance in the western half of the continent, their influence on Native groups had already long been felt through their acquisition of the horse, trade goods and fire-arms, and by the effects of disease. The resulting increase in group mobility, coupled with periodic population decline as a result of unfamiliar virulent diseases, scrambled the pattern of traditional Native land occupations, rendering later historical reconstruction highly tentative.[21] The nature of the longevity of the Blackfoot, and other groups on the prairies, is subject to much speculation.[22]

As the use of the horse spread throughout the plains after 1500 A.D., certain centres, first in the southwest, and later further north, took on importance as trade mart areas. During the early eighteenth century, the Mandan country, in contemporary North Dakota, became just such a focus. In the words of Ewers: "at the horticultural villages of the Upper Missouri the expanding frontier of the horse met the expanding frontier of the gun."[23] This probably happened intermittently in the middle decades of the eighteenth century, for when La Vérendrye journeyed to the Mandan country and beyond in 1748, the horse and the gun appear to have been absent among the sedentary farming tribes of the upper Missouri country. The gun frontier expanding from the northeast and the horse frontier from the southwest gradually came together in those same trading villages on the upper Missouri, and, in time, this meeting had an energizing effect on the Blackfoot tribes. They were introduced to guns by their trading partners, the Cree and Assiniboine, well before they had horses.[24] They may have finally obtained horses from two sources: the Assiniboine of the plains and the Kootenay of the southern Rockies.[25] Once possessed of guns and horses, the Blackfoot rapidly mastered the use of both for the bison hunt. Their increased mobility allowed them to greatly expand their geographic zone of influence and to keep unwanted people, European or Native, out of the western prairie zone. This advance in hunting methods undoubtedly rendered obsolete the older technique of running bison over jumps such as those found at Waterton and at "Head-Smashed-In."

Horse-adapted plains groups, such as the Blackfoot, developed their own trade priorities as European influences increased. In the beaver-scarce zone of the dry belt of southern Alberta, Blackfoot hostility may have derived partially from tribal anxiety to retain control of the bison lands and to preserve the conditions of long-established Native trading patterns.[26] After 1730, cooperative relationships developed between the Blackfoot peoples, the Assiniboine and the Cree, in the interests of facilitating the fur trade to Hudson Bay and Montreal. By 1800, when traders such as Peter Fidler and David Thompson were seeking ways across the mountains, the Blackfoot had become a formidable force in the lands of present-day southern Alberta, representing a barrier to any outsiders seeking entry to the Waterton country.[27]

Two groups that the Blackfoot sought to isolate from commercial contact with European traders were the Kootenay and Salish-speaking Indians residing on the western slopes of the mountains. The Kootenay in particular had, for many years, made periodic use of the eastern slopes of the Rockies and the adjacent prairie, but their ultimate place of origin remains a mystery.[28] In 1912, James Teit gathered information about the Kootenay that indicated that earlier they may have been centred on the Sun River in the headwaters region of the Missouri River.[29] Yet only the most fleeting glimpses of the Kootenay and the Blackfoot can be gained for the years before 1800. It is clear that both groups continued to make regular use of the prairie bison, that the Waterton area served as an important border zone between the two groups, and that each made periodic resort to and through these mountains.[30] In 1858, James Hector described the way in which new trade relationships with the Europeans eventually led to the development of the Kootenay Plains, on the eastern slopes, as a traditional mart area. It was here that the Kootenay ventured to deal first with middlemen traders sent by the fur traders of the Saskatchewan River country, and, after 1799, with representatives from Rocky Mountain House.[31]

Following the successful American exploration of the upper Missouri River and the Pacific Northwest in 1804-6 by Lewis and Clark, the pattern of Native-European trade relations become more complicated. America and British fur traders steadily encroached upon the southern plains from the north and south in the early nineteenth century. Many old Native alliances became strained, as between the Cree and the Blackfoot. After 1806, the tribes of the so-called "Blackfoot Confederacy" became more unified in an effort to set the rules of trade within their territories.[32] The conditions of the fur trade changed radically after 1821, both in terms of organization and in terms of resource interests. The rise of demand for bison hides added weight to the pressure on plains tribes' subsistence resources. While the American trade absorbed most of the bison hides between 1821 and 1870, the Hudson's Bay Company did not neglect this resource.[33] As the nineteenth century unfolded, bison numbers started to decline, a trend recognized by many after 1850. As the bison contracted, their numbers, in relative terms, became ever more concentrated on the high plains. In 1846, the Belgian-American priest of the Oregon country, Father Pierre de Smet, noted that "the different Indian tribes find themselves closer and closer together," and he correctly forecast that the territory of the Blackfoot would represent "the last retreat of the

Buffalo."[34] These pressures on the availability of what many Native peoples called "the staff of life" ushered in the period of what J. S. Milloy has described as the "buffalo wars" after 1850, when a time of troubles between Cree and Blackfoot peoples became quite acute. This culminated in a great pitched battle in the autumn of 1870 along the Belly River.[35] The old "buffalo commons" had all but disappeared and new forms of land use economy would soon take form under the auspices of the new Dominion of Canada.

Chapter Two

Intrusion of the European

A systematic review of mid- to late-eighteenth-century cartography of the western half of North America will show a consistent gap in the region around Waterton-Glacier Park. This area remained obscure on European charts for a number of reasons, not least of which was the strong barrier to entry posed by the Blackfoot Confederacy in its territory east of the Rocky Mountains. Fur traders from Quebec and England had, since the 1730s, been establishing fur posts inland, west from Lake Superior and southwest from Hudson Bay. The natural lines of transit were along the great prairie river systems, which had their sources in the Rocky Mountains. Through this process, a continuous motion seems to have been induced amongst the western prairie tribes. As late as the 1780s, some tribes, particularly in the mountain and plateau areas, had still never encountered a European trader, although most were aware of the advantages of European trade goods.[1] This motion was partly a response to a newly found desire for trade goods and partly to a related wish by the tribes to define for themselves a "middleman" position with respect to other Native groups. It was also a response to the spread of European diseases. The expansion out onto prairies by the Cree has been viewed as one major expression of this ferment.[2] The argument has been advanced that many of the Native groups who first gained access to European goods often became anxious to prevent rival or traditional enemy tribes from obtaining these same items directly. Thus, the Cree expansion onto the plains represented a kind of vanguard of the Europeans, undertaken to safeguard their own favoured position in the trade ring. The European traders from the north and east gave the Cree consistent access to powerful trade goods such as fire arms.[3]

Prior to 1800 the mountain barrier was being broached by Euorpean traders. In 1792, with the assistance of the Blackfoot cartographer, Ako-Mo-ki, Peter Fidler of the Hudson's Bay Company gained an initial impression of the Waterton-Glacier country.[4] In 1795, Fort Augustus was founded by the Nor'westers near present-day Edmonton, and Edmonton House shortly thereafter by the Hudson's Bay Company. The traders were already aware that the large territory to the south controlled by the Blackfoot confederacy would not be penetrated easily for trade purposes. At the same time, the trans-mountain Kootenay Indians (Ktunaxa) let them know that good furs could be found on the western slope of the great divide and in the great valleys of the Columbia watershed. The Nor'westers, from a new base at Rocky Mountain House, soon sought ways around the Blackfoot barrier into this virgin fur trading territory (Map 3).

David Thompson was prominent in finding satisfactory routes through the mountains north of Blackfoot territory. In 1800, he sent two French-Canadian traders named La Gasse and Le Blanc to winter with the Kootenay who had come to trade at Rocky Mountain House. The two men were sent down the eastern slope of the Rockies where they crossed the Waterton country en route to visit this western tribe in their home territory around the Tobacco Plains.[5] The Blackfoot were hostile to the presence of these Montreal traders moving among their traditional enemies. The two French Canadians were killed in 1805 and the Nor'westers retreated from the area. Thompson then decided to pursue other strategies focused on a more northerly route through the mountains via first the Howse and then the Athabasca Pass.[6] The fur traders for many years hence travelled north around Blackfoot country and then worked the western side of the continental divide from the valleys of the Snake, Columbia, and Kootenay Rivers. This continued to be the pattern well after the 1821 amalgamation of the Nor'westers with the Hudson's Bay Company.

Exploiting the western flank of the Rocky Mountains was hard and frustrating work, as Peter Skene Ogden's journals reveal.[7] For instance, the workforce was drawn from all quarters, and it lacked some of the discipline that characterized trading parties east of the Great Divide where a more traditional pool of labour could be tapped. In addition, the Blackfoot remained a persistent source of concern,

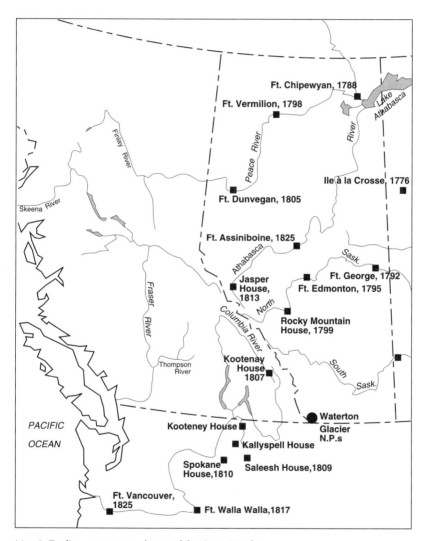

Map 3. Trading posts east and west of the Great Divide.

27

Fig. 8. Peter Skene Ogden (1790-1854). Born in Quebec, Ogden worked for the North West Company. He joined the Hudson's Bay Company in 1824 and became a Chief Trader and worked many regions on the Pacific Slope, including the Snake River, Oregon country, and New Caledonia. He followed British-American boundary issues carefully and is considered to be the author of *Traits of American Indian Life and Character* (1853). National Archives of Canada. C-27147.

even on the western slopes. In 1824, Alexander Ross was assigned to begin a trade initiative south into the Snake Country, replacing Finan McDonald, "that tough old Northwester," who had known the Snakes since he had come there with David Thompson in 1807. McDonald had experienced "Saviral Battils" with the Peigans: he had lost Michel Bourden, the leader of his trappers, along with five of his men; he had suffered badly by having his horses stolen; and he had killed about seventy Indians. His parting comment has become famous: "when that Cuntre will see me agane the Beaver will have Gould Skin."[8]

Ogden (Fig. 8) took over the Snake Country from Ross in 1825 and for several years he ranged widely from Spokane and Flathead Houses, south along the great divide. It is certain that the mountains within present-day Glacier and Waterton were worked for beaver, but most likely this was done by Native people, rather than by the European traders. In Olga Johnson's words: "The Kootenays and Flatheads were learning rapidly enough the tricks of trapping."[9] Non-Native trappers in the area were few in those years. Hugh Monroe, a Montreal-born trader who developed a special relationship with the Blackfoot after 1816, was one of the earliest to reside in the Glacier-Waterton area (Fig. 9).[10]

Flathead Post was the closest trading station to the Waterton-Glacier country, but the severity of winter in the mountains suggested to George Simpson in 1824 that there was little to be gained from staffing Flathead House after November, where "only idleness could occur." He directed that winter trapping would take place only further south in the Snake country.[11] The general strategy pursued on the west side of the great divide was to gain access to the Kootenay and Salish trade at lowland areas along the rivers and lakes. Fur taken by the Indians could then work its way into the hands of the Columbia traders or, by means of a transmountain trade, into the hands of the Blackfoot, who for some time had acted as middlemen traders as well as trappers.

During the post-1814 period of international fur trade competition on the prairies and in the Columbia district, the Waterton-Glacier region remained, if not totally unused, then uncontested by the various interests.[12] The ancient "seasonal round" of activities carried on by Native peoples in Waterton was easily adjustable to the requirements of the greater fur trade.

Fig. 9. Hugh Monroe (c. 1798-1892). Also known among his Blackfoot compatriots as "Rising Wolf" (Mah-kwo-i-pwo-ahts). Born of well-to-do parents at Three Rivers, Quebec, he joined the Hudson's Bay Company as a young man and became one of the first fur traders to work the Waterton-Glacier country. He married Ap'-ah-ki or Sinopah (Kit Fox Woman) of the Pikunis (Blackfoot), and the couple was well known in the St. Mary's Lakes area of Glacier National Park. Montana Historical Society.

Salish, Kootenay, and Blackfoot alike learned how to participate in the venture, making use of the European traps, working the land for beaver when it suited them, and adding to their material existence with other trade goods:[13]

> *The beaver, weasel, muskrat, all of these small residents of their land, they had been accustomed to watch for fun as often as they killed them for meat and fur; and their legendary personifications were as familiar as their present selves. Now when a small animal was sighted, it was apt to look to the native woodsmen less like a fellow creature, and more like a price; in the gleam of eye and fur could be seen the gleam of a musket barrel or a brass kettle or a hank of beads; on the forest air the trapper*

29

could almost sniff the potent fragrance of the White man's tobacco, waiting in ropes to be clipped off for his pipe. Even bears, who already seemed a little less awesome, because of their vulnerability to bullets, the Indians began to regard not so much as reverenced fellow beings, but more as wearers of hides for which the traders might give good exchange.

The question may then be asked: at what price to the ancient ways of life with their well-known seasonal rhythms? Olga Johnson has hinted at an answer.[14]

Bucking the elements was nothing new to the native mountaineers. But the traders seemed to expect that a man should set his traps and walk his line on schedule, even when he was over-hungry, or ill-fed. Suppose he and his companions were not in the mood for hiking that day; suppose they were in the mood for horse-racing or gambling. Suppose there was company in camp, a new wife in the lodge, or a little son ill unto death. How could they bring the furs to the post at a specific time if these intruders set dates that coincided with a traditional tribal festival, or a regular seasonal buffalo hunt? To rush and worry, always to be frustrating the natural flow of a man's impulses, to break the nerve of tradition leading back down through the years through all the ancestors, wounded the spirit or soul "that substance with which a man is lined." What ailed the spirits of these White fur men that they insisted on over-working, quarrelling, cheating, suffering such hardships and losing their lives in the mountains, to possess animal skins which, apparently, neither they nor their people needed to keep them warm.

Yet by the 1830s, European demand for the beaver was in decline in the face of the rising popularity of silk and other fabrics of choice.[15] The fur trade on the Columbia in the late 1830s could still attract new recruits from the old labour supply centres of Scotland, such as Angus McDonald, a kin of that Finan McDonald who had so little good to say about the Snake Country. The subsequent history of the family of Angus McDonald and his wife, Catherine (of Nez Perce and Mohawk background), reveals that west of the great divide, as on the prairies, the fur trade quickly evolved social and economic forms based on the advantages of European and Native fusion.[16] On the eastern slope of the Rockies, the Blackfoot especially were able to adapt their bison-oriented way of life to the new American trade on the Missouri, where after 1832 the demand for the bison hide steadily replaced the demand for beaver.[17] The year 1832 was momentous in terms of Blackfoot-American trade relations. Bull Back Fat, Chief of the Buffalo Followers Band of the Bloods, moved to resolve the long hostility that had prevailed since the violence attending the Lewis and Clark expedition. He concluded a peace with the Americans at Fort Union. Having severely limited European settlement in their hunting grounds, the Blackfoot now moved more easily in a changing, market-oriented, fur-trade world. In 1840, with some of the pomp and ceremony attending a European medieval political marriage, Alexander Culburtson, the veteran American Fur Company trader, married Natawista, daughter of Two Suns, leader of the Fish Eater Band of the Bloods, thus guaranteeing the economic ascendency of this band over the Buffalo Followers.[18]

The 1840s heralded great changes for many Native groups west of the great divide and on the northern edge of Blackfoot territory. Missionary activity increased rapidly, both in British and American territory. The most prominent were the Rocky Mountain missions of present-day Oregon, Washington, Idaho, and Montana initiated in 1841 by the Belgian Jesuit Pierre De Smet and his associates.[19] He ranged widely, visiting Rocky Mountain House in 1845 in the company of two Kootenay Indians, with a view to arranging a general peace treaty between the Blackfoot and the tribes of the western plateau. De Smet travelled by a prudent route, leaving Pend d'Oreille Lake, moving north to the site of Bonner's Ferry, up the Kootenay River through the Tobacco Plains, and then to Lake Windermere. From there, the party moved across the mountains and on to Rocky Mountain House and Fort Edmonton.[20] A map, published in 1846, survives from that trip showing many of the places he visited and also the extent to which the country around Waterton was still "terra incognita." A small cluster of lakes north of Flathead Lake is indicated on De Smet's line of the 49th parallel, suggesting an image of the Waterton Lakes. De Smet's peace initiative was not a success, but the new Rocky Mountain Missions to the Kootenay and Salish tribes on the western slope and in the plateau continued to prosper in the absence of protestant competitors.

Aside from providing us a record of early church activities, the frontier missionaries often left accounts of the local way of life and economy. For instance, De Smet observed the role played by fishing in the economy of the Kootenay during the 1840s:[21]

> *I arrived among the Arcs-à-plats in time to witness the grand fish festival,*
> *which is yearly celebrated; the men only have the privilege of assisting*
> *there at. Around a fire fifty feet long, partially overlaid with stones of the*
> *size of a turkey's egg, eighty men range themselves; each man is provided*
> *with an osier vessel, cemented with gum and filled with water and fish.*
> *The hall where this extraordinary feast is celebrated is constructed of rush*
> *mats, and has three apertures, one at either extremity for the entrance of*
> *guests; the middle one serves for transporting the fish. All preparations*
> *being complete, and each man at his post, the chief, after a short ha-*
> *rangue of encouragement to his people, finishes by a prayer of supplication*
> *to the Great Spirit, of whom he demands an abundant draught. He gives*
> *the signal to commence, and each one, armed with two sticks flattened at*
> *the extremity, makes use of them instead of tongs, to draw the stones from*
> *the embers, and put them in his kettle. This process is twice renewed, and*
> *in the space of five minutes, the fish are cooked. Finally, they squat*
> *around the fire in the most profound silence to enjoy the repast, each*
> *trembling lest a bone be disjointed or broken – an indispensable condition*
> *of a plentiful fishery. A single bone broken would be regarded as ominous,*
> *and the unlucky culprit banished from the society of his comrades, lest his*
> *presence should entail on them some dread evil.*

During the last half of the eighteenth century, several imperial powers vied for a foothold on the Pacific Northwest coast. By 1800, the Spanish interest had been eclipsed, and, by 1850, the viability of Russian claims were on the wane.[22] The two great remaining imperial powers, Britain and America, had commenced, by means of the Oregon Treaty of 1846, to settle their long-standing differences over the proper positioning of the boundary between their two jurisdictions. The geographic character of the western mountain ranges in 1850 were, from a

Fig. 10. Lieutenant Charles Wilson (1836-1905). At age 22, Wilson, a member of the Royal Engineers, was appointed as secretary to the British Boundary Commission Survey party of 1858-62. Wilson was a many-faceted individual who in addition to his official duties, completed watercolours of the boundary country and also published an important account of the Kootenay in 1865. B.C. Archives. No. A-01625.

European point of view, still poorly understood except to a handful of "mountain men" and fur traders. It was into this undefined ground that the members of the British North American Exploring Expedition, the famed "Palliser Expedition," advanced in 1858, as part of their assignment for the Royal Geographical Society and the British Crown. In terms of mid-century reconnaissance, this party had been preceded only by American government surveyor, James Doty, who in 1854 had attempted to determine the northern limits of American territory along the eastern slopes of the Rockies. He noted that "my survey shows that the Chief Mountain Lake and its environs, as well as the tract of fertile country extending south to the Marias Pass, belong to the United States."[23]

At this time, the Hudson's Bay Company's lands were coming under intense scrutiny by Royal Commissioners in England. Officialdom sought to obtain better information on the lands south of the Saskatchewan River. While members of Palliser's expedition were still working their way across the prairies, the United States and British governments took other initiatives. They jointly appointed a commission to survey the border between British and American territory along the 49th parallel from the Pacific coast to the continental divide, in accordance with arrangements agreed upon in the Oregon Treaty.[24] As the boundary surveyors worked their way eastward from New Westminster along the 49th parallel, Lieutenant Thomas Blakiston, having separated from the main body of the Palliser expedition, set a course southwestward into the very heart of Waterton Lakes National Park. In 1858, he criss-crossed the present park lands via the middle and south Kootenay passes, the latter commonly known as Boundary Pass. It was in the course of these border explorations that Blakiston bestowed several geographic place names in the area of today's park, including that of Waterton (Map 4).[25] By the summer of 1858, Blakiston had departed the Waterton country for Fort Carlton, and so he did not meet the boundary surveyors. By 1861, the British survey party had completed its assignment. Just west of Cameron Lake on the great divide at Akamina Station, the survey party erected a "Pyramid of Stones" to mark the eastern terminus of the line from the Gulf of Georgia (Fig. 10).[26]

The signing of treaties in 1855 between various tribes south of the 49th parallel and the American government cleared the way for an influx into Montana of miners, bison hunters, and merchants of many stripes (Fig. 11).[27] Significant

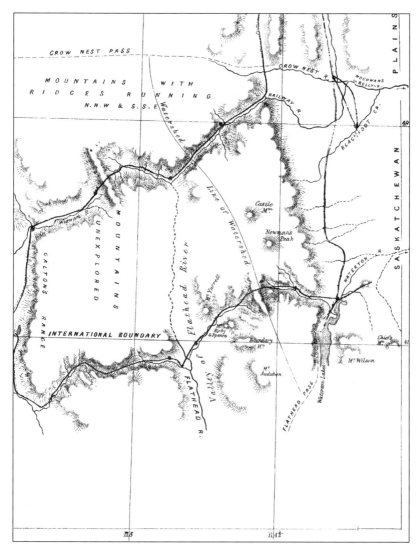

Map 4. Blakiston's map of the border region of Waterton-Glacier country. 1858. This map is a portion of a larger map published by the Palliser Expedition with its final report.

Fig. 11. Chief Many Spotted Horses of the Blood Tribe. This leader of the Lone Fighters Band signed the 1855 Blackfeet Treaty on the American side and the 1877 Treaty at Blackfoot Crossing on the Canadian side. Sketch by Gustavus Sohon, 1855; Glenbow Archives, Calgary. NA 360-14.

mineral strikes were made in Idaho as early as 1861. Rumours of precious metal had circulated around Montana for many years.[28] In 1864, the American Fur Company, sensing the final collapse of the fur and hide trade, sold out to the North West Fur Company and abandoned the upper Missouri basin to the free traders.[29] By 1865, Fort Benton, on the upper Missouri River, was taking on significance as a frontier entrepôt. From this isolated outpost, commercial probes, legitimate and illicit, were made into British territory by means of the Whoop-Up Trail, which extended into the vicinity of modern Lethbridge.[30]

As the Whoop-Up Trail became increasingly well used by traders and wolfers, there was some urgency for a final definition of the boundary east from the mountains. A second phase of the boundary survey was therefore authorized in 1870, charged with establishing the line between the Lake of the Woods and the continental divide. The British party commenced its work in 1872 under the direction of Major Cameron, who was assisted by Captain Samuel Anderson, Lieutenant Galwey, Lieutenant Rowe, and Captain Featherstonhaugh, some of whose names have persisted as geographic place names in Waterton Lakes National Park. The young George Mercer Dawson was also in the party as geologist.

The lawlessness and illicit liquor trade with the Native peoples along the Whoop-Up Trail came to a head at about the same time the boundary surveyors were completing their work. In the spring of 1874, the newly formed North West Mounted Police force was dispatched from Fort Dufferin on the Red River to establish Canadian sovereignty over the western territory north of the 49th parallel. The force followed the Boundary Commission party's trail on this "great trek" west and established Fort MacLeod. They were accompanied by some 235 head of cattle. Although a small herd of cattle had been established by the

Methodist missionary, John McDougall, at Morely in 1873, the arrival of the police's herd marked the practical beginnings of the ranch industry in southern Alberta.[31] More importantly perhaps, the fixing on the ground, by 1874, of the approximate international boundary line allowed for the commencement of land surveys on either side of the border. This fact had urgent social consequences.

On the Canadian side, the long-standing British Imperial practice of extinguishing Native title by means of treaties, in advance of any granting of title to intending settlers, became a public task of the highest priority. The various "numbered" treaties of the Northwest Territories had been unfolding sequentially from the Lake of the Woods country westward since 1871. The Blackfoot and Sarcee (TsuuT'ina) Indians of this quarter came to terms with the Crown in 1877 at Blackfoot Crossing on the Bow River. After the signing of this treaty, cattle were steadily driven into southern Alberta from Montana. One frontiersman who had been a steady witness to these events from both sides of the border was already resident at the Waterton Lakes at the time of the 1877 treaty: the Irish-born soldier, frontiersman and "mountain man," John George "Kootenai" Brown (1839-1916).

"Kootenai" Brown was one of the first of European background to settle in the vicinity of Waterton Lakes National Park. He was a figure about whom legend continued to build during his lifetime, and well after. Born of a military family in County Clare, Ireland, in 1839, he was orphaned in the mid-1840s during the course of the great Irish potato famines. He was then raised with great care in his grandmother's household.[32] Her persistence with the War Office finally obtained a commission in the military for young Brown and initial service in India, where he was probably associated with his Irish compatriot and neighbour, Arthur Vowell.[33]

The life of the military in the days of the Indian Mutiny did not appeal to either Brown or Vowell. The latter resigned in 1860 as a senior lieutenant and Brown in November of 1861, during a period when Brown's Company of the Eighth Regiment was being recalled home from India. The reasons for their resignations were undoubtedly economic.[34] Brown and Vowell decided to seek their fortunes on other frontiers. The two men departed for the west coast of America via the Isthmus of Panama. They arrived at Esquimault and Victoria in early 1862, and by the summer, having replenished their "grub stake" through labouring jobs, they reached the Cariboo Goldfields of British Columbia. Vowell was not impressed by the prospects for fortune, and he returned to Victoria at the end of the first season, where he went on to a long and distinguished career in the Civil Service of British Columbia as Gold Commissioner and Superintendent of Indian Affairs.[35] Brown persisted for another two years. Before redirecting himself to the Wild Horse Creek area of the East Kootenays, he summed up his experience: "I had no money when I went into Cariboo and I had none when I came out in 1864, but I had a little fortune for awhile in between."[36]

At Wild Horse Creek, he took another crack at making his fortune. He then turned his hand to a variety of jobs over the next few years, and in 1865 he went into service as a constable in the employ of Gold Commissioner Peter O'Reilly. The Wild Horse Creek area was essentially an American enclave in British territory and a man with Brown's experience in the military was valuable to those charged with maintaining law and order. Brown went to New Westminster briefly, where he was entered on the civil service payroll and then assigned to Wild Horse Creek. Brown soon resigned his post on account of reduced wages and turned to prospecting once again. The Kootenay goldfields were depleted quickly, however, and Brown sold his claims and headed east towards the plains, a journey that took him through the South Kootenay Pass and past the Waterton Lakes. His next twelve years on the prairies were packed with adventure, some of it inglorious. Effectively adopted as a member of a migratory Métis community, he was soon captivated by the rough and tumble of prairie life. He married Olivia d'Lonais, a woman of considerable beauty, with whom he had two children, and became expert in the ways, languages, and customs of prairie peoples. He lived dangerously on occasion, particularly while engaged in work as a wolfer and trader in liquor.[37] This phase of his life ended in the vicinity of the Teton River in May, 1877, where he reportedly killed a fellow wolfer, one Louis Ell, following a bitter dispute over debts and Ell's seizure of some of Brown's furs. Records of the legal proceedings in Fort Benton in November of that year are scanty, but a verdict of not guilty was handed down on the basis of Brown's plea of self-defence and a lack of evidence to the contrary. Brown, with his family, quickly took his leave of Montana and entered the southern Alberta country to settle down once and for all.[38] He arrived at the Waterton Lakes, the place that he had seen over a decade earlier en route out of the Wild Horse Creek mining area, and to which, according to his first biographer, he had vowed to return.[39] A fatigued and harried Brown decided to settle his family near the lakes, safe inside Canadian territory.

He was preceded there only by H. A. "Fred" Kanouse (d.1920), an American trader of the Fort Benton area, who had built a cabin on the eastern shores of Upper Waterton Lake about 1874.[40] He had moved across the border for reasons curiously similar to those which had motivated Brown. The claim of self-defence was used by Kanouse followng the death of trader Jim Nabors near the Marias Pass. Kanouse was the Sheriff of Choteau at the time, and one wry observer in Montana stated that "he has not up to the present been arrested."[41] After that date, Kanouse remains a somewhat shadowy figure in the historical record. He had been frequenting the Bow and Oldman River country since 1871. He built Fort Warren in the foothills "where he had established trading relations with the Kootenay."[42] Kanouse's cabin may have been at either Fort Warren or Kootenay Post.[43] These composed part of the overall complex of trade facilities associated with the Whoop-Up Trail running from Fort Benton into British territory.[44]

Kanouse was identified by one Louis Watson as being among the earliest traders in the Fort Mcleod area.[45] His connections remained significant on both sides of the border. When Natawista, the aunt of Chief Red Crow of the Bloods, separated from her husband, trader Alexander Culbertson in 1869, she returned from Fort Benton to the land of the Bloods to live with Red Crow's people, and she eventually married Kanouse.[46] By 1871 his trading had taken him as far north as the Elbow River in present-day Calgary, but hostility from the Bloods eventually drove him south again to the Waterton Lakes, where Brown found him (Figs. 12-14).[47]

Brown appears to have quickly worked out an arrangement with Kanouse, for in late 1877 he gained use of the cabin for his wife Olivia and their two daughters.[48] Shortly after, Brown established his own place on the western shores of Middle Waterton Lake, which he operated, with Kanouse, as a trading post and a headquarters for his guiding and hunting expeditions. The two men operated a varied trade with Kootenay, Peigan and Blood Indians, involving whisky, furs, and general trade goods. Owing to the rapid change in the land situation for the Indians after 1877, brought about by the treaty settlement, the Brown and Kanouse commercial operation

Fig.12. Alexander Culbertson, Montana-based trader of the American Fur Company and his wife, Natawista or Medicine Snake Woman, aunt of Chief Red Crow, along with their son (c. 1863). After 1869, Natawista and Culbertson parted, and the former came north to live among the Bloods. Later, she met Fred Kanouse and became one of his wives. Montana Historical Society.

Fig. 13. H. A. "Fred" Kanouse. (d. 1920) This legendary trader of frontier Montana and Alberta was an associate of "Kootenai" Brown after 1877 in the Waterton country. Originally active in Fort Benton, he was the pioneer trader of early Calgary between 1871 and 1874. Glenbow Archives, Calgary. NA 31-1.

Fig. 14. Red Crow (1830-1900). As Head Chief of the Blood Tribe from 1870 to 1900, this influential leader of the Fish Eater's Band saw his people through the difficulties of the transition from life on the old buffalo commons to sedentary life on the large Blood Reserve north of Waterton. Glenbow Archives, Calgary. NA 3281-1.

Fig. 15. "Kootonai" Brown's homestead. 1883. This structure was shared and then taken over by Brown from Fred Kanouse and was located on the flats near the Waterton River and Lower Waterton Lake. A. S. Hill, 1883.

was short-lived. The partnership was dissolved by 1882, following which Kanouse spent most of his time around Fort Macleod undertaking ranching and other commercial ventures. The cattle Kanouse drove in from Montana in 1877 mark the beginning of commercial ranching in southern Alberta.[49]

In order to help sustain his family, Brown took to farming on lands at the mouth of Blakiston Creek. He was not long alone in his chosen paradise. By 1882, a few other settlers appeared along the Belly and Waterton Rivers. W. A. Henry obtained a lease to graze cattle on the grasslands surrounding the Lower and Middle Waterton Lakes, while the area to the north became part of the lands leased to the large Cochrane Ranch interests. A year later, Frederick W. Godsal, soon to become a friend of Brown, established his South Fork Ranch in the vicinity of Cowley, in the Castle River area.[50] In his entertaining memoir of travels in North America, Arthur Stavely Hill, indicated that he was a guest at Brown's cabin in 1883, a site which the author photographed (Fig. 15):[51]

Early in the afternoon of Monday, Sept 11, 1883, we arrived in sight of the house of Kootenai Brown, an old settler, who had been there for many years.... Brown was occupier of the log hut belonging to Kanouse, in which he lived with a rather delicate wife and some children.

41

In 1884, Olivia died, not long after the birth of the couple's third child, leaving Brown devastated. He placed his children in better hands and allowed himself to be swept into the dramatic and momentous frontier events of 1885 associated with Louis Riel and the Métis resistance at Batoche on the North Saskatchewan River. In the course of these events, Brown took up duties as a guide with the Rocky Mountain Rangers, the paramilitary force established to defend the fledgling settlements of the far Canadian West.[52] With the end of hostilities at the close of summer, 1885, Brown resumed life in the Waterton Lakes area, where he continued to occupy the Kanouse cabin. Brown's biographer, William Rodney, refers to him returning "to his cabin on the eastern shore of the middle Waterton Lakes" to resume his solitary life.[53] Brown was now a man of greater means nonetheless, for he had been recognized for his services during the Riel troubles. Major Stewart, leader of the Rocky Mountain Rangers, had argued the case for his men in Ottawa, and in time members of the force were declared to be entitled for award of the North West Medal. They were also made eligible to receive 320 acres or $80.00 scrip money in payment. Brown opted for the land and was granted a half section in the south half of Township Nine.[54]

Brown did not do much with his land over the next five years, being too busy in the employ of the North West Mounted Police, work which took him far afield on many occasions. He had however, taken a second wife, Isabella – "the Flash of Blue Lightning" – a Cree woman whom he presumably met in the Medicine Hat area when he was serving with the Rocky Mountain Rangers. While Brown undertook some small scale agriculture for his own needs, the labour involved coupled with the rise of large ranching units nearby, did not recommend farming as a viable way of life. Between 1885 and 1890, he had experienced some illness as well as a broken leg, and these afflictions may have helped persuade him in late 1890 to sell his half section to a man named McArthur.[55]

The following autumn, he took out a new patent for land that was "much more advantageously located near the junction of Pass Creek and the Lower Waterton Lake."[56] This quarter section included a fine hay meadow and sufficient grazing for Brown's horses and provided timber enough for a new cabin (Figs. 16, 17).[57] This area later provided the focus for the park farm in the 1920s and 1930s. Over the next ten years, Brown's activities reflected three main interests:

Fig. 16. "Kootenai" Brown (c.1898). By the 1890s, Brown was starting to achieve romantic status as a veteran of the frontier. Photographs such as this helped to foster such an image. Glenbow Archives, Calgary. NA 2539-19.

Fig. 17. Isabella Brown (c. 1898). Of Cree background, Chee-pay-qua-ka-soon – "the Blue Flash of Lightning" – was Brown's second wife and a sure shot. She did much to provide a comfortable domestic context for Brown in his role as a forest, game and park guardian. Parks Canada.

pursuit of his guiding business, an interest in oil speculation; and work as a packer and guide in the Crowsnest Pass area. This last mentioned was mainly after 1897, during construction of the new CPR line through the pass.

The arrival of Mormon settlers at Lees Creek and in the Cardston area after 1887 provided the first tangible expression of what the future was likely to hold in terms of human pressure on local wildlife resources.[58] Throughout these years, Brown's attempts to find a reliable source of game, first in the Edmonton bush country, and then closer to home in the Waterton area, stimulated a personal interest in schemes for forest reservation.[59] These concerns were reinforced by the demands now being made upon him as guide, following the completion of the Crowsnest Pass Railway, which had opened up the mining country of Southeastern British Columbia. Brown's services were now being sought less by fishing and hunting enthusiasts, and more by persons connected to mining and oil interests.[60] Hunting and fishing, as aristocratic pursuits, were giving way to the demands made by everyman.

Chapter Three

Ranchers, Resources and the First Waterton Park Reserve: 1895-1930

"Kootenai" Brown had chanced to arrive in the Waterton country on the eve of one of the great historic changes in western prairie land use: that marking the shift from the old wild buffalo landscape to that of modern cattle-grazing. Under the new confederation arrangements, land in the western prairie territories was administered from Ottawa by the Department of the Interior. Grazing leases on such crown lands were sanctioned through the regulations provided under the Dominion Lands Act of 1873. The amendments of 1881 allowed leases of twenty-one years for ranches of up to 100,000 acres at a cost of one cent per acre. The first great experiment in large-scale ranching was initiated by Senator Matthew Cochrane of Compton, Quebec, whose venture centred on the Bow River west of Calgary.[1] The interplay of early snow and local topography proved disastrous over the first two winters and so in 1883 the Cochrane interests took out ranch lands to the north of Waterton Park.[2] At this time, only a few individuals, including "Kootenai" Brown, were making use of the future parklands for agriculture and grazing purposes.

Intending settlers soon began to filter into the region, and by 1891 the ranching community was experiencing social strains in the wake of "squatting" farmers seeking to establish themselves on the large ranch leaseholds. The North

Fig. 18. William Pearce (1848-1930). Called by some the "Czar of the West" and the father of prairie irrigation policy, this veteran land surveyor played an important role in the establishment of natural resource and park policy within the federal Department of the Interior. He remained an important influence on western settlement after joining the CPR in 1899. Here he is shown in his CPR office in Calgary. Glenbow Archives, Calgary. NA 325-1.

West Mounted Police were increasingly pressured to give more time to disputes arising between ranchers and settlers and to the promulgation of eviction notices.[3] At the same time, officials of the federal Department of the Interior, with the strong urging of Superintendent of Mines, William Pearce, worked hard to adjust the character of the original ranch leaseholds in a way that would suite both the cattlemen and the settlers. The main policy advanced towards this end was the so-called Stock-Watering Reserve System, put in place by Pearce in 1886 and expanded in 1892.[4] The policy intended to prevent squatters from taking up favourable positions on essential watering sites and grazing bottom lands, locations considered essential to the ranchers. There was considerable opposition to the Stock-Watering Reserve System, but the cattlemen were well organized in both the West and in Ottawa, where Senator Cochrane had the ear of the Conservative Party. Pearce's system survived the defeat of the Conservatives in 1896 and was essentially left in place by the Liberal administration of Sir Wilfrid Laurier (Fig. 18).[5]

The introduction of the system of stock-grazing reserves and revisions to the system of large grazing leases received mixed reactions from cattlemen and intending settlers alike. The forces behind the British-owned Walrond Ranch, north-west of

46

the park, remained hostile to any changes in the status quo, and on occasion violence threatened to break out in connection with the Walrond methods of ranch operation.[6] Others north of Waterton, such as Godsal, the enterprising rancher from Cowley, took a much more conciliatory approach (Fig.19).[7]

The grazing-settler conflict was perhaps, the first major land use debate in which water was the central issue. The importance of the nearby mountains as a source of headwaters, fish, and wildlife brought together apparently disparate individuals in a discussion of public reserves and their ideal nature. Along with F. W. Godsal, "Kootenai" Brown was one of those

Fig. 19. F. W. Godsal (1853-1935). Born in Shropshire, England, Godsal was well educated and connected. Following a period in Ceylon, he came to Canada where the Marquis of Lorne encouraged him to try ranching in the foothills country. From his ranch at Cowley, Godsal became an important advocate for the establishment of Waterton Lakes National Park and was active in the Alpine Club of Canada. Parks Canada.

who reputedly participated in the conversation, gradually becoming an active proponent for the establishment of a public reserve at Waterton in the mid-1890s.[8]

Establishment of Special Reserves in the Waterton-Glacier Country

The initial suggestion that a public reserve should be set aside around the Waterton Lakes appears to have originated with William Pearce. On noticing the success of the park reserve at Banff Springs, Pearce made the following observations in his 1886 Annual Report:[9]

> *There are many other points in the Rocky Mountains which, in the near future, it would be well to reserve, among which may be mentioned the vicinity around the lakes which rise near the 49th Parallel and empty by the Waterton River into the Belly River.*

Pearce's suggestion for additional reserves failed to generate action for a number of years, even though, in 1887, letters and editorials appeared in the *McLeod Gazette* drawing attention to the need for improvement in the game guardian system in that quarter.[10] In 1893, however, Pearce had his memory jogged by Frederick Godsal, who wrote to him, anxious to revive interest in the park reserve idea.[11] Pearce happily sent Godsal's suggestions on for consideration. Some opposition was met at upper levels, but this time it was countered by Minister T. Mayne Daly, who in 1894 authorized establishment of a park reserve around the Waterton Lakes.[12] The action took effect the following year when the greater portion of two townships was set aside as the Waterton Lakes Forest Park.[13]

It is significant that the forest park was established during the brief tenure of MacKenzie Bowell as prime minister of Canada. In 1890, as minister of customs, he made a tour of inspection of facilities in Alberta and British Columbia. "Kootenai" Brown served as packer and guide for Bowell's party and its NWMP escort, which travelled by horseback through the Crowsnest Pass into British Columbia. It is likely that Bowell thus learned first hand the views of the locals about the need to set aside lands in the Waterton area.[14] It came as something of a relief to the aging Brown when, in 1901, he was appointed fisheries officer. His job was to look after the resources of the Waterton Lakes Forest Reserve, a position he held until 1912, after which he was appointed as, effectively, the first superintendent of Waterton Lakes National Park.

The large forest park reserves created in these years, such as Yoho and Waterton, had been established under an 1884 Dominion Lands Act Amendment. These reserves did not enjoy the discretionary protection that had been extended to the Rocky Mountains Park (Banff) under the special act of 1887. They were essentially forest reserves "without special supervision or protection." Their "timber was available to settlers under permit and the prevailing regulations permitted prospecting for petroleum and the reservation of potential oil-producing lands."[15]

The creation of a distinct identity for national parks, as opposed to forest reserves, owes much to the work of Frank Oliver, who in 1905 replaced Clifford Sifton as the Minister of the Interior. In 1906, local M.P. John Herron sponsored a new name for the park unit called the Kootenay Lakes Forest Reserve, no doubt to the joy of Canon Middleton, the advocate of traditional place names. For the next five years, the reserve was under the control of the superintendent of forestry in Ottawa. On Herron's recommendation, "Kootenai" Brown was nominated for an enhanced officer position, that of chief forest ranger, an appointment formally approved in 1910.[16] Under Oliver's guidance, a new Dominion Forest Reserves Parks Act was passed in 1911, legislation in which distinctions were made between "forest reserves" and "parks." The former were withdrawn from settlement but allowed certain controlled resource usages under permit; the latter were to be used mainly as "public pleasuring grounds." With the subsequent establishment of the Dominion

Fig. 20. James B. Harkin (1875-1955). Harkin became the first director of the new National Park system in 1911. A former journalist, he had served as secretary to both Clifford Sifton and Frank Oliver, successive ministers of the Department of Interior. Thus he knew the personalities and mechanics of the department intimately. He remained the director of parks until 1936. National Archives of Canada.

Parks Branch, and the appointment of a vital young director, James B. Harkin, the development of a national system of parks was underway (Fig. 20).

Events seemed to be moving in the direction favoured by park proponents. Ironically, the passage of the 1911 Act reduced, rather than increased, the size of Waterton. To many, this seemed a retrograde step, despite the rationalizations offered, which suggested that the lands around the park proper were still in forest reserve status and that protection to wildlife and trees was still being given.[17] This shrinking of the boundaries took place shortly after the United States had established the extensive Glacier National Park directly to the south of the Waterton boundary.[18] Canadian park policy, in this case, appeared to be moving in a direction opposite to what was appropriate. The federally sponsored Commission of Conservation, established in 1909, moved to exercise its influence by putting pressure on Ottawa to review the reduced boundaries. J. B. Harkin exercised his authority to

Fig. 21. John F. Stevens (1853-1943). A graduate engineeer from New England, in 1889 he was commissioned by James J. Hill to find a route for the Great Northern Railway across the Rockies from the railhead at Havre, Montana. Stevens found such a route via the Marias Pass. He later went on to become the chief engineer on the Panama Canal project and then served as the head of the American Railway Mission to Russia in 1917-18. Great Northern Railway.

alter the arrangements of 1911. The Dominion Forest Reserves and Parks Act was amended in 1913 so as to allow additions to the park system from lands other than those defined as forest reserves.[19] In 1914, the park was expanded once again, this time to its largest historic size of 1095 square kilometres (about 423 square miles).[20] At this time, the park's name reverted back to "Waterton" from "Kootenay."[21] Over the next seven years, a number of other adjustments were made between Waterton and local forest reserves, and the 1921 exchange left Waterton with about 220 square miles. These boundaries did not change for close to forty years.[22]

In Montana, the development of the special park reserve at Glacier developed out of more complex circumstances. The mining frontier unfolded with great speed in the 1870s.[23] As one historian noted: "Montana was famous as a mining community long before its agricultural possibilities were even suspected."[24] Mining interests gained easier access into the old "boom and bust" placer mining areas from the south by the completion of the Union Pacific and the Northern Pacific Railways after 1869. The Butte area was the main focus. The assault on reserved Blackfeet lands in the northwest part of Montana came after the final push by James J. Hill's Great Northern Railway through the Marias Pass in today's Glacier National Park. The existence of the Marias Pass had been suspected ever since the years of the Lewis and Clark expedition, but its exact location remained elusive until the late 1880s, following the survey work of John F. Stevens.[25] With completion of the railway in 1892, this great wilderness was suddenly vulnerable to many of the usual frontier pressures (Fig. 21).

The lands set aside in 1910 as Glacier National Park had been part of the Blackfeet Reservation defined under the 1855 Treaty.[26] As early as 1883, Lieutenant John T. Van Orsdale had urged that some of the area along the Great Divide be set aside as a national park.[27] With the urging of George B. Grinnell and others concerned about the rising tide of miners invading the Indian lands, the western belt of the Indian reservation was purchased back by the U.S. government in 1895, with a view to opening the lands to a more controlled form of prospecting. This proposal was just the latest in a series of land cessions made in the "shrinking Blackfeet territory" others having been made in 1873 and 1888.[28] By early 1896, this latest "ceded strip" of Indian land had been set aside as the core area of the Lewis and Clark Forest reserve.[29]

For many years, G. B. Grinnell had been expanding his views beyond considerations of mere headwaters and wildlife conservation. His article "The Crown of the Continent" finally appeared in *Century Magazine* in 1901, eight years after its submission.[30] Thereafter, he started to part company with influential forester Gifford Pinchot and other "progressives" in his view of the aims of conservation. Pinchot strongly favoured multiple-use philosophies, such as grazing in forest reserves.[31] Grinnell, on the other hand, became a steady influence towards the 1910 establishment of Glacier National Park (Fig. 22).[32]

In comparison with Waterton Lakes National Park, even at its greatest geographic extent in 1914, Glacier was a much larger reserve, amounting to over one million acres.[33] The need to patrol this great wilderness was an urgent priority and some experienced men who had been employed in the forest reserves continued on in the new park, shifting their interests towards wildlife protection and predator control. Included in the new park establishment were some seasoned veterans of the frontier.

Glimpses of the last few years in the life of Albert "Death-on-the-Trail" Reynolds are revealed in his diary for the years 1912 to 1913. In 1901, he had worked as a forest ranger in the Flathead Forest, based at Lake McDonald. He guided geologist Bailey Willis, who called him "a fine old woodsman." Some tourists who encountered him in 1903 observed that he could "climb like a mountain sheep."[34] In 1912, he was based at Camp Creek, some two miles south of Waterton Lake, from which he executed lengthy and regular patrols. He was

Fig. 22. George and Elizabeth Grinnell at Glacier National Park, 1923. G. B. Grinnell (1849-1938), naturalist and editor of *Forest and Stream* after 1876, became an important proponent for Glacier National Park establishment after he started to visit the area in 1885. Glacier National Park Archives.

hosted on the Canadian side on many occasions. In the course of their parallel duties, he and "Kootenai" Brown became associates and friends. His rambling abilities were legendary, but in the end, he lived up to his name after experiencing a foot injury on the trail.[35] On February 4, 1913, Brown recorded in his own diary: "Mr. Reynolds, U.S. Ranger, Messrs Hazzard and Carpenter here. 32 degrees below zero... Reynolds very sick. Up all night with him."[36] Reynolds was taken to Pincher Creek, where he died on Feb. 8, 1913 (Fig. 23). Time was now short for Brown as well. From 1910 to 1914, he

Fig. 23. Albert "Death-on-the-Trail" Reynolds (1847-1913). An experienced woodsman, Reynolds came to the Flathead Valley from Wisconsin with his wife Sarah, in 1871. In 1901, he "retired" and became a forest ranger in the Lake McDonald area. With establishment of Glacier National Park, he became a park ranger and was active in the northern areas. He regualarly came into contact with "Kootenai" Brown. Glacier National Park Archives.

served as chief forest ranger at Waterton. A symbol of the park in its early days, the grand old veteran of the Canadian-American frontier died in 1916 and was buried along the western shore of Lower Waterton Lake, next to his first wife, Olivia.

Boundaries and the Adjustments of the Native Peoples

The years from 1877 to 1920 were difficult ones in terms of adjustment for Native peoples on both sides of the international boundary. As in earlier times, the U.S-Canadian border – "the Medicine Line" – was of little significance with respect to ties of kin and lifeways, but the border was taking on significance with respect to legal entitlements and future prospects.[37] Various land disposition issues found their origins in these years, such as the Timber Limit "A" issue in the Waterton Lakes National Park. The ecological conditions which for centuries had supported traditional hunting, gathering, and knowledge, started to alter rapidly in the 1870s, including the long economic interplay between mountain and prairie. The rapid manner in which the cattle-grazing range replaced the old bison landscape after 1880 had momentous consequences for Native peoples.

Fig. 24. Haying on the Peigan Reserve, north of Waterton. c. 1892. The Peigan and Blood peoples took to agriculture rapidly after the disappearance of the bison herds, but great difficulties were put in their way with respect to the marketplace by the strictures of the Indian Act. Glenbow Archives, Calgary. NA 4461-4.

Fig. 25. Blackfoot Woman wearing HBC blanket. c. 1885. This photo reveals the important role played by the European trading companies in supplementing the mode of garb among prairie Native peoples. With the decline of the bison herds after 1860, the shift to European materials was reinforced. Sir Alexander Galt Museum and Archives. P19770156000-GP.

Fig. 26. Two Salish-speaking Indians of the Lake McDonald area. c. 1909. Abraham Isaac (L) and Michel Kaiser. Helen F. Sanders, 1910.

Fig. 27. Hide lodges on the shore of Two Medicine Lake, Glacier National Park. c. 1914.
Glacier National Park Archives.

The Native reserve and reservation systems in Canada and the United States evolved under different conditions. On the American side, between 1855 and 1877, it was severely complicated by a legacy of anti-tribal war and periodic community removal. On the Canadian side, the years following the signing of Treaty 7 in 1877 saw rapid impoverishment and economic adjustment for the Blackfoot, Sarcee, and Stoney peoples, all of whom had participated in the treaty ceremony at Blackfoot Crossing. Subsequent social adjustment was not made easy, owing to legal, economic, and religious discrimination.[38] During the treaty negotiations, the famed Blackfoot Chief Crowfoot remained sceptical about the Treaty Commissioner's claim to be able to provide for the Indians during times of famine: "I don't think you can. You will run out of breath."[39]

Many of the Indians on the new Peigan and Blood Indian Reserves north of Waterton did take to agriculture, but the restrictions imposed by the Indian Act and the agency system, complicated otherwise satisfactory economic performance and the effective marketing of produce.[40] Others moved into natural resource work associated with mining and lumbering, or participated in the nascent tourism industry, particulary as fishing and hunting guides (Figs. 24-27).[41]

Fig. 28. Charcoal (1856-1897). This Blood Indian was executed for murdering a fellow tribesman in what was considered a crime of unusual passion. In his desparate state, he temporarily sought refuge in the Blood Indian Timber Limit of Waterton Forest Reserve. Glenbow Archives, Calgary. NA 118-54.

Some were left behind, stretched hopelessly between past and present. Such was the fate of the Blood Indian "Charcoal" whose "world" has been so sympathetically described by Mike Mountain Horse and Hugh Dempsey. In 1896, conflicting thoughts of custom, tribal honour, religion, and ritual murder all circulated uneasily in Charcoal's mind. A cuckold once too often, he took violent action as he saw fit. On the run from the police, he finally disappeared into the relative cover afforded by the Blood Timber Limit along the Belly River, thereby temporarily eluding Major Sam Steele's North West Mounted Police. Eventually apprehended, Charcoal was hanged at Fort Macleod in 1897 (Fig. 28).[42]

The Natural Resource Frontier in the Early Waterton Park Reserve Period

The notion of a park reserve in 1895 was considerably different from what it became after 1930 when the first powerful National Parks Act was passed into law in Canada. The business of Canada in the late years of the nineteenth century was development and settlement, and the motives behind special land reserves were distinctly utilitarian. Godsal, Brown and others sensed a real threat to wildlife in those years, but the suggestion that special reserves should be viewed as anything more than places to guarantee future fish and game supply was still some years away.[43] Productive land uses were seen to be compatible. One of the first economic resources to gain attention in the Waterton-Glacier country was oil.

Native peoples in the vicinity of Waterton Lakes, particularly members of the Kootenay and Stoney (Nakoda) tribes, had known of the "stinking waters" on Cameron Creek for many years. "Kootenai" Brown and others were quick to learn of it and of its past and potential applications. Brown was accustomed to gathering the dark substance by soaking it up with fabric bags and then using it as a general lubricant, as a medicine for horses, and perhaps as a fuel.[44]

Interest in oil was such that in 1891 William "Smooth Bore" French and William Fernie decided to obtain some old drilling equipment from Petrolia, Ontario. They tested to a depth of 230 feet, but struck only water.[45] A more concerted effort was then mounted after 1896 by Allan P. Patrick, a Dominion Topographical Surveyor. French directed him to lands along Cameron Creek

Fig. 29. The geology of the Lewis Overthrust is well illustrated at Cameron Falls. The wife of Col. Macleod of the North West Mounted Police is seated on the left, c.1892. Glenbow Archives, Calgary. NA 4461-28.

Fig. 30. Allen P. Patrick, founder of the Rocky Mountains Development Company in 1901 and promoter of Oil City in Waterton Lakes National Park cruising in the foothills in 1922. Glenbow Archives, NA 88-1. Calgary.

about eight kilometres from the present Waterton townsite along the Akamina Highway. By 1901, Patrick had formed the Rocky Mountains Development Company, with John Lineham and Arthur Sifton as associates. Lineham would go on to become an important influence in the commercial development of the Turner Valley oil field. Sifton, as the brother of the incumbent Minister of the Interior, Clifford Sifton, had access to influence. The company took out a lease facilitated by an 1898 Order in Council that permitted the reservation of land for the prospecting of oil and its sale.[46]

The subsequent history of Alberta's first "discovery well" at what became known as Oil City was something of a comedy of errors with respect to business practice and human relations. The desire of some individuals to out-finesse their partners by means of subterfuge and sabotage led to the destruction of much of the drilling equipment and a jamming-up of the well.[47] With order restored, drilling undertaken in 1902, this time by experienced men from Petrolia, Ontario, eventually produced a sound, but temporary, flow of some 300 barrels per day taken from a depth of about 311 metres (1,020 feet). Three other holes had been drilled by the end of 1907 but with little to show. Another attempt was made in 1906 at the foot of Cameron Falls in the present Waterton townsite by the Western Oil and Coal Company, also with disappointing results. The smell of oil had nevertheless been sufficient to attract a horde of speculators to the Waterton area. More than half of the forest park reserve had been reserved for petroleum exploration by 1905.[48] This frenzy brought the old group of conservationists together once again for purposes of an appeal to officials in the Department of the Interior. With new legislation for forest reserves pending, however, no remedial action was taken to curb the oil rushers.[49]

Events in the Glacier country often directly mirrored those in Waterton. Just as Alberta's "discovery well" was located within what became a special land reserve, so too in Montana oil was first found on lands that would later be included in Glacier National Park. This took place in 1901 at Kintla Lake, close to the Canadian boundary.[50] The coincidence may be traced to that geological formation which straddles the international border, identified geologically as the "Lewis Overthrust." This structure was given its classic definition in 1902 by American geologist, Bailey Willis.[51] The "Lewis Overthrust" is notable for the way in which older layers of rock have

Fig. 31. Oil City, the setting of Alberta's first oil strike, along Cameron Creek in Waterton Lakes National Park. c. 1915. The location was declared a National Historic Site in 1968. J. C. Holroyd.

Fig. 32. Oil City and Cameron Creek in flood, 1919. Glenbow Archives, Calgary. NA 4089-2.

been displaced, by great lateral pressure, above layers of younger rocks. It is quite visible at the scenic Cameron Falls in the Waterton townsite (Figs. 29, 30).

The oil-bearing capacity of these formations associated with the Lewis Overthrust were not of a type suitable for long-term production, and, hence, the oil boom was short-lived. Most traces of Oil City disappeared shortly after a fire swept through the site in 1919.[52] The oil rush did leave its imprint on the place names of Waterton. When R. A. Daly came to publish his masterly geological survey report on *The North American Cordillera* in 1912, one of his maps identified Cameron Creek as Oil Creek (Figs. 31, 32).

The oil episode provided a certain stimulus towards development of a townsite around the Waterton Lakes. With the continuing entrance of settlers into southern Alberta in the early years of the century, there was no shortage of those anxious to make use of the mountain regions for oil or any other productive purposes. As late as 1914, Superintendent Brown expressed concern about a return of the oil hunters and sought direction from his superiors:[53]

> *I beg to inform you that there is quite an "oil boom" in this district, and land is being taken up all round by prospectors. I have heard that it is the intention of some parties to come on the park to bore for Petroleum and more, that in the event of my preventing them they will hold the Parks Department responsible for all delays. What am I to do?*

The reply from headquarters confirmed that Brown had the power to refuse all such interests through the powers of recent park legislation, enacted in 1911. Over the next half century, there would be much drilling activity for oil in southern Alberta, but it was ultimately gas that became economically important in the area north of Waterton.

While the interest in oil gradually declined along Cameron Creek, other resource possibilities came to the fore. The most important centre of development in the years 1906 to 1911 was at Waterton Mills on the northern edge of Maskinonge Lake. This was the setting for a short but lively episode in the lumbering history of Waterton Park. The development of Waterton Mills, commenced with the incorporation of the Waterton Oil, Land and Power Company in Montana in 1906.[54] Glacier National Park had not yet been founded, and timber exploitation was quite

61

Fig. 33. Waterton Mills. c. 1908. The buildings were located near the bridge at the entrance to Waterton Lakes National Park. In 1905, Waterton Mills became the post office for Waterton Lakes, replacing Oil City. After 1914, the site was converted into a park ranger station. Glenbow. Archives, Calgary. NA 4603-1.

legal in the lands south of Upper Waterton Lake. The new company was controlled by the Hanson Brothers, formerly of Butte, Montana. The brothers had an interest in some 200 million feet of lumber on the United States side. They intended to float the logs through Waterton Lake, mill them at the north end, and then ship the processed wood to American and Canadian markets. To this end, the Waterton Mills were built and commenced production in 1907. Forty-five men were employed and the mills had a capacity for sawing 25,000 feet of lumber per day. After relocating to the site with his family, Henry Hanson applied for permission to open a post office, which took the name Waterton Mills. Another mill for Lethbridge was being contemplated (Fig. 33).[55]

The success of this scheme was dependent on the efficient movement of the logs down the lake to the mills. The first motor launch was underpowered and so the company had P. G. Peterson design a larger craft. This resulted in construction of *The Gertrude,* a sixty horse-power, one-hundred-foot-long paddle-wheeler which drew a mere eight inches, allowing it to navigate the shallow river sections between the lakes during high water periods. *The Gertrude* was everything her owner had expected. In the first year, business had not been as brisk as hoped, but prospects looked good after an Idaho firm placed an order for some 2,000,000 feet of lumber. In the summer of 1908, bad luck struck the Hanson Brothers when one of the largest floods in memory swept through the area. The mills were damaged, the log boom destroyed, and logs were strewn along the Belly and Waterton Rivers all the way to Lethbridge. The important Idaho contract could not be filled, and in the next two years there were few new orders.

A second wave of bad luck then struck the ill-fated company. The brothers had actually leased the Waterton Mills site from the Hudson's Bay Company, but, in 1909, the Canadian government purchased the land, following which, in 1910, Kootenay Lakes Forest Reserve was re-classified as Waterton Lakes Park. While the Hanson's attempted to retain control of their lease, the Parks Branch took the view that the Hanson firm was probably more interested in running commercial tourist operations in the park than in lumbering, and refused to renew the lease.

That same year came more misfortune for the brothers. The United States established Glacier National Park, thus putting into question the Hanson's source of lumber. This was the last straw, and, by 1911, the company was "in such financial straits that its chattels were auctioned by the sheriff and in 1911 most of the buildings at Waterton Mills were seized and sold."[56] Considerable acrimony ensued and legal actions were not finally resolved until 1924.[57]

The Waterton Mills story had involved steam-boating on the lakes, an enterprise in which the proprietors did indeed make an effort to combine lumbering with sight-seeing excursions by means of a motor launch named *The Linnea*, and *The Gertrude*. According to Stutz, this idea "proved to be more a dream than a planned reality."[58] Despite the acrimony between the owners and the Parks Branch over the next few years, *The Gertrude* functioned, with mixed success, as a tourist excursion craft. In 1916, Hanson left the park and leased *The Gertrude* to W. O. Lee and Sons. Lee operated a summer tent village and used *The Gertrude* as a tea room and restaurant. Following a reorganization of the Dominion Parks Branch in 1918, the new officials decided that *The Gertrude* was inappropriate for the park setting and ordered it removed. This being impractical, the craft was scuttled in the centre of a bay, which then became known as Steamboat Bay. This rather accurate name was later changed to Emerald Bay, removing the last tangible reference to this colourful episode in park history.[59] More recently, *The Gertrude* has taken on a new identity, being visited regularly by scuba devotees and by the Parks Canada underwater archaeological unit (Figs. 34, 35).

Fig. 34. *The Gertrude.* This stern paddelwheeler served first in the ill-fated Hanson lumber mill operation before being converted and serving as the largest of the early tour boats on the Waterton Lakes. It was eventually scuttled in Emerald or "Steamboat" Bay. Parks Canada.

Fig. 35. *The Linnea* plying on Upper Waterton Lake, south of the knoll where the Prince of Wales Hotel would eventually stand. c. 1920. J. C. Holroyd.

There is a certain irony attached to the ill-fated attempt at lumbering on the Waterton Lakes. Both the Canadian and American parks shared an institutional past as federal timber reserves from which it was expected that lumber interests would benefit. After 1911, however, the nature of the public interest in park lands was redefined significantly towards the recreational and protectionist side.[60]

Resource extraction associated with mining was only on a small scale in Waterton between 1880 and 1920. An interest in gold, silver, and copper led to the development of the Lineham Creek Mine, the Copper Creek Mine, and a mine on Galwey Creek. Production was minimal and with the achievement of national park status in 1930, these mines were sealed.[61]

Despite steady changes to national agricultural and settlement policy after 1894 – changes which favoured development of irrigation agriculture and mass settlement in the West – ranching also remained an important activity. Grazing was encouraged on crown lands as early as 1881 under the government lease system. Regulations exercised under the Dominion Lands Act provided a basis for the discretionary granting of leases by park superintendents. Despite efforts to control grazing in park areas, over-grazing was prevalent. In 1908, Howard Douglas, Commissioner of Dominion Parks, went on record as opposing grazing leases in parks for reasons that we would today probably call "ecological."[62] Regulations to establish guidelines for grazing in parks were developed in 1914.[63] "The Superintendents were directed to decide what areas should be grazed and wardens were to ensure that the cattle did not exceed the permissible number, or wander outside the designated areas."[64] Ottawa had received notes of complaint from camping parties in the Pass Creek Valley with respect to cattle crowding around tents and "messing up everything."[65] Adjustments to the general grazing regulations after 1914 often focused on the related question of controlling diseases that might be spread from domestic animals to park wildlife.[66]

South of the border, on the fringes of much of Glacier National Park, pressure for grazing also remained an issue after park establishment in 1910. The new park lands had been under the administration of the Forestry Bureau since 1895. The varied duties of a forest ranger in the final year of the bureau's land management responsibility have been preserved in the diary of Frank Liebig.[67] This was a momentous summer, marked by the great fire of 1910. While the late stages of this fire preoccupied newly appointed Superintendent William R. Logan, he did find time in later 1910 to start formulating plans for the park. These stressed road improvements, encouraging tourism facilities within reach of the average American, and setting out a strategy for the repatriation of the more than 16,500 acres that were still in private hands. Some of these homesteaders grazed their livestock and shot wildlife on their property "without regard to the national park surrounding their land."[68] In years of World War I, the military encouraged a continuation of grazing activity as helpful for the provisioning of troops.[69]

On the Canadian side, no exclusive grazing rights were to be granted to ranchers, but those closest to the park were, in fact, given preference, leading to charges of favouritism and lack of regulation enforcement.[70] By 1918, Chief Warden H. E. Sibbald felt the situation required the appointment of a warden as "Grazing and Timber Inspector" who would have "full authority to deal with the ranchers." R. C. McDonald was appointed to enforce the regulations which allowed for a maximum of 3,000 head of cattle in the park. This attempt to keep a close record was "a failure." In 1919, a newly appointed warden expressed the view that the park was severely overgrazed: "the result is that all the winter range for the elk and deer has been badly eaten off" and that once domestic stock entered an area, the wild game tended to disappear.[71] Such observations were confirmed in 1925 when M. O. Malte, Chief Botanist of the National Herbarium, came to Waterton to undertake a study of conditions in the park. He compared his observations with those he had made earlier in 1911. It was his opinion that, while the upland zones were relatively unchanged, the lowlands had been greatly reduced in complexity owing to overgrazing.[72] Malte's report represented one of the earliest efforts at Waterton to introduce scientific observation into park land management.

Land-based resources have not been the only strength of the Waterton country. The fisheries of the many lakes and rivers provide perhaps the strongest link with the ancient past.[73] Europeans entering upon the scene in the last half of the nineteenth century were quick to remark upon the possibilities. The quality of the fishing around the Waterton Lakes was well known to the boundary survey parties of the 1860s and to "Kootenai" Brown, who in the later 1870s made part of his living from guiding activities. In his diary for July, 1861, British surveyor Charles Wilson remarked upon the delight he took in the fishing to be found around the main lakes. Survey party members normally survived on a staple of bacon and were always anxious for a break in the dietary routine.[74]

Fig. 36. Fishing camp at Waterton, c. 1897. Fishing in Waterton country has been important and productive for all time periods. Trout, pike, and whitefish have all been popular with anglers. Parks Canada.

We used to think we had capital fishing in the Cascade Mountains, but this year has quite beaten anything we have seen before; the streams are literally alive with the most delicious trout of all weights, from about 4 oz. to 2 1/2 lbs and they are the most ravenous fish I ever met with. The greatest catch was made by Dr. Lyall (our surgeon), who caught 9 dozen in about four hours.

H. R. MacMillan, a federal forest reserve inspector, observed in 1909 that "Char or Lake Trout weighing as much as 23 pounds are still caught in the Lakes" but "fly fishing has been nearly exhausted." He referred to "wasteful fishing" through the use of "set lines and dynamite" and that with the recent rise in popularity of the park the natural fish stock had "became depleted," one party being recorded as taking 500 fish in one day.[75] Artificial stocking programs, particularly of Brook trout, were introduced in the 1920s, based on fish supplied by the hatchery at Banff and by fry received from a hatchery in Glacier National Park.[76] Commissioner Harkin was moved to observe that "Waterton Lakes Park probably ranks first as a fishing resort."[77] This, it appears, was the popular consensus view, for the Dolly Varden (Bull trout) was selected as the most appropriate symbol for Waterton's automobile promotional bumper sticker (Fig. 36).

The pride in the local fishery prompted petitions from the Pincher Creek area and the local board of trade, received in Ottawa in 1924. These argued in favour of a local hatchery. Harkin was in agreement with the suggestion and sought the support of the influential local journalist, federal politician, and newly appointed Senator, W. A. Buchanan.[78] As a result, in 1926 Department of Fisheries officials approved a hatchery for Waterton. An important site prerequisite was a good supply of fresh water, and a location near the park entrance on Spring Creek was selected. Along with the main works, a handsome dwelling for the hatchery superintendent was designed by Oland and Scott, the builders of the Prince of Wales Hotel.[79] The new facilities opened in 1928.[80] Other facilities had to be constructed, so in 1929 tenders were let for construction of rearing ponds, troughs, an ice-house and garage.

From the very beginnings of the hatchery's existence, beaver activity caused problems along Spring Creek. Beaver dams slowed the water flow and tended to encourage silting in the sluices. This silt could be sufficient to kill the fry in the hatchery. A number of methods were employed to solve the problem, including live-trapping and beaver relocation, but both were time-consuming, costly, and ultimately not very effective. Relocated beaver tended to need a good deal of time to readjust to a new environment. In 1929, following an eradication program, the beaver nevertheless soon returned to the top of the sluices. One local historian observed that "the presence of the beaver continued to plague the hatchery until it was closed permanently."[81] This took place in 1960 when the National Parks Branch decided to consolidate fish hatchery operations at Jasper. The fish hatchery buildings at Waterton were then used for other purposes, but the rearing ponds were kept active for some years and were useful as holding areas for fish about to be transplanted to the lakes of Waterton or as displays for townsite visitors.

Whatever the technical difficulties associated with the hatchery, the program of stocking Waterton's lakes (and many other bodies of water on provincial lands in southern Alberta) was a success. Rainbow, Cutthroat, and Brook trout were the fish most sought by anglers. Some of the interior high altitude lakes such as Crypt, Lone, Lost, and Lineham, were regularly stocked as well, providing many visitors with excellent back-country angling.[82]

The Birth of the Waterton Townsite: 1895–1918

The earliest non-Native places of residence around the Waterton Lakes were those occupied by traders Fred Kanouse and "Kootenai" Brown. In his memoirs, Brown recalled starting a store with Kanouse "in a little log shack on the Lower Waterton Lake" on what later became his homestead. Their supplies were all hauled from Fort McLeod "by I.G. Baker bull teams."[83] In the quarter century after their arrival in southern Alberta, the rudimentary ways of the frontier settler were gradually supplemented by town life development. Fort Macleod, Pincher Creek, Mountain View, Cardston, and Cowley were some of the growing communities in the upper Oldman River Valley.[84] A seasonal townsite at the narrows between Middle and Upper Waterton Lakes gradually took on an identity after 1900. Unlike the present focus of the town, initial decisions by early settlers tended to favour locations on Middle and Lower Waterton Lakes in the vicinity of Brown's homestead. Such sites were better disposed towards communication with Fort Macleod, towards natural water power for small industry, and towards minimizing the difficulties of travel in winter, which always sets in early around the upper lake. Following the establishment of Waterton Lakes National Park in 1911, a farm evolved on the lands east and southwest of Lower (or Knight's) Lake, which produced crops for the park horses, thus helping defray certain public costs.[85]

Actual legal land disposition was a slightly different matter. A long-standing bit of Rupert's Land lore holds that the initials "HBC" on the Hudson's Bay Company flag stood for: "Here Before Christ." So it was in the Waterton Lakes area. As a function of the transfer of Rupert's Land to Canada in 1869, certain of the old lands were reserved for the company, and this included some property around the northern edge of the Waterton Lakes. Three parcels amounting to about a section and a half were under company control as late as 1926, at which time the Dominion Parks Branch completed negotiations for transfer to the park.[86]

The "oil boom" in Waterton, while short-lived, did provide a certain stimulus to the development of a townsite around Upper Waterton Lake. The first buildings in the present townsite date from unsuccessful drilling activity in the Cameron Creek area undertaken in 1903 by the J. B. Ferguson interests. Following

Fig. 37. John Hazzard's hotel. c. 1919. The first hotel built in Waterton was close to the lake in what has remained the commercial core of the townsite. The hotel is to the rear of the four men. Ernie Haug.

unsuccessful tests, Ferguson moved his outfit to the Cameron Creek fan (the location of the present townsite) and established a base of operations. The complex included a bunkhouse, blacksmith shop, kitchen, stable, and office.[87] The oil drilling experiments at the Cameron Falls and along Cameron Creek proved no more productive than had those at Oil City further up Cameron Creek.

Following the 1895 forest park reserve establishment, a parallel kind of shift in land use took place around the lakes, driven by the need to resurvey the agricultural lands and distinguish them from the forest reserve which allowed recreational activities and seasonal occupations. In 1905, some of the first photos of the future townsite were taken by H. R. "Bert" Riggall, a recently arrived immigrant from England, then homesteading in the Twin Butte area.[88] The townsite was opened for private commercial and cottage development in the spring of 1911, following the survey of 150 lots along the lakeshore carried out the previous November. Among the first buildings was a small hotel erected in 1911, by Mr. J. F. Hazzard.[89]

Fig. 38. Herbert "Bert" Riggall (1884-1959) came to the Twin Butte area from England in 1905. Rancher and wilderness outfitter, he left an important photographic legacy of early southern Alberta and the Waterton country. He was also a gunsmith and often repaired rifles for members of the Warden Service. This photo portrays one of his high country expeditions. Whyte Museum of the Canadian Rockies. CA 1925 (V.26).

Fig. 39. J. G. Brown in Sarah Luele Nielson's automobile. c. 1912. Parks Canada.

The coming of the automobile age was significant for Waterton, for it altered the one major circumstance that had kept the park's image somewhat subdued within the context of the larger national system: difficulty of access. That the first oil strike in Alberta should have taken place in park territory was highly symbolic of the growing car-dependency, which so quickly changed the character of North American parks and life. Automobile boosterism was not long in developing in the Waterton area.[90] "Kootenai" Brown's biographer has observed how much he loathed the new horseless carriages, even though he was quick to see the virtue of gasoline launches. Marie Rose Smith noted Brown was easily distracted by a pretty face, and it is probably owing to the persuasive abilities of an early resident of the townsite, journalist Sarah Luela Nielson, that a photograph exists showing Brown poised in a car. It is probably the vehicle which "Lu" Nielson had won in a contest, reportedly the first automobile in the townsite (Figs. 37-39).[91]

Years on the range could not easily be removed. In the photograph, Brown still appears to be sitting tall in the saddle. Despite his misgivings, Brown condescended to learn to drive. In 1911, he remained uncertain about the benefits of the automobile, but, two years later, he had adjusted to the inevitable. He wrote to his superiors stating, with some amazement, that officials of the Great Northern Railway Company of St. Paul, Minnesota, had come all the way to the park "in three days in an automobile."[92]

Institutional life made simple beginnings as well. In 1956, Bessie Annand recalled that "Archdeacon Middleton held his first regular services in Waterton Park in the summer of 1911." He used a wagon box for a pulpit and "preached to the worshippers seated on the grass on the spot where the RCMP barracks now stand."[93] In 1915, Arthur Harwood of Twin Butte, well regarded as a cook, both on the open range and among Waterton construction crews, was appointed as a police magistrate and also took on the mail-hauling contract. In 1920, he was appointed postmaster, a position he held until 1948.[94]

Towards New Park Conservation Policies

In the aftermath of World War I, two natural resource issues at Waterton demonstrated the need for the adoption of stronger and more coherent national park protection policies. The first concerned the pressure for impoundment of Waterton Lake for irrigation purposes. The second concerned the continuing removal of what were considered "predatory animals" from the park.

Owing to the severe drought conditions that prevailed between 1916 and 1922 in southern Alberta, Commissioner Harkin had to work to prevent the construction of a dam at the narrows between Upper and Middle Waterton Lakes. Such a structure was favoured by some of his own colleagues within the Reclamation Branch of the Department of the Interior. Such a project would have facilitated a comprehensive irrigation scheme for the adjacent prairies, some-thing favoured by many people on the land.[95] Support for the proposal was not surprising, given the impact of the severe drought of 1919. With dead cattle strewn all across the prairie in the aftermath of that summer, the pressure to open more humid lands to grazing was strong.

An influential Royal Commission Report on Economic Resources and Development had recently been tabled in the House of Commons. One of the commissioners was William Pearce, father of the 1894 North West Irrigation Act and now an employee and advocate for the CPR. Although a strong proponent of parks, Pearce also favoured the use of lakes and streams as sources of irrigation water.[96] Accordingly, in November of 1919, an engineering crew from the Reclamation Branch was sent to the narrows between Upper and Middle Waterton Lakes to assess the feasibility of a storage dam that would control and raise the level of the upper lake. Their report was favourable, and a dam construction project gained wide-spread support from the citizens and commercial interests of southern Alberta. In his defence of the project, P. H. Peters pointed out that (1) Southern Alberta required a sure irrigation supply for dry years; (2) residents had petitioned for the project; (3) Waterton had the capacity to irrigate a very large bloc of Alberta land; and (4) the cost of construction would be low.[97] These were all sound arguments, not easily cast aside.

Initially, Park Superintendent George "Ace" Bevan could see some advantages in the dam project, but Harkin urged caution and developed two strategies: a protracted policy war with his colleagues in the Department of the Interior; and pursuit of what may have been one of the first systematic public participation campaigns on behalf of a park position. The first strategy involved several lengthy commentaries on the Reclamation Branch's proposals.[98] The second was more difficult to achieve. The proponents were well organized along interest-group lines, and so Harkin sought, through Superintendent Bevan, to quickly muster an identifiable park clientele. Bevan was instructed to seek out alternative sites for the dam outside of the park. A further opportunity occurred when L. E. Dimsdale wrote a letter to the *Lethbridge Herald* in 1921 strongly promot-ing the park status quo. Bevan then sought petitions from those who were in agreement with the Dimsdale position.[99] The influential Dominion Surveyor and officer of the Alpine Club of Canada, A. O. Wheeler, weighed energetically into the debate in 1922, lecturing in Calgary and Edmonton on the meaning of the national parks. He made systematic use of newspapers and the new radio system and offered the services of the club in support of his opposition.[100]

An external factor ultimately shifted the focus of the debate. In 1922, United States park officials registered objections to the entire scheme because of the potential effects on the levels of Upper Waterton Lake on the United States side. An issue of the U.S. National Parks Service *Bulletin* for March 6, 1922, stated that the Waterton dam would do "irreparable damage to broad shores and magnificent valleys covering the floor of the Kootenay Valley at our end of the lake at a point that is the key of the entire future development northward of Glacier National Park."[101] Canadian surveyors from the Reclamation Branch were denied entry into Glacier National Park, and a reference to the International Joint Commission was being considered by the Americans.[102] This potential action, along with the public statements made by influential American conservationists such as Grinnell, persuaded the Reclamation Branch to withdraw its proposal. Amid the rains of 1923, the irrigation scheme dissolved. Projects of this kind were not proposed for another fifteen years.[103]

The second important issue of the 1920s concerned lingering nineteenth-century frontier attitudes towards wildlife. After World War I, a longstanding predator eradication program was still being vigorously pursued in the parks, only partially in response to pressures from the ranching community. Today, one notes with some surprise the names on the list of predators which were still current in Harkin's day, and which wardens had standing orders to eradicate.[104] Included on this list were "puma, wolf, coyote, lynx, bear (if nuisances), gopher, porcupine, eagle, hawk, woodpecker and blue heron (for eating geese eggs)." Uneasy with this list, which encouraged a number of abuses, including payment to warden's for the pelts taken, Harkin began to review recent warden practices. At one point he concluded: "we were in the winter time virtually paying them a salary to carry on a general trapping business."[105]

Influenced by discussions with such informed back-country men as Alberta provincial game warden Henri Rivière, Dominion Entomologist Gordon Hewitt, geological survey zoologist Rudolph Anderson, and Hoyes Lloyd, Chief

Ornithologist with the National Parks Branch, Harkin began articulating new policy much more favourable to the conservation of species.[106] In 1924, a new predator list was issued which saw many of the birds removed from the list. This was followed by a statement released by Harkin on Jan 31, 1925, which outlined a comprehensive philosophy of the conservation of species.[107] Not everyone was impressed by this new direction. A prominent Alberta rancher, A. E. Cross, was prepared to debate the implications of any scheme aimed at restoring the so-called balance of nature. The new policy direction was confirmed, however, and W. W. Cory released a new statement concerning the status of predators in the national parks in May, 1925.[108] By 1928, the department had banned the use of traps by wardens and cancelled the right of wardens to retain the furs of predators for sale.[109] This all followed upon some eight years of different approaches to coyote eradication by wardens and deputized locals. In the early 1920s, for example, nine ranchers and one wolf hunter, Henri Rivière, had been made honorary wardens. In the 1922-23 season, 118 coyotes were killed by ranchers and 22 by wardens.[110] By the time Harkin approved the new list, some observers were making connections between past predator policy and a developing elk problem (Fig. 40).

Continuing policy review at the national level in the United States and Canada, indicated that official attitudes in both countries were in harmony. By 1930, both countries had revised their attitude towards predators in the parks.[111] It took some years to consolidate this non-consumptive view of wildlife in the two national park systems, but the actions taken by Harkin and his associates were fundamental to that process.[112]

Harkin's battles in the 1920s for more effective park management policies represented a shift towards the concept of national parks as sanctuaries. His task in Waterton was compounded by the area's on-going role as a focus for commercial activity, including grazing, oil and mineral exploration, logging, and sport fishing. All of these activities were accommodated within loose policies, first outlined in 1887, which held that parks and reserves served commercial as well as recreational interests.[113] The recreational opportunities offered by the park after World War I became increasingly linked with the townsite, and the main appeal of the townsite was its relationship with scenic waters (Fig. 41).

Fig. 40. Members of the Waterton Park and Warden statff. c.1920-24. From left to right: Andrew Bower, warden, J. C. "Bo" Holroyd, warden, uncertain, L. S. "Mac" McCallister, (a future warden, probably working as a stock rider at this time), and Steven Harwood, mechanic. Parks Canada.

Fig. 41. Looking at the the townsite from the east from Sopha Mountain. c. 1920. T. J. Hileman. Glenbow Archives, Calgary. NB 32-1.

The lengthy negotiations conducted during the 1920s concerning the transfer of land and natural resource ownership and administration from Ottawa to the prairie provinces came to a conclusion in 1930.[114] Part of these negotiations had concerned the role to be played in the future by national parks policy and which policies should prevail with respect to the control of water rights in the parks. The scope of the debate went back to 1919 when a draft for a new National Parks Act had first been produced. The early promoter of parks, William Pearce, had in the meantime altered his loyalties somewhat on becoming an employee of the CPR and a strong proponent of southern Alberta development. He now favoured even greater public control of water resources for the general economic good.[115] His main adversary became J. B. Harkin of the Dominion Parks Branch. The latter staunchly defended an extension of the authority of the Parks Branch over resources under its jurisdiction. Harkin had his work cut out for him for his advocacy put him up against a number of Albertans who held contrary views concerning the desirable scope of powers to be given to national parks. Included in this group of Albertans was R. B. Bennett, M.P., the man destined to become prime minister in 1930. The new National Parks Act came into effect in 1930, the same year as Bennett's political victory, as did the Natural Resource Transfer Agreement. As a part of the process, previous federal park legislation was codified and given new form and powers.[116]

Post-War Tourism and Expansion of the Townsite: 1918-1930

The architectural legacy of the old prairie frontier in southern Alberta started to disappear rapidly after World War I. Around Waterton, the process started in 1919 when fire swept through the log village of Oil City on Cameron Creek. In the townsite proper, a number of other older buildings were lost to fire in the 1920s. What replaced them often reflected a certain pioneer rusticity, but there was also a trend towards greater individuality, as befitted a growing summer tourist community. Reflected in this "roaring twenties" attitude were certain strong expressions of alpine architecture of which the Prince of Wales Hotel was merely the most flamboyant. Randomness was being replaced by a certain sense of order in the planning and architectural sense.

At the onset of war in 1914, developments in the Cameron Creek fan on the west side of Upper Waterton Lake were few, but, in 1918, a second survey of 80 villa lots was prepared. There was nothing that could be mistaken for a formal "town plan" in the early 1920s, but certain broad zoning guidelines were put in place, enforced at the discretion of the park superintendent. In 1919, for example, lots 1 to 9 in Block 26 had been reserved for official departmental purposes. The new lots were not thrown open until 1921, providing new lease opportunities for those who wished to build a seasonal camp or cottage. The delay can be attributed to the rise of the irrigation lobby in those years and the flooding of the townsite that would have resulted from any proposed dam across the narrows between Upper and Middle Waterton Lakes. Superintendent Bevan, wisely chose to curtail new lot leases and the issuing of building permits until this question was resolved.

This freeze on development was a considerable frustration to Canon Samuel H. Middleton who, since 1915, had been attempting to finance the development of a church and school in the townsite for the people of the Blood Indian Reserve where he was active as a clergyman and educator at St. Paul's School.[117] The slowdown in development was also of more general concern to national park administrators. "Tourist revenues were a primary source of justification for national parks, and Waterton was clearly a weak link within the system before 1923."[118] As part of a general reorganization, Bevan had been appointed as park superintendent in 1919. He subsequently devoted much time to promoting new

Fig. 42. Children in playground at Waterton. Parks Canada.

development in the townsite. New cottage lots were surveyed under his direction, and a sawmill operation established to facilitate building activity. New administrative facilities were also built, including a work camp and staff dormitory above Linnet Lake, playground facilities for children, and a new park headquarters building on a lake front lot in the townsite (Fig. 42).

Waterton townsite underwent a considerable building boom in the 1920s. The resident population expanded from a mere handful in 1921 to about 300 persons.[119] Many lots were taken up and buildings put in place according to the national park leasing rules. A prominent cottage-owner was the politician and journalist William A. Buchanan, a steady defender and proponent of the park.[120] The building boom led to a shortage of cottage lots facing the lake. C. M. Walker was instructed to begin further surveys in 1924, and, by 1926, a new plan for Waterton was completed.[121] Some of the support facilities that had grown up alongside the vacation tents and dwellings included hotels and rooming houses, a town campground with shelters, the dance hall, a swimming pool, community house, restaurants, food services, and a town garage (Fig. 43).[122]

Many of these post-1923 developments in the townsite may be viewed in the context of an initiative taken in the Ottawa headquarters, where an internal unit known as the Town Planning Division was established in 1921. Subsequently known as the Architectural Division, the staff members exercised a tight control

Fig. 43. W. B. Foster residence. Parks Canada.

on design standards for new park buildings. Liverpool-born William D. Cromarty (1884-1960) joined the Department of Interior as director of the new division in 1921. A talented architect, he had been associated earlier with the University of Alberta. He was brought onto the scene at Waterton in 1924 in order to guide the general plan of development for the townsite, and he served as acting park superintendent between 1925 and 1929 in order to supervise implementation. Even though Cromarty "inherited a townsite plan" in 1924 "he imposed a series of zones upon it." In this way, "commercial development was channelled onto Waterton, Mount View and Windflower Avenues."[123] Thus, "the development of new facilities at Waterton Lakes" became some of the "first major priorities for this unit."[124] Architectural motifs for buildings were devised during his tenure and some of the parks most attractive new buildings were designed by Cromarty personally.[125] One such design was prepared for Walter B. Foster on Evergreen Avenue (Fig. 44).[126]

There were other factors influencing design in the closing years of the decade. Some of the new buildings reflected contemporary changes in the building trades in which brick was starting to replace wood. Some outstanding designs were executed in which wood craftsmanship was mixed with half-timbered gable treatments and stone. An attractive stone and half timbered dwelling accommodation for the Royal Canadian Mounted Police

Fig. 44. 303 Evergreen. c. 1927. Parks Canada.

Fig. 45. Our Lady of Mount Carmel. Roman Catholic Church. c. 1930. Before 1925, Oblates from Pincher Creek occasionally visited Waterton. In 1925, Bishop John Kidd of Calgary, initiated a project for establishment of a church which was completed by 1929. Parks Canada.

was added to the townsite in 1928. This handsome house still retains much of its original character.

Religious sentiment and the attractions of the Waterton Lakes coalesced early in the century. Adherents of the Church of Jesus Christ of Latter-Day Saints (or Mormon Church) became regular patrons of the park after 1900, sometimes using the park for large outdoor gatherings. When, following ten years of careful construction, the long-promised temple in Cardston was dedicated in 1923, a large contingent of guests visited Waterton townsite, where they were hosted by Luela Nielson at her cottage, one of the first in the vicinity of Cameron Falls.[127] In the beautiful "Telestial Room" in the new temple, art murals, executed by Edwin Evans of Utah, portray various wilderness themes, including Cameron Falls in the Waterton townsite.[128] Members of other faiths added churches to the townsite. All Saints' Anglican Church was erected in 1928. This was followed by the attractive log Roman Catholic Church built in 1929 by J. and B. Morris (Fig. 45).[129]

The main architectural event of the 1920s was clearly the construction of the Prince of Wales Hotel. On the books of the Great Northern Railway since 1913, the project came and went in different forms until Louis Hill finally made a firm decision. The contract was an encore for the builders, Oland and Scott of Lethbridge, who were still basking in praise for their completion of the much-admired Waterton dance hall in 1926.[130] Architectural drawings had been prepared for the hotel earlier in that same year by Great Northern Railroad architect Thomas D. McMahon – plans which outlined a much more extensive structure than the one actually completed.[131] The decision to proceed with the building of the Prince of Wales Hotel was taken in August by Louis Hill, president of the Great Northern since 1907, having succeeded his father, James J. Hill. The board members of the Great Northern were aware that their other hotel facilities in Glacier National Park had become "saturated" and that a natural extension of their market lay just to the north in Waterton Park. They were also aware that by opening this new hotel, their American patrons would have a place to repair in order to escape the restrictions of U.S. prohibition laws.[132] The striking new alpine-style hotel opened in July, 1927, some two months behind schedule, but remarkable enough given the frequency of the work-order changes made by the owners. In the words of one student of the building "the principle man-made difficulty arose from the personality of Louis Hill."[133] When the hotel opened, it imparted to Waterton some of the flavour of the larger mountain parks to the north, more favourably located on the transcontinental railways. For the builders, Oland and Scott, Mr. Hill's frequent changes of mind represented serious constraints, given the shortness of the desired deadline, the difficulties of site access, and the considerations that the architect had to give to high winds off Waterton Lake. On occasion, these were known to rise as high as 130 kilometres per hour. J. B. Harkin has been at pains to point out these difficulties to Hill in 1925.[134] The designers worked with such wind velocities in mind, and the finished structure had considerable flexibility at the top. The late request for peaked dormers, as a change order, might have been tolerable, but then Hill decided to add two more stories after building construction was well under way. The building season in the fall of 1926 was very wet, and high winds forced the standing frame of the building off its foundations by about 20 centimetres. Getting the frame realigned was very difficult, and some permanent imperfections were sustained. Finishing carpenters had many problems to contend with as a result of the shifted frame (Plate 4).[135]

The completed hotel seemed to please most people, nevertheless. As a gesture toward its Canadian location, Louis Hill had passed through Winnipeg in order to purchase furnishings for the hotel. The interior featured Native American pictograph motifs. More in keeping with the exterior, however, the waitresses wore Alpine costumes. By many accounts, the new hotel represented the "largest frame building in Alberta."[136]

As an adjunct to the new hotel, the Great Northern Railway moved to improve the quality of boat excursions available on Upper Waterton Lake. The sleek motor launch *The International* was built at the American end of the lake at Goat Haunt Landing and was launched in 1927 for the convenience of those at the new hotel, as well as other park visitors. The craft was one of several that plied the lakes of Waterton-Glacier country, built for Great Northern Railway by J. W. Swanson.[137] *The International*, with its 200 passenger capacity, is still in operation (Fig. 46).

Outside of the townsite, there were other forms of architectural expression, associated with recreation and sport fishing. In 1921, William Thompson, golf professional at the Banff Springs Hotel, laid out the first nine holes of a course at Waterton Lakes. He selected an area on an open bench south of Pass Creek and

Fig. 46. *The International* was launched in 1928 by Canadian Rockies Hotel Ltd., a subsidiary of the Great Northern Railway. It is still in operation as the main tour excursion boat on Upper Waterton Lake, plying between Waterton townsite and Goathaunt Landing in Glacier National Park. T. J. Hileman. Glenbow Archives, Calgary. NB 32-17.

east of Crandell Mountain.[138] Given the drying nature and frequency of the chinook winds and the lack of water supply, the greens in these early years consisted of smooth oiled sand.[139] The attractive and rustic clubhouse, built in 1924, was expanded in 1929, but lost to fire in 1953. The golf course itself was extended to 18 holes as part of the relief projects of the 1930s (Fig. 47).[140]

Another important addition was the fish hatchery complex, opened in 1928 at the mouth of Spring Creek on the northern edge of the park. This was another project completed by Oland and Scott, with carpentry by Sandy Dunn.[141] While much transformed, these buildings of the 1920s did much to turn Waterton townsite into an attractive service centre. The automobile was slowly pushing development towards more diverse forms of park access.[142] With the sudden economic crisis of 1929, the mood supporting expansion slowly gave way to one more akin to retrenchment.

Fig. 47. Waterton Golf Course, mid-1930s. The original nine holes were laid out by William Thompson, the Golf Professional at Banff. Expansion to eighteen holes occurred in the 1930s as a relief project. The rustic club house burned down in 1953. Parks Canada.

Fig. 48. Waterton Fish Hatchery. This complex was opened in 1928 following several years of advocacy by local angling associations and promotion by Senator W. A. Buchanan. Located at the northern boundary of the park, it was built by the firm of Oland and Scott, the builders of the Prince of Wales Hotel. Fish stocking programs were popular in Alberta in these years, but today ecological arguments have generally prevailed against continuing such activity. National Film Board of Canada.

Plate 1. Chief Mountain. This great massif has been a landmark for centuries to overland travellers and also an important sacred site to Native peoples. The peak often appeared on early maps as "The King." It is also a sacred site and has great religious significance for the Native peoples of the region. Geologically, it is the most visible expression of the phenomenon known as the "Lewis Overthrust." Photo: Sophie Hicken. Lethbridge.

Plate 2. Entrance, Boundary Pass, from the East by James Madison Alden (1834-1922). This New Englander went west during the goldrush of 1849. He was attached as an artist to the American Northwestern Boundary Survey of 1857-60 and executed this watercolour in present-day Waterton Lakes National Park in 1860. James Madison Alden. Glenbow Collection, Calgary, Canada.

Plate 3a. This large biface was found at the Emerald Bay Site, an extensive stratified campsite occupied for at least 7,000 years. Bifacially flaked tools are common throughout the archaeological record, but it is less common to find one notched so that it can be hafted to a shaft. The clear chalcedony used to make this tool is one of a wide and colourful range of lithic materials found in the Waterton archaeological record, derived from quarry sources in British Columbia, Montana, and the Dakotas.

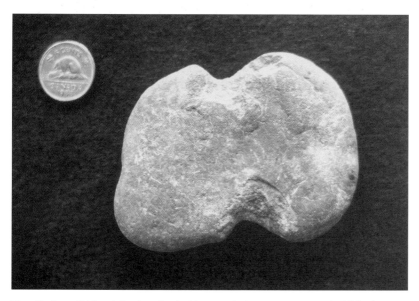

Plate 3b. Stone fishing sinker found at the Narrows site between Upper and Middle Waterton Lakes. This artifact demonstrates the longevity and importance of subsistence fishing by ancient cultures active in Waterton country. Parks Canada.

PHOTO BY HILEMAN

6505   WATERTON LAKES, PRINCE OF WALES HOTEL, WATERTON LAKES NATIONAL PARK, ALBERTA, CANADA

Plate 4. Prince of Wales Hotel. 1927. Post Card. Canadian Rockies Hotel Co. c.1927. Author's Collection.

Plate 5. Pat Bad Eagle, Peigan Indian (approximately 60 years old at time of portrait). Annora Brown. Glenbow Collection, Calgary, Canada.

Plate 6. Waterton Lakes, Alberta. Annora Brown. Glenbow Collection, Calgary, Canada.

Plate 7. Waterton in winter. Parks Canada.

Plate 8. Going-to-the-Sun Road. The road, completed in 1932, is currently at the centre of important planning discussions, owing to the great costs involved in maintaining such a high-level route under greatly expanded tourism demand. Graham MacDonald.

Plate 9. The Waterton Natural History Association has been active since the early 1980s as a friends-of-the-park group. As well as sponsoring projects, the WNHA operates a shop that sells park-related materials and a selection of high-quality souvenirs.

Chapter Four

Waterton During the Years of Depression and War: 1930-1945

The years from 1890 to 1930 were remarkable ones for the middle and financial classes in both the United States and Canada. Despite ups and downs and the dislocations of World War I, both countries were marked by economic expansion and a growth in international prestige. A spirit of financial optimism prevailed in the financial capitals of North America in the last half of the 1920s, although one may recall Desmond Morton's observation that the "roaring twenties" looked "a lot less like paradise to working people."[1] In Canada, this optimism of market capitalism translated into steady pressure from the western prairie premiers to carry through the federal-provincial negotiations aimed at turning control of crown lands and natural resources, then under Ottawa's authority, over to the provincial capitals. This issue had been festering since the creation of Alberta, Saskatchewan, and Manitoba. A close student of these negotiations observed that "Like the siege of Troy, the last phase of the 'Natural Resources Question' had taken almost exactly ten years."[2] The transfer process was significant for national parks, for once Dominion Crown lands were under the control of the western provinces, new park establishments would become much more cumbersome to achieve. Consolidation of policies and legislation on behalf of the national parks was considered pressing in Harkin's mind. The final passage of the Natural Resources Transfer Act and the National Parks Act in 1930, coincided with changes in political power in Ottawa, one in which the Conservative Party under R. B. Bennett, replaced MacKenzie King's long-serving Liberals. Despite the financial shock-waves of 1929, neither the departing government nor its replacement was prepared to suggest the great upward surge of financial prosperity was over. The transfer of resource control to the western provinces seemed to bode well.

In the Waterton-Glacier country, there were resourceful personalities who wanted to give the automobile age a boost through a positive reinforcement of the image of the great parks in the border zone. Foremost among these were Canon S. H. Middleton, William A. Buchanan, and Dr. J. S. Stewart, M.P. for Lethbridge.[3] The Prince of Wales Hotel had already been completed and the great Going-to-the-Sun Highway on the Montana side was well underway. The prospects for enhanced international tourism through road construction looked encouraging. An appropriate diplomatic gesture was required.

Establishment of the Waterton-Glacier International Peace Park

One of the sustaining myths of modern Canadian-American relations concerns the notion of an "undefended border" between the two nations. Since the demise of the American-based Fenian raids in the 1860s, there has been a good deal to support the myth. Canadians and Americans have long displayed a preference for economic rather than military warfare, punctuated by occasional attempts at fostering "free trade." People living in the border zones, however, have often set their own economic and social agendas, regardless of shifting fashions of political policy in Ottawa and Washington.

Complementing this "hands-across-the-border" way of life along the 49th parallel, international institutions and legislation have been designed with a view to accommodating and resolving resource disputes in the border zones. The most significant of these has been the International Joint Commission founded in 1909. This body, as we have already seen, helped resolve the dispute over the proposed Waterton Narrows Dam.[4] Park and wildlife lands, the requirements of migratory birds, and the politics of international fish stock were obvious foci for joint international diplomacy and action in the first decades of the century.[5]

The so-called "Progressive Era" in the United States produced yet another new type of institution in the early years of the century, one which sought to secularize the idea of good works. The faith displayed in the economic system by its most successful practitioners spawned a different approach to collective social service, one based on the free association of businessmen bound by certain stated principles. The Rotary Club, dating from 1905, was the first of these now-large service clubs to be founded. Paul P. Harris, a Chicago attorney, sought to foster the "ideal of service" as a suitable ethic for modern business and the professions and to promote this ideal through an international connection of the like-minded. The name "Rotary" was adopted because the meetings were held in rotation at different offices of the membership. In 1912, the name became the International Association of Rotary Clubs, and in 1922 the present name – Rotary International – was adopted.[6] The branches, as well as those of other similar organizations, grew rapidly, many taking root in smaller centres in rural areas. It was the natural kinship of the clubs in southern Alberta and Montana that allowed them to become an important force with respect to the large national parks contiguous with each other at the international border.

Canon Samuel Middleton of Cardston was an energetic Anglican Clergyman living among the Mormons, a teacher on the Blood Indian Reserve, a Waterton Lakes enthusiast, a proponent of the British Empire, and a Rotarian.[7] The population of Cardston had long been users and promoters of the Waterton Lakes. Cardston presumably stood to be a commercial beneficiary of the new Going-to-the-Sun highway, which would soon bring Montana tourists into southern Alberta in great numbers. Hence, the Cardston Rotary Club initiated a meeting of several regional clubs from Alberta and Montana at the Prince of Wales Hotel in July of 1931 to strike an international committee for general purposes of the Rotary. The Cardston Club sent Canon Middleton, J. E. Low and J. Y. Card as representatives. At this first "Annual good will meeting" discussion focused on many "visionary topics," the principal of which was the desire to foster "a world-wide International Peace Movement." A resolution was put forth and adopted that "the proper authorities be petitioned to commence negotiations to establish the two large national parks of the border zone as a permanent International Peace Park, which shall be definitely set aside for this laudable purpose."[8] In the view of one close student of Peace Park history, it would be inappropriate to credit any one individual with the concept; yet Canon Middleton "emerged as the key personality in the promotion of the peace park idea over the next quarter of a century."[9] Thomas Davis, the president of the Rotary Club, played an important role as well, and a plaque near the Prince of Wales Hotel honours his contribution.

Following acceptance of the resolution it then fell to elected representatives from each country to develop the idea in the political arena. In Canada, the task of negotiation fell to Brigadier-General J. S. Stewart, M.P. In the United States, the Honorable Scott Leavitt of the Montana House of Representatives took up the cause, and he introduced a draft bill into the House of Representatives in late 1931. In January, 1932, Commissioner Harkin received a draft copy of the bill in Ottawa. Premier R. B. Bennett was supportive but took the view that Canada would not prepare parallel legislation until the United States had passed its bill into law.[10] Towards the end of February, 1932, the United States Committee on Public Lands completed a favourable report on the concept. O.D. Skelton of the Canadian Department of External Affairs had already confirmed to U.S. authorities that Canada would be prepared to reciprocate with similar legislation.[11] In late March, the bill was recommended by the Lands Committee for passage, and in April it moved to the Senate for review.[12] A minor tempest in a teapot then delayed matters. Politicians started to complain that this new initiative was stealing thunder from an on-going effort to establish an International Peace Garden in the Turtle Mountains along the Manitoba-North Dakota border. Since efforts had been underway for some time on behalf of the Peace Garden, certain individuals, including the Liberal member from Saskatchewan, W. R. Motherwell, took exception to the timing of the Waterton-Glacier proposal. Members of the peace movement were threatening to go to war! Motherwell, supporting Senator Frazer of North Dakota, and the Manitoba Member for Souris, E. F. Willis, contended that "You cannot have the whole boundary line seeded down with peace parks."[13] It was an odd but short-lived protest. In the end, the forces of opposition had their say, but quickly came to realize that further opposition served no good international purpose, and the complaint was dropped.

Following passage of the bill in April of 1932 in the United States, the Canadian version quickly moved through parliament. In Ottawa, Bill 97 – An Act Respecting the Waterton Glacier International Peace Park – had been in draft form since February.[14] It was passed into law in June, 1932. Robert Scace has

Fig. 49. Prince of Wales Hotel, 1936. This photo shows the celebrations for the establishment of the International Peace Park in 1936. Celebrations were delayed four years owing to depression and political conditions. Canon Middleton on balcony with other dignitaries. In 1993, the hotel was recognized as a National Historic Site. National Archives of Canada. PA58935.

observed that "It is remarkable that during a period of profound economic depression the two governments should introduce and so quickly pass legislation on a matter to which no urgency could be attributed."[15]

With the laws on the books, attention now moved to appropriate forms of dedication and planning for the future. There were in fact two dedication ceremonies. The first took place at the Glacier Park Hotel, Montana, in June 1932. The Canadian ceremony was delayed for four years owing to the depressed tourist trade, which caused the Prince of Wales Hotel to close down in 1933, and then by the federal election of 1935, which would have prevented politicians from attending a dedication in that year. A ceremony was arranged at the hotel in July of 1936 (Fig. 49). In the intervening years, Canon Middleton had become anxious to see some kind of recognition accorded to "Kootenai" Brown. When the ceremony did take place, it was presided over by Alberta Lieutenant Governor W. L. Walsh, and a plaque and cairn for Brown were dedicated in the townsite.[16]

These commemoration initiatives had been eagerly sought by men of good will but also by men who still had something to lose. The optimism that drove them was steadily giving way to pessimism among a broader cross-section of North America's working population. The passage of the International Peace Park legislation coincided with the worst economic crisis in memory. Before the crash of 1929, North Americans were expecting a continued rise in prosperity in which it was assumed that increasing percentages of the working classes would benefit. As late as December, 1928, President Coolidge could say openly that the country might "regard the present with satisfaction and anticipate the future with optimism."[17] The "twilight of illusion" did not come until the summer of 1929, when those relative few who understood the market began to comprehend that all was not well. As the market "came to be considered less and less a long-run register of corporate prospects" and more "a product of manipulative artifice," the speculator was "suddenly required to give it his closest, and preferably undivided attention."[18] For many, it was too late.

Just about everyone in North America underestimated the deep-rooted nature of the crisis, including the Canadian prime minister. Nearing the end of his electoral mandate in early 1930, Mackenzie King stated in the House of Commons, with too much force, that his government would not, with respect to the mounting depression, "give a single five-cent piece" in relief assistance to any provincial government that was not Liberal.[19] It was a statement that would come back to haunt him, and it was quickly seized upon by Calgary millionaire and politician Richard B. Bennett. He used this pronouncement to great effect in the 1930 federal election campaign and led his Conservatives to victory. In September, Bennett called a special session of parliament as a response to the mounting economic devastation. He asked parliament to grant $20 million "for relief of unemployment in constructing, extending or improving public works and undertakings."[20] This request would have consequences for development in many of the national parks across Canada. Meanwhile, the optimism that accompanied the transfer of natural resources to the provinces was suddenly compromised by the realities of the mounting depression economy. The high-minded hopes of the advocates of the International Peace Park need to be contrasted with the mounting demands for urban relief pressures, declining rural population in southern Alberta, and the strife in the coal mines of the nearby Crowsnest Pass, where violent labour protests and severe legal repressions were unfolding.[21] Indeed, for those who had been watching the southern Alberta scene carefully, a foreshadowing of the dislocations of the 1930s was noticeable in the dry "Palliser's triangle" portion of south-east Alberta. James Gray has remarked upon the disturbing features of the previous census returns, which implied that "the movement out of the border country became almost a stampede between 1921 and 1926." The 1926 census indicated that, in Alberta, farm abandonments for the last five years mounted to some 10,000, half of which were in divisions 3 and 5 in the border zone around Medicine Hat.[22] Ways of sustainable life in parts of southern Alberta were threatened well before the onset of the depression.

J. B. Harkin, was a proponent of the post-war optimism. He sensed a rosy future for the parks and an important role for them in the improved lives of the people, and indeed he had waxed eloquent and idealistic on the high purposes of the parks.[23] Through his publicity director, Mable B. Williams, he actively promoted the publication of guide books for intending tourists, many of whom would visit the parks of the future by car and excursion vehicle.[24] Automobile boosters and their clubs had been active on the prairies in the 1920s, and they could point to some victories. The Canadian government had built the Banff-Windermere Highway in 1923 as part of the deal with British Columbia for the establishment of Kootenay National Park. The United States government then set a new standard for high mountain travel with its development of the "Going-to-the-Sun" Highway in Glacier National Park after 1925.[25] Proposed completion of this outstanding scenic road gave southern Alberta tourism promoters renewed reason for requesting further improvements, for it seemed logical that there should be a more direct Canadian link with the Going-to-the-Sun route (Fig. 50). The deepening economic crisis improved prospects for such road developments in both countries, for they were seen as just the kind of labour-intensive enterprises ideal for government sponsorship in getting people back to work. Park roads and facilities would be greatly enhanced by relief labour provided under the unemployment and relief acts of 1932 in Canada, and Franklin Roosevelt's "New Deal" legislation of 1933 (Figs. 51-54).[26]

In Canada, the Bennett administration initiated a wide-ranging program of relief work camps across the land.[27] Two systems were in fact established: one operated by the Department of National Defence, and one by the National Parks Branch.

Fig. 50. Going-to-the-Sun Road. Plans for such a trans-mountain road had been in the air since 1910 and several routes were considered. U.S. National Park Engineer George Goodwin made surveys in 1918 which conformed fairly closely with the final route selection. Congress appropriated funds in 1924, and the road was completed in 1932. T. J. Hileman Glacier Natural History Association.

These two systems absorbed many provincial camps that had sprung up after 1930. The social conditions in the camps, the terms of employment, and the political motives behind the camps, have been matters of interest to historians.[28] At Waterton, we know that at least eight relief camps were in operation during the mid-1930s.[29] These were oriented towards single unemployed males, for the administration did not want to encourage an influx of entire families with the increased costs implied.[30] Wages in relief camps were normally twenty cents per day, the workers being provided with meals and accommodation.[31] The routine of the work camps across the country soon started to wear thin, and the workers dubbed themselves "the Royal twenty-centers."[32] Conditions across Canada were variable, and it appears the camps in the national parks were favoured over the National Defence camps. But the effect on the spirit was near universal. The words of one internee worked their way into the parliamentary record. "It is really the fact that we are getting nowhere in the plan of life – we are truly a "lost legion of youth" – rotting away for want of being offered a sane outlet for our energies."[33]

The general slowdown in the economy had curtailed private initiatives for tourism-related development in the national parks, but under the relief camp program much road-building, campground development, and other general park

Fig. 51. Shovel at work on Akamina Road construction. 1920s. Parks Canada.

Fig. 52. Relief Camp, Akamina Road. 1930s. Parks Canada.

Fig. 53. Piling stumps with gin pole, Akamina Highway, Mile 10. c. 1934. Parks Canada.

Fig. 54. Work on the Belly River Road. 1930s. Parks Canada.

improvements were undertaken. Park managers welcomed the possibilities afforded by the "lost legion of youth" in view of scarce budgets.[34] In Waterton, relief work proper commenced in 1931 when some 170 men were employed on various park improvements, including the main campground and additions to the golf course.[35] By 1932, there were two camps along the Akamina Highway in the southwest portion of the park. Work on the Akamina Road project had been underway since 1924, and this link was completed by relief labour in 1932 "resulting in a marked improvement to this popular thoroughfare."[36]

At least five work Camps were established in the southeast portion of the park from which work commenced on a project that was to greatly increase visitation to Waterton Park.[37] Clearing of the right-of-way for this important link with Glacier National Park began in 1932. In January, 1936, Superintendent Knight reported on the progress made in completing the new Belly River Road, also known as the Chief Mountain Highway. This new link between Waterton and the east side of Glacier National Park was opened to the public in the summer of 1936.[38] The road, which crossed through the Blood Timber Limit, established a more direct link with the Going-to-the-Sun Highway. Previously, tourists travelling from the United States had to take a circuitous route via Cardston in order to reach Waterton.

In addition to road clearing and building, relief labour was used in park-operated sawmills. In 1932, some 80,000 feet of lumber were processed at park-based mills.[39] Some of the camp names familiar from those days were McNeilly's camp at the mouth of the gorge on Cameron Creek, and Crandell Mountain Camp. The present campground located at the north end of Crandell Lake is a vestige of one of these old relief camps.[40] There were programs established for the youth of the country as well. The Conservation Corps sponsored camps along Blakiston Brook in which timber cutting and road clearing were the main activities.[41]

As the depression dragged on, work proceeded on the Red Rock Canyon (or Pass Creek) Road. Knight reported for 1935 that "a few improvements were carried out on the Park roads but new work was necessarily limited on account of shortage of funds."[42] Knight's 1936 reports evaluated the work done on the Akamina Road with the assistance of relief labour and indicated the social benefits provided by which work "was provided for fourteen persons with forty-four dependents, the total number assisted being fifty-eight."[43]

South of the border in Glacier, a parallel but very different process was underway. The new Democratic president, Franklin D. Roosevelt, had tallied seven million additional votes over his Republican opponent, Herbert Hoover. His "New Deal" Congress quickly passed the Federal Emergency Relief Act, which put money into the hands of states and municipalities for direct expenditure. By 1933, Roosevelt's main answer to unemployment came through establishment of the Civilian Conservation Corps (CCC) camps.[44] Between 1933 and 1942, many hundreds of young recruits worked at Glacier on various improvement projects.[45] There were striking psychological and practical differences between the American and Canadian approaches. In Canada, Prime Minister Bennett was a sincere but reluctant interventionist, warming to the task only towards the end of his mandate.[46] President Roosevelt, on the other hand, prodded by his Interior Secretary, Harold Ickes, quickly developed interventionism in his soul. Canadian relief efforts smacked of stop-gap measures, whereas Roosevelt saw the need to assault the depression with a genuine set of long-term programs, thought through carefully from top to bottom. The Canadian effort took men of all ages off the streets and isolated them as minimum wage earners, out of sight of the public, and often far from their families. Men were free to leave, but the overall image of punishment and disapproval seemed to hang over the Canadian camps.[47] Roosevelt aimed his efforts at the young unemployed to a much greater degree than did the Canadians. John Salmond contended that the president "brought together two wasted resources, the young and the land in an attempt to save them both."[48] There were strings attached to the American program: the young men were required to send twenty-five of their thirty dollar monthly earnings back to their families for their support. Immediately, the standard recruit could identify himself with being a breadwinner. The CCC operated in six month shifts so that new recruits were always being given a chance. Locals, with appropriate skills, were hired as work supervisors, partly for reasons of efficiency, and also to deflect local criticism of "outsiders" coming in to do local work at government cost. Other local opposition quickly faded when the local CCC programs were seen to be important stimulants to the surrounding economy. The military was involved in certain aspects of the program, providing one more element of community solidarity with unemployed youth.[49]

A comparison of CCC photographs with Canadian relief camp photos often demonstrates a strong contrast, one which might be described as the evoking of future possibility as opposed to the smell of defeat. The CCC was designed as a great adventure for the young, one in which full community support was sought. The spit and polish associated with Boy Scout outings and the Marines was not lacking in the American camps, as opposed to the badge of shame implicit in the Canadian programs. Many of the normal ingredients of American culture were tacked on, including the baseball diamond and education opportunities, even if the latter were not always carried out effectively at the field level.[50] While much important project work was completed in the Canadian park camps, there was a lack of this larger social direction. In time, considerations of cost seemed to be driving many decisions, with considerable wrangling going on between parks and military camp administrators.[51] The unifying hope driving Canadian policy was that the unemployed, if unseen for long enough, would finally disappear. In Glacier, Superintendent Eivind Scoyen pushed the CCC program to its limits throughout the early 1930s owing to its value in helping him get much needed work done, particularly in burned-over areas where lumber could be salvaged. His successor in 1933, Donald Libbey, was just as interested, but by 1942 the CCC was voted out of existence as war labour demand and other economic opportunities had rendered it redundant.[52]

The difference in the psychology of the relief camp approach was striking in the two countries. Until the early 1940s, there was generally no difficulty in finding recruits in America because of the positive attitude associated with the program. In Canada, the effort tended to succeed only because the unemployed and transient had few other options.[53] Indeed, the park camps in Canada were closed out by 1937. Waiser has noted that after that date "little time was lost removing the structures and clearing the sites." It was as if "the buildings were a blight on the landscape, and any reminder of them had to be wiped out."[54]

Daily Life in the Camps at Waterton

On February 20, 1933, the chief engineer at Banff, J. M. Wardle, sent to headquarters copies of correspondence and a petition from relief workers in Waterton, previously forwarded to General J. S. Stewart, M.P. The petition had raised a number of issues with respect to wages and conditions in the camps.[55] Subsequently, Wardle's office cooperated with Knight in undertaking a systematic inspection and review of the camps by way of response. Engineer C. M. Walker was instrumental in carrying out the review, and in his report of May, 1933, he found little substance to the kinds of complaints presented in the petition.[56] Some improvements of a general kind were initiated, however, and from photographs and official reports that were produced as part of the inspections carried out by the Banff Engineering Office, it is possible to gain an impression of what it was like to live and work in the park camps. From a report on the Akamina Road Project, for example, the basics of camp architecture, provisions, and routine was outlined as follows:[57]

1. Types of Quarters Provided: Tents with board floors, with stove in each tent.
2. *Meals:*
    Breakfast: Cereal, bacon and eggs, hotcakes, syrup, tea and coffee.
    Dinner: Soup, two kinds of vegetables, beef or pork, pies or puddings.
    Supper: Hot or cold meat, two kinds of vegetables, macaroni and cheese, cake, jam, pies.
3. *Beds:* Wooden bunks, two men to a bunk.
4. *Bedding:* Palliasse* and hay, three blankets per man.
5. *Heating:* Wood stove in each tent.
6. *Sanitation:* Each camp has a covered privy, chlorinated daily.
7. *Lighting:* Coleman lanterns and Cold Bals Strom lanterns.
8. *Recreation:* Reading matter and games were received for the camps through the good offices of the "Lethbridge Herald" and other people too numerous to mention.
9. *Provision for Commissary Supplies:* Each timekeeper has a commissary consisting of boots, rubbers socks, underwear, mackinaw coats, mitts, gloves, soaps, tobacco, writing paper, etc.
10. *First-Aid, Medical and Hospital Arrangements:* Each camp has a First Aid man. Dr. Giles is in charge of camps for medical attention, care of injuries, etc. A small bunkhouse at Headquarters has been made suitable for use as a Hospital.
11. *Additional Information:* All local relief workers reside in cottages within the townsite.

These standards were held up as the ideal, and undoubtedly they were not always achieved. The camps varied somewhat in their facilities, according to their

---

* A straw mattress

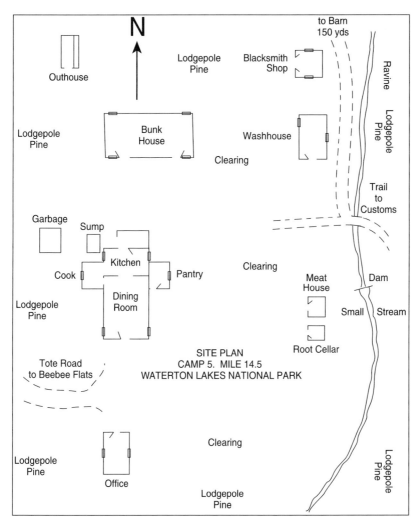

Fig. 55. Plan of a Relief Camp recorded by Frank Goble. Cardston, Alberta.

functions. In reply to a questionnaire in 1935, Superintendent Knight indicated that at Camp 2 "the men are in the permanent log buildings and the canvas has been moved to Camp 4." Buildings at Camp 2 included: a bunkhouse, a cookhouse, an office, a roothouse, blacksmith shop, wash house, a canvas stable, permanent latrines, and a small meat storage house (Fig. 55).[58]

Camp No. 1 in the Waterton Bridge area was the real hub of activity and co-ordination for the park camp program. C. M. Walker reported in February of 1933 that:[59]

The permanent buildings at this camp consist of a warehouse, office, hospital, washroom and root-cellar. With the exception of the hospital building (which by the way, is the frame office building erected during construction of the Waterton River Bridge three years ago) these buildings were quite satisfactory.

At about this time, C. K. LeCapelain, a national parks engineer at Banff (and later Waterton superintendent) took an interest in the adequacy of facilities at Camp No. 1. In late 1933, he argued that he thought it "advisable to erect a building at the Headquarters camp No. 1" in order to accommodate "men going to and from town and the further camps."[60] He noted also that:[61]

Last winter there was a tent camp at Camp No. 1 for some months which served the purpose of a stop-over place. After this was moved, the men in transit were accommodated in the hospital and storehouse which I think you will agree with me as not being advisable to do this winter. Mr. Walker during his visit to the Waterton Relief Camps commented adversely on the disorder of the hospital building, which I may say was due to the fact of it being at the time crowded with men in transit.

While the superintendent occasionally expressed an interest in having additional men to carry out more work, the number of labourers employed at Waterton, owing to its relative isolation, was not as great as at some of the other national parks. In 1933, J. B. Wardle remarked that:[62]

Fig. 56. Group kitchen under construction by relief labour, Waterton townsite campground in 1935. Provincial Archives of Alberta. 69.359/90.

On account of the small number of men in each camp, and the scattered
camps, it would be impossible to supply the same recreational facilities at
Waterton as at Riding Mountain or Prince Albert Parks. The men, however,
are supplied with sufficient reading material and games, such as checkers, to
keep them interested. The meals are uniformly good and well served.

These were desperate times for a large number of Canadians, and inevitably frictions developed in the camps, not just between internees but also between the men and the park administration.[63] The petition of early 1933 can be seen as a reflection of men much aggrieved by general circumstances more than by the immediate ones. A sympathetic humanity informs most of the correspondence of the park personnel charged with carrying out a difficult program under trying financial circumstances. In the end, a great deal of solid and lasting improvement was accomplished by these work forces, many of the fruits of which are silently acknowledged by modern tourists travelling today's park roads or when they use any number of recreational facilities (Fig. 56).[64]

Developments in Forest Communications

With the passage of the National Parks Act in 1930, the mandate for forest and wildlife protection was clarified and strengthened. By 1936, the remaining components of the Department of Interior had been parcelled out to a number of federal agencies and the old agency dismantled.[65] The wardens in the National Parks Bureau, who previously maintained a somewhat ambiguous place with respect to colleagues in some of the other bureaus, were now presented with a clearer work program, one that over-lapped much less with the duties of those in other land management agencies.

Adapting the developments in new communications technology to forest conditions in national parks had been an ongoing process since 1914 when telephone lines were first run from park headquarters to the various warden cabins.[66] A system of warden districts had been defined in Waterton by 1919 and, following adjustments to the park boundary in 1921, a network of cabins and communications was created and refined over the next thirty years. The plan of districts reflected the geographic realities for a given park. The cabins were placed where they might most effectively control general access by tourists or potential poachers. "From 1930 onwards a greatly expanded system of roads, trails and telephone lines helped improve communications between warden stations and park headquarters."[67] As early as 1937, Warden K. B. Mitchell discussed the possibilities of short-wave at the warden school session held in Banff that year.[68] A short-wave system was still some years away despite the cumbersome nature of existing arrangements. The Superintendent for Waterton reported in 1941:[69]

Telephone service was maintained as well as can be expected with our set-up. However, as reported to you before, the reception on our forest telephone system is not satisfactory; and it will take a major expenditure of possibly $1,000.00 to put it in good condition. During the summer months our system is overloaded when hooked up with that of Glacier Park and there is a loud alternating current hum due to the wire in the Townsite being on the electric light poles.

104

Reports such as these reveal that a good deal of energy had to be given over to telephone line maintenance and construction during the 1920s and 1930s.[70] For the parks staff, capitalizing on World War II advances in technology had to wait until the 1950s. The forest grid communication system was still in place in 1952, but after that date, the reworking of forest remote communications was rapid.

This re-tooling of forest communications went hand in hand with the progressive centralization of warden facilities in the townsites and the abandonment of the old district warden cabin system. This centralization gained momentum after the tabling of the *Glassco Commission Report on Government Organization* in 1962. The general recommendations of the Commission were reviewed by officials of the National Parks Branch, who then commissioned a special study on how the recommendations might best be applied to the parks service generally, and to the warden service particularly. The results of this study led to the study sessions carried out at Prince Albert Park under Jim Sime, which resulted in the reforming of warden duties and operations.[71]

Grazing and Irrigation

Several students of Alberta history have noticed that, for the agricultural community, the Great Depression of the 1930s really started in about 1917 when a number of drought years followed in succession.[72] As previously mentioned, the resulting economic dislocations induced a rash of farm abandonments and closures in the dry "Palliser Triangle" portions of Alberta, and this trend was reinforced by the stock market crash of 1929 and the advent of dustbowl conditions in the 1930s. Attempting to rationalize the unpredictability of drought conditions with the economics of providing a reliable water supply through irrigation combined into a recurring policy issue for local politicians in the years leading up to 1935.[73] James Gray concluded that the "whole face of Western Canada had to be radically altered."[74] Requirements of the farm and ranching economies needed to be rethought at all levels, and reinventing prairie economics became a major item on the provincial and federal political agendas. This process culminated in April of 1935 with the passage by the Bennett Government of the important Prairie Farm Rehabilitation Act.[75] Before that date, only the Mormon communities centred at towns such as Cardston, Stirling, and Raymond had fully accommodated themselves to the vagaries of the Palliser

Triangle's climatic conditions by means of irrigation, the cultural mastery of which had been the basis of their initial settlements in southern Alberta, as early as 1887.[76]

The Mormon irrigation communities were on the right side of post-1896 western development policy that favoured filling up much of the ranching landscapes with immigrant agriculturalists committed to mixed farming operations. Cattle remained an important part of the southern economy, but their care remained problematic in dry years. While rains has returned to southern Alberta in the last half of the 1920s, during the dry years of the 1930s, the border lands of Waterton must once again have resembled a land of plenty to stricken ranchers. As a concession to conditions of the drought, the park remained open to ranchers.

From the diary kept by Warden J. C. "Bo" Holroyd, we may learn some of the details of the daily routine of park grazing in these years. On May 15, 1933, he noted that he was "Counting cattle on Park for Jenkins Bros. and the McKenzie Bros." The Jenkins had "approximately 500 head" and "the McKenzie Bros. approximately 350 head." Exactly five years later he recorded that "J. S. Jacobs of Caldwell paid $56.00 for grazing fees for 15 horses, 40 cattle and permit."[77] Revenue generation was one of the advantages of granting grazing permits in those cash-strapped times. Between 1929 and 1942, fees generated from grazing were a substantial park revenue item.[78]

Although the new National Parks Act of 1930 had set a new tone for what was appropriate land use in the parks, local politics still counted for much. Under the new Prairie Farm Rehabilitation Act the first priorities had been to stabilize soil conditions and to encourage the digging of water dugouts on farm and ranch properties. These phases moved quickly after 1936. More problematic was the question of community pastures. The idea was to reclaim abandoned and marginal agricultural land by fencing and the seeding of good forage crops, thus providing a good communal resource. The idea was that the land assembled for such pastures would be assembled by the province and deeded back to Canada to be administered by the Prairie Farm Rehabilitation Administration (PFRA), centred in the various experimental farm stations in the West. This idea played well in Saskatchewan, but not in Alberta. Having finally obtained land and natural resource control from Ottawa in 1930, and incensed by Ottawa's disallowance of some of its economic reform legislation, the Social Credit administration of

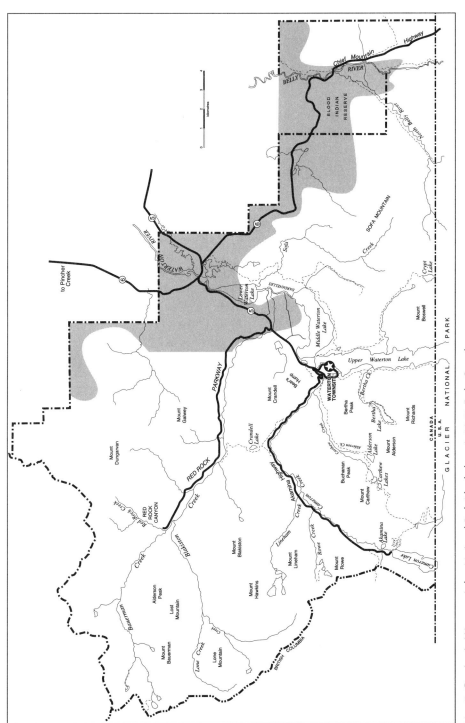

Map 5. Grazing in Waterton Lakes National Park (shaded area). 1947. Parks Canada.

William Aberhardt was in no mood to start handing the land back.[79] From the federal point of view, sites such as Waterton Lakes National Park, already under Ottawa's control, provided an opportunity to demonstrate, not just a good neighbour policy in difficult times, but also elements of the community pasture idea without raising political conflict. The question of grazing was not put to rest in Waterton until 1947 when grazing privileges were ended (Map 5).[80]

Water diversions and impoundments developed by the Alberta Irrigation Company in the early years of the century, using the St. Mary's River, had not become a political issue with Montana, for there were no discernable cross-boundary effects.[81] Concerns that the Americans might themselves, in the late 1890s, divert the upper reaches of the St. Mary River for purposes of irrigation in Montana proved groundless, perhaps owing to the already well-advanced projects of Galt's mining, rail, and irrigation schemes in southern Alberta.[82] As early as 1915, the Province of Alberta had passed its Irrigation Districts Act, which "encouraged the proliferation of small irrigation districts in the hands of the local users."[83] This legislation was in no way offensive to American water interests. The 1923 Canadian proposal to dam the Waterton Lakes, as we have seen, was another matter. By that time, the International Joint Commission had been long established as a mechanism for the mediation of such projects where cross-border effects were implied.

It had taken some time for both settlers and the corporate sponsors of prairie agriculture to discern the appropriate scale of land units such as might support the costs of irrigation.[84] With the establishment of the Eastern Irrigation District in Alberta in 1935, ambitious plans to enhance irrigation in the dry belt of southern Alberta were advanced, involving greater coordination of the St. Mary's, Waterton, and Belly Rivers, all of which had their headwaters in the United States.[85] Under the new PFRA program, these plans were reinforced by A. E. Palmer of the Lethbridge Agricultural Research Station.[86] By the early 1940s, proposals to employ the waters of the Belly and Waterton Rivers for irrigation on areas north and east of the park were in circulation.[87] These appeared to be straightforward initiatives without serious potential for land use conflict.

The proposals were put on hold during the war years, but they came to the fore quickly after 1945. They involved, in part, the systematic tapping of the waters of the Waterton and Belly Rivers starting at points well outside of the park boundary. In a near total reversal of what had taken place in 1923, the United States raised objections of a much different order. The irrigation proposals on the table had no implications for the water levels in Upper Waterton Lake, and all of the proposed engineering work was to influence purely Canadian river flows. American interests, seemingly unconcerned with the mandate of Glacier National Park, sought a ruling from the International Joint Commission on the grounds that some compensation was owing to the Americans for the use of waters that had originated in the United States. The International Joint Commissioners received an official Reference in 1948. Quite logically, the commissioners charged the Americans to demonstrate just how they might possibly make use of the U.S. portion of Upper Waterton Lake and the sources of the Belly River for purposes other than those currently associated with park use. Engineering studies were mounted on the U.S. side, which attempted to show that waters might be run out through a tunnel in one of the surrounding mountains in Glacier National Park, a proposal that was then shown to be geologically quite unfeasible.[88] The American position fell apart as the Chief Engineer for the United States, under cross-examination, was forced to conclude that the Americans had never made use of the source waters and never could. The American and Canadian representatives never did come to any formal agreement. Instead, the IJC Reference was allowed to die a natural death, facilitated by its own lack of coherence. The commissioners finally took the position that there could be no basis for a claim. On the Alberta side, the proposed irrigation works, sponsored by the Prairie Farm Rehabilitation Administration, went ahead on the lower Waterton and Belly Rivers, the large associated St. Mary reservoir being completed in 1956.[89]

Resolving the Confusion Over Blood Indian Timber Limit "A": Treaty Seven and Native Lumber Rights

Since the expansion of the boundaries of Waterton National Park in 1914, the park map included on its eastern side a clearly distinguished land unit within the park, identified as Timber Limit "A," associated with the Blood Indians who lived northeast of the park on one of Canada largest reserves. In the midst of the depression years, a legal decision on the proper status of this land was achieved, although it would be another thirty-five years before all the legal implications were finally resolved.

In 1877, the "Blackfoot Treaty" (Treaty No. 7), to which the Bloods were signatories, made reference to the provision of wood and water for the Indian peoples as a consideration in their selection of reserve lands. A close student of the history of the Blood Indians has described the early circumstances surrounding the establishment of their reserve on the eve of the settling of southern Alberta by ranchers and settlers. This early history is in part the story of several rounds of negotiations between Indian Commissioner Edgar Dewdney and the Natives for a reconsideration of the initial land allotment.[90] The Blood Council decided quickly that the eclipse of the bison no longer justified their initial choice of reserve lands, those lands being mainly on the open prairie. What they now sought were lands of greater diversity, with a view to agriculture and self-sufficiency. Dewdney was agreeable to this, and in 1880 he achieved a formal release from the 1877 conditions.[91] The wording of the new treaty, agreed to by Red Crow of the Bloods, included the following:

> *I, Mekasto, or Red Crow, Head Chief of the Blood Indians, on behalf and*
> *with the consent of the Blood Indians included in said Treaty do hereby give*
> *up all our rights, titles and privileges whatsoever to the lands included in said*
> *Treaty, provided the government will grant us a Reserve on the Belly River in*
> *the neighbourhood of the Mouth of the Kootenai River.*

As the original land allotment assigned to the Blood Indians was quickly seen to be inappropriate, given the continuing demise of bison herds, several adjustments to the Blood Reserve were made over the next thirty years, including assignment of a timber limit along the Belly River. The "Kootenai River" was, in this instance, a reference to the Waterton River. The old reserve lands had been centred further northeast on open prairie.[92]

These were difficult times for the Blood people generally. Many were still in Montana where a last desperate chance to follow the old ways, giving chase to the buffalo, was still possible. At the time of the 1880 renegotiation, there were about

800 people on the Alberta Blood Reserve. By the spring of 1881, over 2,500 defeated, starving, and measle-ridden Bloods arrived back from Montana. "Fences were pulled down for firewood and seed was dug up for food by the new arrivals."[93] By 1882 the Bloods, pending surveys of their new reserve lands, had "spread out along the river from the present town of Glenwood, where the Fish Eaters camped, to the northern-most point near Slide Out, where the Short Men and North Bloods settled."[94] By March, 1883 the Head Men of the Bloods had been satisfied and the new treaty was ratified on March 2, 1885.

In preparing the official surveys for the new reserve, John C. Nelson made thorough appraisals of the qualities of the land. One of his consistent observations concerned the lack of a good wood supply on much of the Indian land.[95] In this situation is be found the origin of the separate land unit identified as Timber Limit "A" established for the exclusive use of the Blood Band by an Order in Council in 1889.[96] In exchange for this new limit the Bloods gave up some 440 acres from their reserve.[97]

This arrangement for provision of a wood supply area, in accordance with the 1877 treaty, was made in advance of the establishment of the Waterton Lakes Park Reserve in 1895. Timber Limit "A," located on the west bank of the Belly River, was confirmed by a federal order in council on June 12, 1893, as being included as part of the Indian Reserves withdrawn under the Dominion Lands Act.[98] Timber limit 776 (adjacent to Timber Limit "A") was established in 1897, since much of the land in Timber Limit "A" had recently been swept by fire.

No particular conflict in the arrangement was noticed until the extension of Waterton Lakes National Park's boundaries in 1914. At that time, the boundaries "enveloped" the Timber Limit "A" lands.[99] Park officials then made the assumption that the timber limit lands were merely a limit, and not a part of the Blood Reserve as such. With the passage of time, the view of wardens and other park officials stressed the notion that all park regulations, with the exception of those respecting the right to take wood, applied to the members of the Blood community. In 1917 and 1934, charges were laid against local Indians for breaches of park regulations.[100]

Only with attempts to resolve these court charges through due process did the ambiguities of the ownership of Timber Limit "A" begin to unfold. As early as 1917, park officials had made requests to the Solicitor General for a ruling with respect to the merits of the court charges. A definitive judgment finally came down in 1936 in favour of the Blood Indians.[101] After lengthy negotiations and land exchanges involving the Province of Alberta and the two main parties to the dispute, a settlement was achieved. The negotiations and the clarification of title also allowed for completion of the Chief Mountain Highway across what was now clearly Indian land. The park boundary then assumed its current shape, indicating the Blood Indian Timber limit clearly excised from the park by the early 1970s (see Map 6).[102]

Developments in the Waterton Townsite: 1930-1945

The completion of the Prince of Wales Hotel in 1927 held out much promise for enhancement of the tourist trade at Waterton. The depression years quickly took their toll on the new establishment, and it had to close its doors temporarily between 1933 and 1936.[103] Numbers of visitors to the park were down. If these were not particulary lucrative years in terms of revenue-generation, the public relief programs at least allowed for a considerable amount of housekeeping and facility improvement. This was true for the townsite as well as for back-country park developments. Following the passage of the National Parks Act in 1930, Commissioner Harkin reviewed the old sub-division plans for Waterton Ttownsite and then asked the Surveyor General to withhold from lease those sites identified on the 1926 consolidated plan located on Middle and Lower Waterton Lakes.[104] This represented a first move towards systematic zoning of the townsite area, a process that would continue over the next forty years. In the early 1930s, zoning practices displayed an *ad hoc* history, but one based on common sense decisions by architecturally sensitive park superintendents, such a W. D. Cromarty, who in the absence of formal guidelines, had concentrated various residential, commercial, and public functions in appropriate areas.

Many post-war structures gave way to attractive peeled log buildings or to combinations in frame, log, and stone (Figs. 57, 58). Through the relief programs, which got into full swing in 1932, Waterton Park sponsored the development of a number of attractive new buildings and facilities and expanded and replaced some of the older ones. This included the handsome new registration

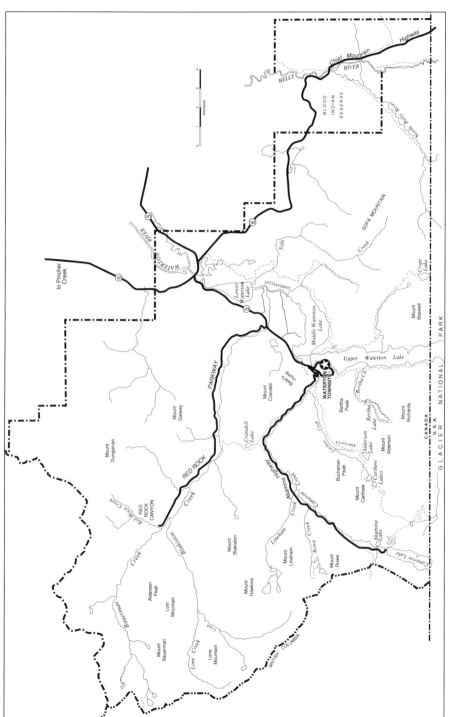

Map 6. Waterton Lakes National Park: modern boundaries. Parks Canada.

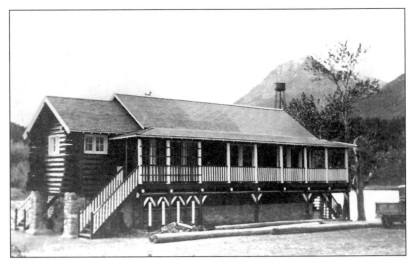

Fig. 57. Bath house at Lake Linnet in 1936. Provincial Archives of Alberta. 69.218/154.

Fig. 58. RCMP building. This handsome structure was built between 1928 and 1930. National Archives of Canada PA 58930.

Fig. 59. Superintendent Herbert Knight in front of the new park headquarters building. 1938. Provincial Archives of Alberta. 69.218/159.

kiosk at the park entrance, the revamped administration building, and structures in support of recreation. The designs were prepared under the direction of Cromarty, who had returned to his duties in the Ottawa office of the Architectural Division. Improvements were made to the work compound. These included a garage, workshop, bunk house and kitchen-dining hall erected on a bench over-looking Linnet Lake. The superintendent's office, first erected along the town waterfront in 1919, had been modified in 1925 and 1928. A large wing was added in 1936, doubling the working space (Fig. 59). For the town visitors, the relief workers completed a series of new kitchen shelters, lavatory buildings, and a large group facility, which projected a fine rustic quality achieved through the use of half-log siding and large stone chimneys. These designs clearly provided a continuity with what had been achieved under Cromarty's direction in the 1920s.

Despite the stagnant economy, a certain amount of commercial and institutional development still took place during the 1930s, reflecting perhaps the situation whereby automobile trips to parks still provided one relatively economical family vacation in bad times. Erik Hagglund's Bungalow Cabin camp near Cameron Creek was established in 1933.[105] Much of rustic Kilmorey Lodge, built in 1928, was destroyed by fire in late February of 1933, but was rebuilt in 1934.[106] The attractive Crandell Mountain Lodge

115

Fig. 60. Waterton's first dance hall. c.1912. Ernie Haug.

Fig. 61. Waterton's second dance hall was destroyed by fire in 1938. Ernie Haug.

Fig. 62. View of Waterton Motors. 1930s. Parks Canada.

was built between 1937 and 1940.[107] One of the great landmarks of Waterton, the large dance hall, burned to the ground in 1938 (Figs. 60, 61). It was a significant loss to the recreational life of the townsite and indeed, to much of southern Alberta. A journalist for the *Lethbridge Herald* lamented:[108]

For years this beautiful building – the largest dance hall between Winnipeg and Vancouver – has been the pride of the park. Year after year it has drawn thousands of tourists and weekend visitors who have enjoyed dancing on the spacious floor. Year after year Waterton residents have eagerly awaited the opening of the hall on May 24. For them it has meant the definite end of a long, secluded winter, and the beginning of a period of good times and renewing of friendships. Now, not a square inch of the beautiful hardwood floor remains. The windows are masses of moulten glass, and only the centre cement pillar and charred oak pillars which supported the mezzanine floor remain, gruesome evidence of the holocaust, and Main Street looks strangely empty.

The steady increase of public facility improvements came to a temporary close in 1937 when the relief camp programs were ended and the Ottawa Architectural Division Office was dismantled. From that date until the late 1940s,

117

Fig. 63. Flooding in the Waterton townsite. 1937. Provincial Archives of Alberta. 69.218/170.

building requirements were few. The main initiative in the war years was the construction of a series of staff houses, the largest of which was on Cameron Falls Drive, and which bore a similarity in design to the house built for the fish hatchery superintendent in Jasper in the same year.[109] If the dismantling of the Ottawa Architectural Division led to a relaxation of design standards for private dwellings, the tone set by Cromarty and his associates over the previous two decades nevertheless left an imprint evident in much of the town (Fig. 62).

Municipal Improvements

Other post-1930 townsite improvements included the upgrading of the electrical system. Until 1942, much of the electrical power was purchased from the Glacier Park Company, which operated a small power house in order to supply the Prince of Wales Hotel. By 1942, war oil shortages had forced the hotel to shut down. The park superintendent first rented, and then purchased generating equipment for installation at the park headquarters garage in 1945. Anticipating great increases in post-war use of the park, arrangements were made in 1947 with Calgary Power Ltd. to supply all townsite needs.[110]

With the general rise in demand for tourist accommodation and facilities after 1925, questions of municipal water supply had to be addressed. A 1926 plan shows the general features of a water system put in place in the townsite over the previous two years.[111] The water supply was drawn from Cameron Creek at a spot some 500 feet above the falls in 1924, and the system was regularly upgraded over the next thirty years.[112] Oversupply of water in the townsite by other forces has been a periodic difficulty owing to the coming together of climatic events. In 1937, the townsite was seriously flooded by the swollen waters of the lake and spring run-off. It was not the first flood nor would it be the last (Fig. 63).

Chapter Five

The Literary and Artistic Response

There were individuals in late nineteenth century Waterton-Glacier country who played their part as witnesses to the last phases of the disappearance of the old buffalo commons. The high plains world was in transition and people such as James Willard Schultz (1859-1947) and Walter McClintock (1870-1949) understood the drama about them. Both found themselves in social circumstances among the Blackfoot of Montana and Alberta in which they were eventually welcomed as intimates, sympathetic recorders of traditional knowledge, and spokesmen and defenders of Native rights.[1] McClintock was adopted in 1896 by Chief Mad Wolf of the Pikuni Branch of the Blackfoot, a man of great oratory skill and a guardian of the sacred Beaver Bundle. McClintock then spent several years recording the ethnographic details of traditional Blackfoot life and culture on both sides of the border. He later took authentic materials on tour in Europe, and wrote several books including two which have become lasting contributions, *The Old North Trail* (1910) and *Old Indian Trails* (1923).[2]

James W. Schultz, or Apikuni, as the Blackfoot called him (meaning Scab-Robe), made a name for himself as a recorder of Native tradition. The eighteen-year-old ex-military student from New York had gone to St. Louis in 1877 and then on to Fort Benton, where he worked as a trader, rancher, guide, and hunter. In the early 1880s, he married a Peigan girl, Nahtaki (Fine Shield Woman) and relocated to the Blackfeet Reservation. It was with publication of *My Life as an Indian* in 1907, which recorded a version of his biography down to

Fig. 64. John Willard Schultz (1859-1947). New York-born Schultz arrived at Fort Benton in 1877 and later married a Blackfoot woman, Nahtaki. He gradually came to take an interest in Native lore, particularly after the death of his wife in 1902. Encouraged at the start by George Bird Grinnell, his writings have become an important part of Pacific Northwest history. James Willard Schultz Papers, Collection 10. Image number 360.

the time of Nahtaki's death in 1902, that Schultz came to public attention. He then began publishing stories about the Glacier country in *Forest and Stream* in association with George B. Grinnell, whom he had guided on occasion. In such titles as *Blackfeet Tales of Glacier National Park* (1916), he successfully promoted ancient lore to a wider public (Figs. 64, 65).[3]

Literary effort on the Canadian side was associated more with those who followed in the wake of the North West Mounted Police: the cattlemen, farmers, and particularly those of more genteel background. A good deal has been written about the imprint left on the cultural and economic life of southern Alberta by the English "remittance men," who were so prominent among the new invaders of the land. The "remittance men," as a class phenomenon, were not restricted to the Canadian side of the border.[4] Of the 311 ranchers in Wyoming in 1880, 52 were British.[5] Early accounts tended to lead to a stereotyping of this group as a whole. In essence, they were deemed to be socially well-connected back in the British Isles, seldom short of funds from home, and habitually short on prudence. In the Pincher Creek area, the life of Lionel Brooke (c.1850 – c.1930) did indeed help to foster the stereotype of the man who had been "sent out" in order to "make good" with the help of a family bankroll.[6] A more comprehensive view of these "privileged" settlers has since been established.[7] The survival of the 1890s letters of Claude Gardiner (1870-1942), who gradually developed his Wineglass Ranch north of the Peigan Reserve, provides a more accurate view of the life of many of the "remittance men," revealing something about the conditions they faced, their character, and some of the contributions they made to local institutional life.[8]

122

Fig. 65. Walter McClintock (1870-1949). Pittsburg-born McClintock came to the Pacific Northwest in 1896 in the party of Gifford Pinchot, Chief of the U.S. Forest Service. After working on surveys for new forest reserves, he stayed on in the Glacier area where he was adopted by Chief Mad Wolf of the Blackfeet tribe. Over the years he gathered much information of an ethnogical nature which he published and became a defender of Native rights. He is shown here listening to Brings-Down-the-Sun. Walter McClintock, *On the Old North Trail* (1923).

Alberta historian Lewis Thomas has suggested that the notion of "privilege" played an important role in the thinking of late nineteenth-century eastern politicians and businessmen, just when they were searching for a way to settle and exploit the West in an orderly fashion.[9] As has American writer Wallace Stegner, Thomas has been at pains to point out that the western frontier was seldom a social vacuum and that the ideas settlers brought with them were of the greatest importance in the fashioning of a new but recognizable way of life.[10] The well-known guide, writer and rancher, Andy Russell, a long and watchful resident of Waterton country, has left a fond personal recollection of the "remittance men." He focused not just on the often humorous elements of financial folly, but also on their importance as an influence on frontier education, particularly with respect to literary sensibility. It was in the fine personal library of Harold Butcher that, as a small boy, Russell was first exposed to Kipling and Dickens, and where, because of his promise, he was given exceptional borrowing rights.[11] Russell's books on wildlife have become classics of Canadian literature and his name is now attached to an award given at the periodic meetings of the Waterton-Glacier Writers' Workshop.

123

The beginnings of landscape painting in the Waterton-Glacier country, may be traced to the work of Charles Wilson and James Madison Alden, military men attached respectively to the British and United States wings of the International Boundary Survey of 1857-61 (Plate 2).[12] Their styles of documentary painting, inspired by the pragmatic need for land delineation, marked a transitional phase from the period of the great romantic painters of Native personality and events represented in the work of artists such as Karl Bodmer, Paul Kane, and George Catlin. An extension of such documentary recording surfaced in some of the early members of the North West Mounted Police and among other military men on the American side.[13]

Despite the heightened awareness fostered by the conditions of frontier life, the opportunities to think about art and literature, much less execute productions, was still rare in the early years of frontier settlement. Hard, regular, backbreaking, and sometimes heartbreaking work was the usual offering to men and women of the first generation. A mix of privilege, talent, personality, and opportunity sometimes overcame the limitations imposed by the life of labour. Such was the case of a young ex-American who joined the North West Mounted Police as a surgeon, just in time for the "great trek" of 1874, which ended in the establishment of Fort Macleod on the Oldman River. Between his official duties, Richard Nevitt found time to execute impressions in watercolour of the prairie and mountain landscape and of the social life about him.[14] As a class, the early police force members, like the "remittance men" played a part in the development of community art in southern Alberta.

Many of these first North West Mounted Police members did not return east after their terms of duty but stayed on in various capacities as ranchers, settlers, surveyors, railway builders, guides, and administrators.[15] Having had opportunities to become familiar with the country and its possibilities, and to put by a sum of money for investment, some made sound economic choices upon leaving the force and became leading members of the new western communities. Such was the case with Edmund Forster Brown who left behind the depression conditions of England in 1885 for western Canada. After two years spent on a ranch near Moosejaw, he joined the North West Mounted Police and was assigned to Fort Macleod. For eight years, Brown patrolled the settlements of

Waterton country. About 1890, Brown married Elizabeth Cody, a young teacher in Fort Macleod, recently arrived from Newmarket, Ontario. The Brown's daughter, Annora, would become an outstanding artist and writer. She studied at the Ontario College of Art under the stimulating influence of certain members of the fledgling Group of Seven. Returning to Alberta, Annora Brown managed, through sheer force of will and persistence, to produce art of an exceptional quality, the difficulties of looking after ill and aging parents notwithstanding.[16] The mountains of Waterton-Glacier country and the prairie environment dominated by the Oldman River were her most important sources of inspiration. Her book, *Old Man's Garden,* is a contribution to the interpretation of Native lore concerning plants and their place in a vanishing way of life.[17] Brown also completed some fine portraits and pictures illustrating life and culture on the Blood and Peigan reserves (Plate 5).

On the American side of the border, the clash of the frontier with the homelands of the Blackfoot and Nez Perce, had attracted the attention of writers and artists of some influence. Charles M. Russell achieved fame after his arrival in the Judith Basin of Montana in 1880.[18] He appears to have spent much of 1888 in Canadian territory, particularly in the High River area, and his experiences among the Blackfoot and Sarcee (Tsuu T'ina) exerted an important influence on his work and his view of Native peoples.[19]

Native identity in the early twentieth century, on both sides of the border, tended to be at the mercy of administrators of many types, although there were those in the larger community who objected.[20] Before 1920, Francis E. Leup, the American Commissioner of Indian Affairs, became determined to resist the considerable influence of business interests and Christian reformers on the Bureau of Indian Affairs (BIA) schools. As early as 1905, he had contended that "the Indian is a natural warrior, a natural logician, a natural artist" and that "we have room for all three in our highly organized social system." Let us not "make the mistake" of "washing out of them whatever is distinctly Indian."[21] This kind of thinking permeated the ideas of John Collier when he became director of the Bureau of Indian Affairs in Washington in the early 1930s. He was a strong promoter of the recent Wheeler-Howard Bill which reformed Indian Affairs administration towards enhanced local reservation leadership and economic opportunity, and away from the piecemeal severance of reservation lands through the allotment provisions of the 1887 Dawes Act.[22] In the 1920s, Collier became heavily involved in resisting allotment efforts in the southwest, where traditions of art had been in a state of modest revival since shortly after 1900, largely through the interest of artists and philanthropists not associated with the Bureau of Indian Affairs schools. The BIA actively opposed training in traditional arts and crafts until 1930.[23] As a result of this outside influence, fresh air blew through the system in 1932 when an art studio was established in the Indian Bureau School at Santa Fe.[24] This provided something of a model for others, and such thinking would find fertile ground in Glacier National Park.

When the English sculptor and writer Clare Sheridan first came to the American and Canadian West in 1937, she was quick to notice that, despite the harshness of the environment, there were forces favourable to art for "prairie life is apt to make poets of sensitive men."[25] Sheridan, the scion daughter of Moreton Frewen, and a first cousin of Winston Churchill, had come to work with the talented Winold Reiss of New York, at St. Mary's Lake, where three years earlier Reiss has established an art colony school with the support of the Great Northern Railway. It was here that Reiss made not only his own outstanding contribution to portraiture of many of the aging Blackfoot leaders, but also helped to foster the careers of several Blackfoot artists of the younger generation.[26]

Sheridan had stopped to interview John Collier before travelling to St. Mary's Lake and thus became conversant in the radical shifts in policy that Collier had done so much to foster.[27] The new policies that sought to facilitate a renaissance in Native-produced arts and crafts were of particular interest. Her arrival in Glacier National Park was timely. Willard Schultz's second wife, Jesse Donaldson Schultz, had recently arrived in the area with a view to establishing a craft guild at Browning under the auspices of the Works Progress Adminstration.[28] Clare Sheridan quickly became associated with Jesse Schultz and also with the members of the Blackfeet and Blood communities.

In the summer of 1937 she met Chief Sakoyena Tailfeathers and his wife Estochomachi, who had come to St. Mary's from Alberta to be near their young son, Gerald, who, along with his brothers, had developed a strong interest in art. This interest had been inspired by the example of the self-taught and

Fig. 66. Big Bull by the young Gerald Tailfeathers (charcoal drawing). This work was purchased by Clare Sheridan during her period at the St. Mary's Lake Art Colony in Glacier National Park. Hastings Museum and Art Gallery.

entrepreneurial artist of the Bloods, Two Gun (Percy Plainwoman), who was accustomed to sell his art works to passers-by at Standoff.[29] Winold Reiss had arranged that there should be no charge at the St. Mary's Art Colony for Native students of promise. Later in the summer of 1937, Sheridan was invited to stay at the Blood Reserve as the guest of the Tailfeathers family, and it was there that she exercised a certain positive influence on young Gerald by purchasing his charcoal portrait of Big Bull (Figs. 66, 67). In a prophetic statement, she judged that young Gerald "was an artist, as truly as anyone can be." He was far more so "than many a student" studying art in Paris. "Alone he did it" and "there was no teacher who touched it." Sheridan gave him five dollars for the work: "the first picture he ever sold, and not likely to be his last."[30] Gerald Tailfeathers (1925-1975) was inspired by the legends he had heard from his elders, and with encouragement from Canon Middleton, the Canadian Handicrafts Guild of Fort Macleod, and John Laurie in Calgary, he went on to become one of the important artists in the post-1950 flowering of North American Native art.[31]

Before returning to England, the independent and radically minded Sheridan, who had already done sculptures of Lenin, Trotsky, the Canadian war hero, Billy Bishop, and Ghandi, completed a Native series including Turtle, Shot on Both Sides, Big Bull and Mrs. Blackplume with her "papoose." Her sensitive account of Blackfoot country and of her time spent on the Blood Reserve, adds valuable information to a little-known phase of Canadian reserve life, and the experience exercised a profound influence on her work (Figs. 68-70).

The Waterton country has continued to act as a magnet for landscape artists in the post-war period, but this has been supplemented by the influence of the Native revival in the arts. The larger connection between the mountain and prairie landscapes and indigenous art and religious sensibility has been made clearer, through the fruits of interview, the recording of oral tradition, and the results of comprehensive archaeological survey. This includes a developing awareness of the importance granted by generations of Native peoples to spiritual sites such as Chief Mountain (Plate 1).[32]

Fig. 67. Canon Middleton (arm on table) and Blackfoot Cadets. c. 1930. Blood Reserve. Canon Middleton was tireless in his efforts to open up to the youth of the Blood Reserve opportunities for them to participate in the institutions and economy of the wider Canadian community. Waterton Park was an important setting for many of his initiatives. The young Gerald Tailfeathers is located in the second row of boys, third from left. Glenbow Archives, Calgary. NA 1811-43.

Fig. 68. Clare Sheridan (1885-1959). Named Kokotosa by the Blood Indians, this talented English sculptor and writer left an important legacy of work based on her residency in Glacier National Park and on the Blood Reserve in Southern Alberta in 1937. Here she is pictured with a cottonwood sculpture near St. Mary's Lake in Glacier National Park. Jonathan Frewen.

Fig. 69. Mountain Horse, modelled by Clare Sheridan. Mountain Horse sat for Sheridan at the St. Mary's Lake art colony in Glacier. Hastings Musuem and Art Gallery.

Fig. 70. Mrs. Blackplume and papoose. This work was done on the Blood Reserve in Alberta by Clare Sheridan. Jonathan Frewen.

Changing Ideas of Wildlife, Parks, and Tourism: 1945-1975

The policy of the Canadian National Parks towards wildlife in the post-war years was influenced by the 1930s ferment of thought concerning predator-prey relationships. The new ideas reflected several decades of work in academic biology, zoology, and in that particularly complex area of synthesis known as "ecology." The term "ecology" was recognized at the 1893 meeting of the International Botanical Congress, although fundamental ideas had been in the air since the German, Ernst Heakel (1834-1919) coined the term in the 1860s.[1] In 1913, an early practitioner of the new science, Charles Adams of Chicago, had a warning for the students of his day: he stated that ecology was still "a science with its facts out of all proportion to their organization or integration."[2] In the 1930s, there were those who still felt that to be the case. Yet, significant shifts in point of view had been introduced by practitioners of the young science, particularly with respect to the importance of time in natural history studies. Wildlife cycles were coming to be seen as an important factor in any discussion of the so-called "balance of nature." Many ecologists suspected there was no such thing. Rather, nature's ways were understood to be time-bound, dynamic, and cyclical.[3] Such a shift in viewpoint, away from a rather static reading of nature towards one that was inherently historical, had implications for wildlife management.

In its early twentieth century phase, public wildlife management in North America had developed with a view to the sustaining of certain specific game populations of interest to the hunter and angler. The state of the art was comprehensively articulated by Aldo S. Leopold in his 1933 text, *Wildlife Management*.[4] This text was, perhaps, the ultimate statement summing up theory from a time in which species were still viewed somewhat in environmental isolation. Leopold was aware of this, and, in his later years, he made a great contribution to what we are here calling the "ecological" point of view.[5]

The new biology was being taken up in Canada as well, where significant work had been underway since the end of World War I by the English ecologist Charles Elton, the Dominion entomologist, Gordon Hewitt, and the very original William Rowan at the University of Alberta.[6] A dawning awareness that wildlife management was not a straightforward activity was strongly foreshadowed in the controversies surrounding the public movement of bison populations between 1904 and 1935. The lessons learned contributed to a greater understanding of the complexities of wildlife management.[7] After 1935, the ideas of men such as Ian MacTaggert Cowan and C.H.D. Clarke would start to exert an ecological influence on wildlife policy in the headquarters unit of the National Parks Branch.[8] The parks provided an excellent series of laboratories for the field ecologist.

Montana's Glacier National Park had long provided a focus of attention for a number of influential thinkers and advocates of wilderness conservation. The superintendents at Glacier inherited a tradition of advocacy that stretched back to the early visits made by George Bird Grinnell. In January, 1927, Superintendent Charles J. Kraebel sent a letter to the director of the National Parks Service, attaching a copy of an article by the naturalist at Mount Rainier National Park, entitled "Call off the Dogs." The article was a plea for a review of the predator-control policies in the national parks. Kraebel had already been thinking in these terms. "Naturalist Schmoe ... has touched briefly on a matter of no small importance," Kraebel noted in his letter, and he further stated: "I have expressed the idea in various reports and correspondence during the past three years and am now executing it to some extent in Glacier by cessation of special efforts to destroy cougar and wildcats."[9] With confidence, the superintendent asserted that "during fifteen years of forest life, I have become convinced of the importance of maintaining the 'biological balance' in the fauna of wilderness areas, and nowhere is this more important than in the National Parks which purport to be great museums of primitive natural conditions."[10]

Kraebel's letter worked its way into the hands of the influential young forester, Aldo Leopold, who responded at length and in support of Kraebel's views.[11] Others, including G. B. Grinnell, were brought into the discussion, with the result that by 1932 the U.S. National Park Service had affected a radical shift in its policy towards wildlife, one based strongly on ideas being advanced by the new ecologists. By the end of World War II, these ideas had taken hold in other segments of the wildlife management community and among professional biologists. Many of those in the public service, or advisory to it, started to advocate policies quite different from those that had prevailed before 1930 when both the United States and Canada passed new national parks legislation.

Fig. 71. Elliott Coues (1842-1899). This important American ornithologist and historian of the North American West accompanied Major Twinning's American Boundary Survey party of 1874 and made notes on the local flora and fauna in the Waterton Lakes area. E. Coues. 1897.

Ecology as a Point of View in the New Park Management: Of Elk, Fire, and Wolves

Systematic notations on the flora and fauna of Waterton had been made since the visit of Thomas Blakiston in 1857. Comparable materials were probably recorded by the naturalists of the American North West Boundary Survey of 1857-60, but the reports of this expedition were regrettably lost.[12] The cumulative series of observations made since Blakiston's time does allow for some assessment of the ways in which wildlife and botanical patterns have changed in the park over the last century and a half. Following the submission of Blakiston's information to Captain Palliser, other systematic reports soon followed. During the International Boundary Survey period of the 1860s and 1870s, several outstanding naturalists visited the area including

133

the noted American biologist and historian Elliot Coues. Some of his catalogues provided the basis for descriptions of new forms (Fig. 71).[13] In 1895, W. S. Spreadborough made a collection of mammals for the National Museum of Canada as did C. H. Young in 1922 and 1923. A survey of wildlife in the mountain parks was conducted in 1938 by R. M. Anderson.[14] These studies have provided a context for our understanding of wildlife and the growing knowledge of population dynamics. As in the long era of Native use, human actions of the more recent past were becoming recognized as important in shaping the patterns of wildlife.

In North American pioneer and frontier society, the wisdom of predator eradication or "control" was long thought to be an almost self-evident tenet. It permeated the thinking of farmers, ranchers, and the official policies of many a government agency. In the United States, park rangers in Yellowstone destroyed the last known denning area of wolves in 1924, and, by 1930, it was assumed they had been eliminated from the area.[15]

It will be recalled that, as early as 1925, J. B. Harkin was starting to question the assumptions behind Canadian federal park policy on predators. On both sides of the border, professional momentum for a reconsideration of predators and their relationship with other forms of wildlife in the national parks started to build in the 1930s. Prior to his commencement of wildlife surveys in Waterton and other parks in 1938, R. M. Anderson received a memo from F. H. Williamson in which it was noted that "the policy of the Bureau is to regard the Parks as wildlife sanctuaries" ones in which "predators have an important function in maintaining a natural balance."[16] This trend in policy did not sit well with officers of the Alberta Fish and Game Society. In a letter to federal minister T. A. Crerar, W. C. Fisher vented against both Anderson and the park directors. The latter "have a theory that nature will balance itself, and are opposed to killing off predators. This, I believe, is absolutely wrong."[17] Fisher had seemingly missed the argument of the new thinking, however. The senior officers in the Parks Branch were contending that if there was a "balance of nature" it was not something static; it was something that could only be recognized in cyclical time, and that to foster any such a long-term balance was to accept an invitation to manage not just the immediate park but the larger landscape as well. The policy tide had in fact turned, and throughout the war years staff wildlife specialists worked not only to convince external interest groups of the value of the new policy, but also to convince the older style of warden of its virtues. When in 1942 there seemed to be some concern expressed over the presence of a cougar in the Radium Hot Springs boundary area of Kootenay National Park, headquarters wildlife biologist C.H.D. Clarke observed that "we have had trouble in one park after another with excessive numbers of elk" and hence the "advent of a cougar with a taste for elk meat is certainly not a cause for regret."[18] As early as 1937, these ideas had started to influence policy.[19]

Armed with a clear policy on predators now, headquarters officers saw a need to gain information on more general ecological relationships. Towards the end of the war, A.W.F. Banfield and Ian McTaggert Cowan were asked to look into certain wildlife issues in Waterton, particularly that of the rising elk population.[20] Their surveys proved useful. Towards the end of the decade, Waterton was to undergo its last major boundary adjustment, one in which some sixteen sections on the eastern side were excised from the park. An exchange of letters between the National Parks Branch and the Alberta Fish and Game Association explored the issue of habitat for deer and elk.[21] The park position was that the sixteen sections in question were not considered to be critical habitat for elk and deer. The association took the view that these were "wintering grounds of elk and deer long before they were leased to farmers in the vicinity."[22] Both sides were perhaps correct, it being a matter of what particular historic time period was under discussion.[23] In replying to the Alberta Fish and Game Association, the Parks Branch reviewed the reports by Cowan and Banfield, and concluded that "it is not felt that a further investigation is called for at this time."[24]

Historical land use information and reliable wildlife statistics were clearly starting to play a role in park and wildlife management. Here was not just the beginnings of a new deal for predators, but such animals were becoming the subject of study in their own right. Warden Hubert U. Green produced a report on *The Wolves of Banff* in 1951, thus ushering in the beginnings of a preoccupation with "matrices" in wildlife research, in which major ecological factors could be grouped together for analysis.[25] Subsequently, park studies bearing upon the relationships of predators, prey, and important environmental components, such as fire, climate, and human interactions, have become normative.[26]

The changing pattern and control of elk numbers was a significant question for Waterton Lakes managers for much of the twentieth century. The context of the elk controversies was outlined by George A. MacKenzie in his historical review of fire ecology at Waterton Lakes.[27] MacKenzie saw a connection between the rise of the elk population and the history of fire-suppression policy in the national parks on both sides of the international border. In the early years of the twentieth century, elk had been largely unknown in Waterton. In 1912, twenty-nine elk were transported from Yellowstone National Park into Glacier, having been released at Belton. By 1940, over 3,600 animals had become established in the winter ranges of Glacier National Park. Natural reforestation of old forest fire burns gradually decreased the area of winter range, and the elk stabilized at about 1,800 animals.[28] In 1920, F. H. Riggall reported seeing a few elk drifting up the Belly River area.[29] By 1932, elk had increased substantially and had started to move out of the park onto farm lands, leading to the resource-use conflict debates that culminated in the studies of Cowan and Banfield in the 1940s.

In retrospect, it has become clearer that the general proliferation of the elk in this period also coincided with the war on the wolf between 1912 and 1930, and with a vigorous fire-suppression policy. The climatic and soil conditions at Waterton, despite the high winds, does not favour frequent large fires. MacKenzie indicates that there have been only two major fires since 1910. The first was the Cameron Creek and Oil City fire of 1919, and the second was the boundary fire of 1935. The latter was started by lightning on the Glacier side and then swept up the west side of Waterton Lake, threatening the townsite. These two fires accounted for 60 percent of the total area burned since 1910. The five other largest fires consumed less than 400 acres.[30] The relationship of past fires to the increase of elk in the twentieth century was established by MacKenzie through a consideration of those trees that require a helping hand from fire in order to propagate.

There are two main species of tree in Waterton that are fire-generated, which is to say, the cones of these trees require fire to induce germination. These are the aspen and Lodge Pole pine. MacKenzie mapped out in broad time periods, the pattern of fire-regenerated areas of Lodge Pole pine in the park since about 1830:[31]

Dates	Land Area (%)
1830–1870	12.8
1871–1890	23.3
1891–1910	36.1
1911–1965	15.1

Figures such as these, supplemented by historical data on the movement of elk, suggested that fire suppression since the early years of park establishment had probably contributed to reduce prime elk grazing habitat. On the Stony Creek Flats, figures indicated heavy overgrazing by elk after 1945 among aspen clones that had not been burned for many decades.[32] Similarly, there were several Lodge Pole pine stands in the Blakiston Valley undergoing successional change, leading to degradation of the Elk winter range.[33] MacKenzie concluded that the combination of the long-term elimination of predators with increased pressure of an increasing elk population on declining grazing habitat, produced the initial spill-over of elk onto ranch lands in 1932.

Banfield's report of 1947 had looked in a number of directions by way of general recommendations. Domestic cattle grazing was still allowed in the park and questions were being asked about the relationship of domestic cattle to natural forage required by elk. "It would be naive to believe" Banfield stated "that if no grazing of domestic stock were permitted in the park, the elk would cease their depredations on the surrounding ranches. In the long run however, with good natural ranges, population controls and salt blocks, the depredations of elk could be kept to a minimum."[34]

The policy most actively pursued over the next two decades was population control, an approach being taken in other parks as well. Establishment of an abattoir or "slaughterhouse" was approved in 1947 and erected in 1948 in the Cedar Cabin area.[35] While awaiting funds for construction, Superintendent H. A. de Veber chose to obtain an interim facility for use in the winter of 1947-48. This proved to be one of the prisoner of war camp "sectional huts obtained recently from the internment camp at the Kananaskis Forest Experiment Station."[36] Between 1947 and 1969, 1,577 elk were slaughtered, the meat and hides given to the Indian Affairs Branch for local distribution to Native peoples. Despite construction of a new abattoir at the upper compound in 1962, activity was unofficially suspended after the slaughter of 1963 in favour of a policy that would give greater attention to habitat management. Officials had come to take the view that the national parks should not be in the business of the systematic slaughter of wild animals.[37]

The steady shift towards a more ecological view of park resources had implications for the administrative staff and warden organization. Those who had previously been asked to administer the national parks on the ground and to protect wildlife from poachers had tended to be practical men of a military, hunting, farming, guiding, or forestry background.[38] A different type of training and experience became ever more important in post-1945 recruitment. Intimations of a shift in preference towards professional credentials had come as early as 1935 when Dr. B. I. Love was appointed superintendent of Elk Island National Park, east of Edmonton. As a trained veterinarian, it was anticipated that he would be able to find remedies to the recurring complications brought on by too many wild animals confined on too small a territory.[39]

The new developments in remote communication available after 1945 were at least partially responsible for the progressive centralization of warden facilities in townsites or at park headquarters stations and for the gradual revision of the boundaries of the old decentralized district warden cabin system. Centralization as an idea gained momentum after the tabling of the *Glassco Commission Report on Government Organization* in 1962. The report of the commission was reviewed by officials of the National Parks Branch, who then commissioned a special study on how the recommendations might best be applied to the parks service generally, and to the warden service particularly. The results led to a series of warden conferences and proposals so that, by 1968, reform of the warden service was well under way.[40] Essentially, the warden service redefined itself in terms of a greater range of duties and broadened the training and credentials required of wardens.

One witness to the changes of these years was Frank Camp, born in the Jasper area in 1926. On returning from the war, he joined the warden service in Jasper where his father had previously been employed. In 1946, he was sent to Waterton. In the late 1950s, the wardens were engaged increasingly in wildlife studies and Camp has recalled the reaction of one seasoned wildlife watcher, Andy Russell, to some of the wildlife study projects of the day. In Russell's view, there was not much "wildness" left, in sheep "that had been trapped, ear-tagged and horns painted red."[41] These were the early days of attempts to systematically monitor wildlife movements (Fig. 72).

Fig. 72. Lee Creek wardens' cabin. c. 1942. Parks Canada.

Post-War Industry and Waterton

Oil, gas, and mineral rights in Waterton Park were a matter of general commercial interest since the earliest days of park establishment. Such interests remained in the post-war period, but the passage of the 1930 National Parks Act gave greater capacity to the branch to resist such pressures. J. B. Harkin, as we have seen, served notice, in 1925, that the parks were not for hire. The 1930s revival in exploring for oil around the old Oil City location was abortive, but provided a long-term stimulus to the National Parks Branch towards regaining title to all in-park patents. In the years after World War II, the success of Turner Valley helped to maintain a certain stubborn interest in tapping any oil and gas potential in Waterton by whatever means might be acceptable to the government of Canada. In one instance, this led to a complicated proposal by which in-park subterranean petroleum resources would be drained off by an elaborate system of engineered networks introduced from outside of the park boundary. This 1958 proposal also suggested that the park would be given royalties, thus making it a silent partner in the petroleum industry. The response from officials in Ottawa park headquarters to this ingenious idea was decidedly negative, as it had been to other related proposals over the years.[42]

Following this latest of a series of consistent refusals by the federal government to allow any compromise with the regulations on mineral extraction in national parks, the time seemed right to examine the long-standing myth of a resource bonanza in Waterton. In 1963, S. A. Kanik published an oil and gas evaluation based on a summary of current geological knowledge and a history of past performance.[43] In the course of this review, it became apparent why the history of oil extraction in Waterton had been essentially the history of commercial failure. The key was to be found in the dynamics of the famous rock movements, so visible at Cameron Falls, known to geologists as the "**Lewis Overthrust.**"[44] Great layers of ancient rock, responding to lateral pressure from the west, had been forced upwards at a slant, overriding rocks that were much younger in terms of geological time. Thus, according to Kanik: "The Rundle Group of Mississipian age comprises the main reservoir rocks of the oil and gas fields in proximity to the Waterton Lakes Park, and is composed of competent limestones and dolomite rocks." Unfortunately for the oil interests, the "Precambrian complicates the reservoir capacity" and since "all the wells on the subject lots were drilled in Precambrian sediments, oil shows and small recoveries in them had apparently migrated along fault planes which the wells intercepted." In other words, no truly coherent reservoirs of the type characteristic of major strikes had ever been tapped, even though in places oil escaped to the surface and appearing as seeps or as "oil springs."[45]

In the early 1960s, the theoretical basis for an interest in an oil bonanza in Waterton had been thoroughly discounted. It remained only to commemorate as a "site of National significance" the original site of Oil City, and its apparent influence on the later discoveries in Turner Valley and other gas fields north of Waterton.[46] This commemoration effort coincided with the successful conclusion of a long effort at repatriation of the old Oil City (or Lineham) properties in the park, completed by a purchase from the owners in 1961.[47] The oil industry, meanwhile, had established a number of productive fields to the north of Waterton, based on geological sub-structures of an appropriate kind.

140

Proposed Park Expansion: The Elusive Kishinena Country

When viewed on the map, the Waterton-Glacier International Peace Park composes something of an incomplete whole with respect to watersheds and topography. The anomaly is even greater as one moves northwards from Waterton into country where both sides of the great divide have been set aside as great public reserves. The missing piece on the map is in the East Kootenay District of British Columbia. For many years, voices had been raised in favour of a "rounding out" of the Waterton-Glacier country by means of an addition from the Province of British Columbia. Such an addition would have been sympathetic to the developing notion that parks should be conceived of as ecological wholes.

Fig. 73. William A. Buchanan (1876-1954) This influential editor of the *Lethbridge Herald* had a long career in politics as a member of parliament and then as a senator. He was a strong proponent of protection, development, and expansion of Waterton Lakes National Park. Sir Alexander Galt Museum and Archives. P1993102065-GP.

Senator W. A. Buchanan was a strong proponent of this idea. On 7 September, 1948, he wrote to the Honourable J. A. MacKinnon, the federal Minister of Mines and Resources: "For thirty or more years I have been hammering away, trying to get an arrangement made with British Columbia, to have the south-east corner of that Province turned over to the Dominion and added to Waterton Park."[48] Over the years, the British Columbia position had been one of great caution, since it wished to complete a thorough resource inventory of the area, particularly with respect to oil and minerals. In 1948, Senator Buchanan was of the view that there were no real prospects in the southeast corner of British Columbia, and that it was time to renew the Dominion interest in park expansion. The reports back to MacKinnon from civil service resource economists revealed that the East Kootenay country was still riddled with gas and mineral leases and that there was still considerable interest in British Columbia in the commercial exploitation possibilities (Fig. 73).[49]

Federal representations continued to be made throughout the 1950s, particularly following the coming to power of the Conservative administration of John Diefenbaker. The Honourable Alvin Hamilton, Minister of Northern Development, supported by Senator Mike Mansfield of Montana, took a keen interest in forging an agreement with British Columbia for a national park expansion. However these efforts were to no avail.[50] In February of 1961, H. G. Greenway, president of the Waterton-Glacier International Peace Park Committee, wrote to the Honourable Walter Dinsdale, indicating support from Alberta and Montana Rotarians for road improvements. Dinsdale felt that, in view of past lukewarm responses from British Columbia, the issue should not be raised at that time.[51] In 1964, however, the Honourable Arthur Laing, minister in the Liberal Pearson administration, did revive the matter, but, like his predecessors, he failed to get an agreement.[52] In a round-about way, some of the objectives have become realized in the absence of major road improvements. In 1986, British Columbia moved to set aside much of the desired land in the form of a public reserve known as the Akamina-Kishinena Provincial Recreation Area. There are some outstanding wilderness landscape values associated with this reserve, but it enjoys only limited protection from resource use, and the lower reaches of the reserve have been subject to logging activity.[53] While the Canadian Parks Service and the U.S. Glacier National Park still favour the merging of the B.C. corner into a heritage classification complementing the Waterton-Glacier country, the interest in actual road links is no longer viewed as essential to the concept.

People and Parks: Adjusting to Post-War Prosperity

Since the days of Superintendent Herbert Knight in the 1930s, there were various expressions of interest in park museum development and expanding the opportunities for public education and awareness.[54] Such ideas, expressed as formal park initiatives, had to await more opportune times, from a financial point of view. The depression and war put severe limitations on development expenditures of all kinds, yet the statistics on park attendance in those years revealed that an eager population of visitors was at hand. Despite the economic difficulties, numbers of visitors had been on an upward sloping curve with only minor setbacks. Superintendent C. K. LeCapelain's report on the general increase in park visitors between 1940 and 1941 reflected the emergence of society from economic depression at precisely the moment when severe limitations imposed by war were about to curtail vacation travel and expenditure once again.[55]

A positive note was also reflected by the superintendent's reference to a film being made by Fitzpatrick Travelogue Films, scheduled for release by Metro-Goldwyn-Meyer in 1942.[56] Noting that both the International Rotary and Kiwanis had chosen the Prince of Wales Hotel to hold major banquets, LeCapelain summarized the general positive trends of the last few years:[57]

The International aspect of Waterton Glacier International Peace Park is getting to be an important item and contributes considerably to the large increase in American tourist traffic that we have enjoyed, which has arisen from 7,757 in 1935 to 59,778 registrations in 1941.

Similarly, the superintendent stated that golf course revenues had risen and that local Auto Bungalow Camp operator Erik Hagglund reported a successful operating season. To conclude his review, he noted that there had been no fires and that one mile of new trail along Rowe Creek to Upper Rowe Lake had been completed.[58] The only sour note concerned the children's playground, which had been "in constant use" until it was closed in August, owing to a ban placed on gatherings of children under 18 years of age, due to an epidemic of infantile paralysis (polio).[59]

Waterton had undergone a great deal of recreational development, both in the townsite and in the greater park by 1941. A 1938 report tabulated work on a network of forty-two trails throughout the park area.[60] The road system had been substantially upgraded under the relief work program of the 1930s; the golf course had become a great success, although the attractive rustic clubhouse built in 1921 was lost to fire in 1953.[61] The townsite offered more recreational activities to visitors who, as consumers, were starting to recover from the wartime austerity. Special groups, such as the Boy Scouts Association, developed programs well beyond the townsite in areas such as Cameron Lake, where the association maintained a special campground.[62]

Fig. 74. Ski tournament, 1952, Cameron Lake area just outside of Waterton Lakes National Park. The talented photographer, skier, and mountaineer of Banff, Bruno Engler, sponsored a number of tournaments for the Akamina Cup in the early 1950s. Photo: Bruno Engler.

Local civic sentiment was, by this time, building in favour of road upgrading in order to become competitive with the American system. A brief presented by the Lethbridge Chamber of Commerce on "Behalf of All the People of Southern Alberta" made a request for improvements and for greater attention to tourism promotion.[63] Many tourists of the day were so disgusted with the roads leading to and within Waterton Park that they quickly returned to the United States. Statistics provided by the chamber sought to display arguments in favour of bringing Waterton's roads up to the level of Banff. Discounting some of the claims as exaggerated, the episode nevertheless reflected the general tide of rising expectations that marked public opinion in the early 1950s.

An instance of post-war trends in recreation can be noticed with respect to skiing. A survey had been conducted in 1948 to assess the potential for a downhill ski development. By 1953, a slope had been opened on the north side of Bertha Peak, near the townsite. The Waterton Park Lion's Club constructed a rope tow, and then lights were added for night skiing. Another rope-tow was put in place on Mount Lineham near the old Oil City site later in the decade. Studies of general feasibility for more ambitious ski developments were conducted a few years later, but the recurring conclusion of planners in the parks branch was that the weather patterns at Waterton made skiing both unpredictable and hazardous. By 1977, ski operation leases were no longer being renewed by Parks Canada (Fig. 74).[64]

For somewhat different reasons, mountaineering, which had been such an important attractive force for many of the mountain parks on the CPR route, did not become important in Waterton.[65] The lower aspect of the peaks, combined with the development of horse and hiking trails into country approaching the 9,000-foot level, appear to have reduced the challenges associated with this activity.[66] Charles Stokes captured the appeal of Waterton's scenery in 1923 when he oberved that: "Rising abruptly from the plains, the mountains are at once impressive and friendly; and lifting to not too difficult heights, they seem always to be an inviting mood."[67]

Predictably, that most muscular Christian, Cannon Middleton, undertook some climbs, including Glacier's Mount Cleveland, a peak under eleven thousand feet, southeast of the Waterton Lakes. Luela Nielson, an experienced trail rider of the Glacier country, was persuaded to climb Cleveland with Middleton shortly after World War I, and she left an account of the episode.[68]

Waterton and Natural History for the Public

As early as 1946, Superintendent de Veber had raised the question of facility improvements and revived an earlier interest in a museum development.[69] Park natural history programming was given a start between 1948 and 1950, when the future biographer of "Kootenai" Brown, William Rodney, worked in the park as a publicity officer.[70] A display herd of bison was established in the north end of the park in 1952 close to the place where Brown had come out from the mountains in 1865 at the mouth of Pass Creek. He recorded his impressions of that day. "The prairie as far as we could see east, north and west was one living mass of buffalo."[71] Park staff pursued the idea of a park museum, centred on the community shelter in the townsite campground in 1954, although it did not materialize.[72] Over the next few years, discussions and staffing actions were conducted at national park headquarters with a view to increasing public interpretation and naturalist services. This movement was given a strong boost in 1958 following the visit of Northern Affairs Deputy Minister Gordon Robertson to Glacier National Park in Montana. Robertson was impressed with the scope and quality of the interpretive programs, which had an organizational history going back to the early 1920s during the time of Stephen Mather's leadership.[73]

Robertson's tour happened to correspond with a headquarters review of park facilities which resulted in the development of information bureaus, the operation of which was coordinated with provincial and non-government organizations. While museums were important in principle, Alvin Hamilton, the minister in the Diefenbaker administration, was anxious to cater to the needs of the travelling public as a first priority.[74] At Waterton, this meant the development of a new Information Bureau building on the main road into the townsite near Lake Linnet. The first coherent beginnings of a park interpretation program may be identified with a program offered at this new building in 1958. The superintendent noted that "Mr Enright, a teacher from Calgary, commenced his duties on July 1st, as Public Relations Officer" and that his duties included the "development of Information data about the park for staff guidance." This was a position reporting to the chief warden. In that same report, it was noted that Leonard Gladstone, who had served many years in the warden service previous to a motor car accident in 1956, had been retained to work at the information bureau. Gladstone went on to prepare a valuable record of the park's history, which he regularly updated between 1961 and 1968.[75]

At about this time, efforts were underway in Ottawa to more systematically bring ideas about natural history to the notice of park visitors. Partially in response to Gordon Robertson's observations, Dr. George M. Stirret, the former Chief Biologist of the Canadian Wildlife Service in Ontario, was appointed as Parks Branch Chief Naturalist in 1959. Seasonal field naturalists were then regularly hired at the larger national parks. At Waterton, Frank Sudol served on a seasonal basis until 1965. The first fulltime naturalist, E. B. "Buck" Cunningham, was hired in 1965, and, following Cunningham's transfer to Banff, Kurt Seel was appointed in 1966.[76] After that date, regular park interpretive programs continued to develop under the direction of the park naturalist. This tradition has been continued down to the present under various administrative job descriptions.

As in many national and provincial parks, an outdoor amphitheatre carried the main burden of public education along with a series of organized guided hikes. Proposals for development of a museum-interpretation complex were made in 1969 and a concept plan for a development overlooking Lower Waterton Lakes was acknowledged in the departmental estimates for 1972. This project was cancelled by headquarters, however, and, instead, a new indoor theatre was constructed near Cameron Falls, close to the popular fish-rearing ponds. This facility replaced the outdoor amphitheatre, which had been in use for many years, in close proximity to the group campground.[77] The demand for public interpretation and the desire by local park staff to provide improved facilities reflected the importance which the townsite continued to have as a focus for activity at Waterton Lakes National Park.

Waterton Townsite Developments: 1945-1975

J. B. Harkin's belief in a future for automobile tourism had certainly started to come true before the great depression set in. "Auto-courts" had appeared in many of the national parks before 1930. Declines in park visitation figures had been few over the years, coming only in the early years of the 1930s and during World War II.[78] In absolute terms, tourism demand had remained relatively low before the war, for distance travel was still the privilege of those with extra income.[79] With victory in Europe and the Pacific, the North American economy quickly prospered, and, by the 1950s, the war generation of parents, babies in hand, were prepared to travel by car and relax for a week or two in the year. This mounting democratization of the parks fostered a demand for accommodation more modest than that provided by the Prince of Wales Hotel or the rustic Kilmorey Lodge. Tourists were still very cost-conscious in the 1950s. In the United States that year, close to 43 percent of tourist travellers stayed with friends or relatives rather than in commercial accommodation.[80] Commercial demand was rising, nevertheless, and, by 1953, Harry Reeves had established Waterton's second group of tourist cabins. A new form of stop-over place, the "motel" soon gained permit approval as well. First came the Franklin, and then the El Cortez, followed in 1961 by the Emerald Bay.[81]

There were other recreational initiatives at Waterton after the war. The Waterton Lakes are fed from cold, high mountain melt-waters. Places for natural outdoor public swimming have consequently always been in short supply. The pond-like Lake Linnet, near the Prince of Wales Hotel, was one of the few suitable places for a beach, and the park had established attractive change rooms and public lifeguarding there in 1924. A more suitable place for swimming was required for year-round use, and, in 1924, Isaac Allred opened a covered swimming pool in the townsite. Acquired in 1931 by D. H. Ellison, it became known as the Crystal Pool. Water for the pool was heated by a steam plant, and the pool operated successfully for over twenty years. Difficulties in keeping it up to regulation standard, along with snow build-ups that placed stress on the roof, led to its closing after the 1948 season. Interest in the property was surrendered in 1956, and the building was demolished to make way for a liquor store and the new travel bureau.[82] A new pool was built by the National Parks Branch and officially opened in 1960 by the Honourable Alvin Hamilton.[83]

On the institutional side, the town saw the addition of a community hall when the Lions Club purchased a surplus building from the Alberta Air Training Centre and relocated it to the townsite. The Roman Catholic Church building was replaced in 1951 and, in 1962, the United Church of Canada completed an attractive church, built in the rustic style. One year later, the Church of Jesus Christ of Latter-day Saints erected its first church in the townsite.[84]

Despite the significant rise in popularity of park vacation touring after the war, the townsite at Waterton retained a certain sense of scale, owing to the relatively short summer season, the lack of physical room for expansion, and the heavy snows that congested the streets, often as early as October. Issues connected with development and infrastructure improvements in national park townsites were sufficient to prompt a number of studies. The *Crawford Report* (1960) reviewed leasing policy and rates and sought to determine the demand for citizen participation in local government.[85] When asked to express their wishes, the residents of Jasper, Banff, and Waterton all decided against the idea of local government and for a continuation of national park local government authority. The chambers of commerce and residents had undoubtedly carefully considered the financial implications of self-government. The citizen "advisory committee" approach was continued.

In the aftermath of the serious flood of June, 1964, a review of the earlier zone concepts of 1952 was considered necessary and national park and consulting planners completed a number of conceptual plans for the townsite between 1966 and 1969.[86] The professional planning function within the national parks had been expanded considerably since 1957, and, in the fall of 1964, planners became armed with a formalized statement of park policy.[87] With the election of the Trudeau administration in 1968, the national parks would soon embark on a period of more detailed park inventory, planning and expansion under the new minister of Indian and Northern Affairs, Jean Chretien.[88]

Chapter Seven

Towards Cooperative Relationships: Waterton and its Neighbours, 1975-2000

Armed with a national park policy that reinforced the notions of planning and public "interpretation" programs, headquarters officials in the early 1970s started to shift their attention towards an improved knowledge of the resources under their control. Park naturalist Kurt Seel had prepared a valuable guide to the avi-fauna of the park in 1969.[1] Staff members of the Canadian Wildlife Service, who had enjoyed a long relationship with the National Parks Branch, continued to undertake studies within the parks.[2] In 1973, J. Dewey Soper, an acknowledged authority on Alberta wildlife, prepared a report on the mammals of Waterton Lakes that gave particular attention to the role of the smaller and less visible members of the mammalian order in the park.[3] In the 1970s, veteran wildlife biologist Job Kuijt continued working steadily on his monumental book, *A Flora of Waterton Lakes National Park*.[4]

On the cultural side, knowledge of the archaeological aspects of the past were supplemented by the 1968 designation of the Oil City site as a national historic site, giving recognition of the importance of the first oil well in Western Canada.[5] The following year, a former park naturalist and military historian, William Rodney, published his excellent biography of "Kootenai" Brown. These events helped to stimulate a broader interest in the park's past. Shortly after, historian Ian Getty was retained to prepare an important summary of the park's administrative and land use history.[6] The fruit of such selected research and an agency orientation towards formal planning and policy came together in the form of an approved park management plan in 1978.

The decision taken in the late 1970s to suspend ski facility development at Waterton helped ensure that the townsite did not face the steady development pressures that had turned Banff into a year round resort.[7] Nevertheless, park townsite planning was still recognized as an important undertaking at Waterton following the destructive flood of 1964.[8] Water and its control has indeed been a recurring theme in park history, one that has had implications for settlement. Fergus Lothian had recalled the essentials of the local topography: "Prior to the successive surveys which established Waterton Park Townsite, the large alluvial fan on which it was built comprised an undulating area divided by Cameron Creek. The central portion was a grass-covered flat, fringed along the lake and the stream with growths of poplar and pine."[9] This description reveals the vulnerability of human settlement to flooding occasioned either by an excess in Cameron Creek, a general rising of Waterton Lake, or both. Severe floods in fact did occur in the townsite in 1937, 1964, 1975, and 1995, causing severe damage to park administration buildings and private establishments.[10]

The earliest settlers of this quarter lived considerably closer to the prairies, partially to escape the vagaries of local climate. With considerable ingenuity, E. R. Reinelt has sought to impose some order on the genesis of Waterton's chaotic weather.[11] Through the abstraction of charts, he has demonstrated what local residents have long understood, that there is a curious relationship between slope, wind, and convection in the Waterton country, one that can make for difficult domestic living for much of the year, particularly in the vicinity of the Narrows. The ancient Kootenay had a more poetic version, given in a tale in which the warming chinook wind is personified.[12] The seasonality of life at Waterton, now as in the ancient past, may be attributed to its alpine character and the excessive accumulations of snow, which may begin as early as October (Plate 7). This limiting quality has worked to keep the townsite small and free of those forces which have produced ever-busier, year-round townsites in some other national parks.

Spring, especially early June, is the season of watchfulness in Waterton. In the most recent flood visitation, that of 1995, events were triggered by heavy rains across southern Alberta. Between the fifth and eighth of June, close to 175 millimetres. of rain were recorded at the Cameron Falls weather station. The townsite was quite cut off from the rest of Alberta, owing to an extensive channel cutting across the main park entrance road. Emergency funds of well over $1 million was voted for repairs and clean-up.[13]

The destructive role of water has helped shape recent planning efforts, particularly with respect to the location of park facilities and park records. The old park administration building on the lake has now taken on more of a storefront aspect for the giving out of basic information, and much of the park administrative establishment has been relocated to the drier elevations of the Blakiston Creek fan, where the warden office has been located for many years.

The year 1982 was notable for a development that refocused interest on the international heritage represented by Waterton-Glacier. A pavilion was opened on the shores of Upper Waterton Lake near the town campground in recognition of fifty years of the International Peace Park designation. Other initiatives in the 1980s demonstrated how town planning was embracing a recognition of the architectural values of townsites. Equipped with a new heritage policy on federally owned buildings, efforts were made to conserve important older structures and to implement visual standards for the townsites.[14] A study of Waterton's requirements for the conservation of its architectural elements was prepared by the firm Gowling and Gibb in 1987.[15] In 1991 and 1998, assessments of the architectural values of structures in the townsite and outlying areas were prepared by the Canadian Parks Service.[16] In 1993, the grand Prince of Wales Hotel was designated a national historic site, the second in Waterton Lakes National Park.

The economics of heritage conservation of older federally owned buildings has posed difficult budget questions for park staff in the 1990s. Managers have been asked to balance increasing policy demands with declining budgets. The historic gatehouse that stands at the entrance to Waterton Lakes National Park is a case in point (Fig. 75). Long without a function, it is nevertheless an attractive rustic structure in stone and wood, dating from the 1930s, one that acts as a kind of boundary entrance landmark for the park. It is representative of a host of similar structures under federal ownership that many people would like to see survive the ravages of time. Managers may view such structures, often justifiably, as just one more asset for which maintenance funds cannot be found. The dilemma becomes more apparent when put into the context of something as extensive as the historic Going-to-the-Sun road in Glacier National Park. The costs associated

153

Fig. 75. Old Waterton Park entrance gate house. This attractive building, located at the Highway 6 turn-off, close to the old Waterton Mills site, was built under the Relief Works program of the 1930s. Parks Canada.

with adapting a road built for 1930s driving conditions and demands, and which now enjoys national historic landmark status, to the travel expectations of the 1990s, have become prohibitive under the current rules and goals of public finance in the United States (Plate 8). Post-2000 solutions to many similar park management situations that involve a need to balance preservation and use will in many cases, presumably lie in the direction of limitations on past principles of use.[17]

An important aspect of post-1975 park policy at Waterton concerned improvement of external relationships with the public and industry. The growth in public environmental awareness was a significant force behind this initiative. The United States provided a useful model for one aspect of this effort. A variety of citizen-sponsored park cooperating associations had come into operation since the 1920s as auxiliaries to the United States National Park Service. Ottawa park headquarters initiated a major review of the approaches being taken in the United States and other nations, a review which culminated in the tabling of the Mosquin reports between 1978 and 1980.[18] Subsequently, on the strong guiding initiative of Waterton Park Superintendent Bernie Lieff and Chief Naturalist Duane Barrus, the Waterton Natural History Association was established in 1983, a citizen organization mandated to sponsor programs sympathetic to national park objectives.[19] The WNHA has given practical support to the Waterton interpretation and education programs through the production and sales of publications, calendars, post-cards, special events promotion, and general fund-raising for park purposes. It was one more link in the chain that sought to bind the park and citizen groups together in the pursuit of the public purpose. This achievement started to take the Canadian national parks further along a road already travelled by the parks of Europe and the United States.[20] The Glacier Park Natural History Association, based at Lake McDonald, for example, had been organized in 1946.

Other forms of organization were on the horizon that would take the park further into extension relationships and the mobilization of science in the name of special protected areas. It has been noted how the landscape of Waterton slowly freed itself from various claims of resource use. Grazing, oil, mining, and water rights had all been contended for, but by 1945 a park of some integrity had been established in both the legal and practical sense.[21] By 1950, use of the parks was increasing as a result of growing automobile ownership. The priority given to road improvement aided this process and hence a need for larger general budgets. These tendencies started to register in the later 1950s when proposed cottage development on the northeastern side of Waterton led to pressure for a new road into the park. Superintendent T. W. Pierce was requested by headquarters to report on the status of lands located near the northern entrance to the park:[22]

> *You may recall that for many years the Province of Alberta had an agreement with the Department to maintain buffer zones outside park boundaries at the eastern entrance of Banff and Jasper National Parks. Within these zones no development of any kind was permitted. Within the past two years the agreement was amended limiting development to a point within half a mile of the park boundaries instead of the one mile limit that had previously existed.*

Shortly thereafter, National Parks Director J.R.B. Coleman recommended to his deputy minister that the Chief Mountain extension road not be approved.[23]

This reference to "buffer zones" is of significance for it foreshadowed an important initiative of the 1970s that would revive this concern about conservation issues in the park boundary areas. Through the UNESCO-sponsored program, Man and the Biosphere (MAB), Waterton Lakes National Park achieved Biosphere

Reserve status in 1979.[24] Glacier National Park had been designated under MAB three years earlier.[25] The objectives of MAB are to facilitate the long-term conservation of special designated areas through a cooperative system of land-use in the border areas adjacent. In the first two decades of MAB, many of these special designated areas were represented by previously established parks or other protected areas. As of 2000, there were over 340 biosphere reserves established around the world in eighty-two countries.[26] In consideration of the actual scope of surrounding land-use pressures in the Waterton-Glacier region, the designation took on significance as a tool for building up a park constituency and fostering joint-management regimes.[27] The significance of the new designation was acknowledged by the 1987 management plan review team, which concluded that Waterton Lakes National Park was a protected "island" surrounded by lands managed for a wide variety of purposes. These lands were managed by such diverse agencies as Glacier National Park, the Alberta Forest Service, the British Columbia Forest Service, British Columbia Parks, the Blood Indian Tribe, the municipal districts of Pincher Creek and Cardston, extractive industries, and private landowners. Probably no other Canadian national park was so concerned with the jurisdictions of so many different land management agencies.[28]

The main intent of the MAB designation was to muster a variety of volunteer arrangements with industry, educators, local landowners, and scientists, by which a consensus on appropriate buffer zone policies could be continuously fostered. The MAB idea was then strongly oriented towards voluntarism and grassroots involvement by citizens and local organizations.

A review of the minutes of the Waterton Biosphere Reserve Association after 1981 reveals the energy and wisdom that a few interested citizens of a locality can bring to bear on park and general environmental matters.[29] At the March 1982 meeting of the main committee, local rancher Charlie Russell reinforced the importance of the initiatives being taken by ranchers and other private groups on behalf of the association.[30] Following a symposium on biosphere reserves held at Kalispell, Montana, in 1982, the Waterton group pursued a number of strategies aimed at education, information exchange with other related groups, and practical research and test projects. A technical core committee was established to help the association in its research and project work. The Waterton Biosphere Reserve

Association has stressed research on projects that are likely to capture the imagination of the local ranching community, such as the development of new upland grass species appropriate for forage, large mammal studies, predator compensation schemes for ranchers, petroleum industry monitoring, infectious disease studies (particularly with respect to elk and cattle), pine beetle and knapweed infestations, and general environmental education.[31]

The contextual state of Waterton-Glacier country was reviewed in 1987 by *National Geographic* magazine, which identified some fifty examples of potential land-use conflicts distributed around the borders of the parks. These included:[32]

Access Roads	Mines
Amusement Parks	Oil/Gas wells
Grizzly Bear Hunting	Poaching
Home Subdivisions	Scenic Helicopter flights
Livestock trespassing	Seismic blasting
Logging	

The review drew attention to conditions that were not atypical of what was going on in much of North America. The rural areas in much of the continent had been undergoing urbanization of a sort or hosting developments keyed to the needs of expanding cities. Modern transportation by car had reduced the isolation of many areas previously frequented only by wildlife, the Indian and the rancher. This was certainly the case along the eastern slope of the Rocky Mountains in Alberta and Montana. Land use conflicts generated by other public land agencies, such as the Flathead National Forest, contiguous to Glacier, were also of some importance.[33]

The resource extraction frontier at Waterton has been drawn quite firmly at the park boundary since World War II, with in-park lease holdings all re-purchased on behalf of the Crown. Programs such as MAB assist in maintaining sound working relationships with firms such as Shell Resources Canada, which maintains a sizeable gas field operation north of Waterton. The actual success of the MAB model is still open to question. One observer contends that the vision of integrated resource management, outside of the core areas, has not been achieved with any consistency and that "few biosphere reserves fit the ideal model."[34]

Nevertheless, within the context of global concerns over biodiversity as an issue, the larger significance of MAB may be the manner in which it has fostered continuing discussion on the search for models of integrated land use and protection of special areas.[35] As a seed bed of ideas for better land management, MAB has been important. The Third International Conference on the Science and Management of Protected Areas, held in Calgary in 1997, was organized by individuals, many of whom had experience in promotion of the MAB program in the past. Included in this group was former Waterton Superintendent Bernie Lieff.[36]

Just as challenging in the 1990s was the question of the definition of "wilderness." Governments have continued to wrestle with decisions to erode or strengthen, through legislation, the capability of wild animal populations to maintain an independent existence.[37] For example, the integrity of longstanding efforts to provide a safe haven for international herds of migratory elk in Montana and Alberta is now questioned by some who see a threat in the rise of elk-ranching legislation on both sides of the international border.[38] The legislation enabling elk ranching has had the effect of eroding the distinction between animals that range freely and those that are considered to be domestic.

Such considerations led the Canadian Parks and Wilderness Society to sponsor a seminar at Waterton Park in June, 1990, to consider the legal and institutional requirements of the "Crown of the Continent" ecosystem, a term derived from the term coined a century ago by George Bird Grinnell. The expression describes the makeup of the high country, which constitutes the headwaters of rivers and streams straddling the Alberta, British Columbia, and Montana borders. The goal is to link the existing protected areas in a consistent manner and to better rationalize special protected area boundaries with the actual borders of the ecosystem. Despite the special protection status given to much of the land defining the "Crown of the Continent," there are still problems confronting wildlife populations owing to lack of uniformity of policy. Waterton warden Kevin van Tigham observed that bears are now subject to serious identity crises:[39]

In one year, the same grizzly can find itself being shot at legally by hunters in B.C.'s Akamina-Kishinena wildland, avoiding hikers' bear bells in Waterton, pursued by armed game officers on the leased grazing lands or

Alberta's Poll Haven area, and protected by an Endangered Species Act just south of the border in Montana. All this in one bear's home range and the same ecosystem. The same bear is variously an endangered treasure, an agricultural nuisance, a legally hunted trophy and a park resource, depending on where it happens to be at any given time.

Predator control remains a contentious issue in cross-boundary situations in both Canada and the United States, but this area too has seen a shift in public understanding over the last thirty years. Mention has been made of the elimination of the wolf from Yellowstone in the 1920s. The policy of restoring ecosystem elements in the American Northern Rockies now extends to the wolf and the effort has borne fruit in a way that demonstrates the great advantage of the existence of the large international park landscape of Waterton-Glacier. In 1985, wildlife biologists noticed that wolves from Canada had moved south into Glacier and and denned there. According to one writer, this was the first re-establishment of wolves in the American West since the 1930s.[40] On the American side, Robert Ream had spent many years pondering the relationship of Glacier National Park with the large wilderness areas to the north where wolves were to be found. In noting the appearance of the so-called Magic Pack of twelve wolves from the Alberta-British Columbia border zone, Clifford Marktinka, supervisory biologist at Glacier, was moved to remark that "I think this is the biggest thing that has happened there since the creation of the park itself."[41] The Magic Pack – so named because it has sometimes been hard to locate – appears to have grown from the mating of a female named Kishinena and a black male wolf. The pair had denned in Canada just north of Kishinena Creek. The seven pups of this first litter were resident in British Columbia and two subsequent litters expanded the pack to about twenty. At this time, perhaps in response to resource development on the Canadian side, the pack then moved down into Glacier. The 9,065 square kilometres (3,500 square miles) of territory, rich in game, was considered an ideal wolf recovery area, although the sudden reappearance of wolves represented something of an unknown with respect to effects on some of the other animal populations.[42]

Over the last twenty years, the prominence given to biodiversity issues, to defining the proper scope of human use, and to the potential of environmental

159

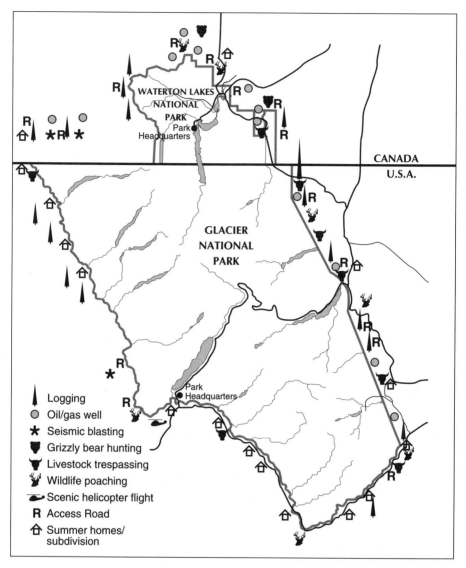

CANADA
U.S.A.

WATERTON LAKES
NATIONAL
PARK
Park
Headquarters

GLACIER
NATIONAL
PARK

Park
Headquarters

Logging
Oil/gas well
Seismic blasting
Grizzly bear hunting
Livestock trespassing
Wildlife poaching
Scenic helicopter flight
R Access Road
Summer homes/
subdivision

Map 7. Envionmental impacts surrounding Waterton-Glacier country, 2000. Parks Canada.

science has stimulated thought about integrated land-management concepts in light of the knowledge that chemical and biological forces are not respectful of cartographic lines on the land. As the need for accurate knowledge of the range requirements of large mammals and other species becomes more acute, new techniques of evaluating population numbers and movements are being ushered in, aided by new techniques in measurement such as DNA testing.[43] Even within the confines of park boundaries proper, management practices may retain a certain ambiguity towards the periodic and specialized use of pesticides, and with respect to the spread of new botanical intruders such as knapweed.[44] Thus, in the future, the notion of park integrity is likely to reflect not only debate over the conditions of tourist use, but also contending ideas of economics and science and the continuing debate about the appropriate scope of human mastery over that most elusive concept known popularly as "nature."

Notes

References in these Notes are given in abbreviated form, i.e., author's surname followed by part of the title of the work cited. Full bibliographical details for these items are provided in the Bibliography. Items in the Bibliography are arranged by author, title, and date. Where the author is unknown, items may be found by title.

Introduction

1. Grinnell, "Crown of the Continent" (1901), 660-71; and Thane, *The Majestic Land* (1950), p. 198.
2. George Catlin, "Letter 31. Mouth of Teton River," *Letters and Notes* (1995), Vol. 1, p. 294.
3. See Lothian, *A History of Canada's National Parks*, Vol. 1 (1976), pp. 30-32.
4. Of particular interest in this sense is the on-going work of the Alberta archaeologist Brian Reeves and his associates in Montana. See Reeves, *Waterton Lakes National Park Ethnoarchaeological Study. Preliminary Report. 1994.* (1995), pp. 2-9; and *Glacier National Park Archaeological Inventory and Assessment. Annual Field Season Reports. 1994-1997* (1995-1998).
5. Reeves, "Executive Summary" (1997), p. 5.
6. See Chief Mountain, *"Kootenai Brown"* (1954), Ch. 8.
7. See Irene Spry, ed. *The Papers of the Palliser Expedition* (1968), pp. 577-78; and Haig, *In the Footsteps of Thomas Blakiston* (1980).
8. On Blakiston, see E. J. Homgren, "Thomas Blakiston, Explorer" (1976), 15-22; "Thomas Wright Blakiston" in *Foreign Pioneers* (1968); "Obituary" *The Auk* (1892), 75; *Dictionary of National Biography* (1910), pp. 214-15.
9. See Spry, *Papers of the Palliser Expedition* (1968), p. xxii; pp. 569-71. Galton was a cousin of Darwin and interested in statistical approaches to the theory of heredity. See Nordenskiold, *The History of Biology* (1928), pp. 585-90.
10. Aldington, *The Strange Career* (1949); Jenkins, *The Naturalists* (1978), Ch. 8; Blackburn, *Charles Waterton* (1989).
11. Rodney, *Kootenai Brown* (1969), pp. 195-98; Chief Mountain, *"Kootenai Brown"* (1954), p. 41.
12. Chief Mountain, *"Kootenai Brown"* (1954), p. 41.
13. Ibid., p. 42.
14. Rinehart, *Through Glacier Park in 1915* (1983), pp. 67-9.
15. In Canada, the Geographic Board of Canada was established in 1897. Part of its mandate was to standardize geographic names, or toponyms, for the entire country. This body became

known as the Canadian Permanent Committee on Geographic Names, consisting of a committee composed of federal and provincial representatives. See *Canada's Geographical Names* (n.d.).

16. Hunter, *Glencoe and the Indians* (1996), pp.130-35; 178-9; Josephy, Jr. *The Nez Perce Indians* (1997), pp. 675-6.

17. Aldington, *The Strange Career* (1949).

18. *The World's First Nature Reserve*. (1989); and Richard Bell, Middleston, Wakefield, West Yorkshire, to J. D. Collinson, Director General, National Parks, Ottawa. July 6, 1989. Waterton Lakes National Park Library.

19. Waterton, "Preface" to *Essays on Natural History*, (1866), pp. iii-iv; and Matthews, "Introduction" to Charles Waterton, *Wanderings in South America* (1973), p. xiv.

20. Jenkins, *The Naturalists* (1978), Ch. 8; Aldington, *The Strange Career* (1949), p. 118.

21. Maltby, "Charles Waterton"(1982); "Proceedings of a Symposium" (1983).

22. Dawson, *Report on the Region in the Vicinity of the Bow and Belly Rivers* (1884), p. 21c f.

23. Schultz, *Blackfeet and Buffalo* (1962), p. 70.

24. Hanna, *Stars Over Montana* (1988), pp. 25-38.

25. *Report of James Doty*. (1854) "... but my survey shows that the Chief Mountain Lake and its environs, as well as the tract of fertile country extending south to the Marias Pass, belong to the United States." See also Josephy, *The Nez Perce Indians* (1997), pp. 308-11.

26. See Lothian, *A History*, Vol. I (1976), p. 31.

27. See Chief Mountain, *"Kootenai Brown"* (1954), p. 41.

28. Goble, *Waterton Park History* (1981), p. 145.

29. NA. RG 84 Vol. 226 W. 326.

30. Quoted in Jenkins, *The Naturalists* (1984), p. 65.

31. Ibid.

Chapter One
Beginnings

1. NA. RG 84 Vol. 2226 W. 320. R.G. Forbis, University of Calgary, to John Rick, National Parks Branch, July 3, 1968.

2. See Milne-Brumley, *The Narrows Site in Waterton Lakes National Park* (1971); Reeves, *The Prehistory of Pass Creek Valley* (1971); and the series of reports reporting on field work undertaken between 1993 and 1997 for Glacier National Park. Reeves, *Archaeological Inventory and Assessment* (1995-98).

3. Reeves, *Archaeological Inventory and Assessment. 1994 Field Season, Final Report. Part I. Inventory* (1996), p. iv.

4. Reeves, "Early Holocene" (1975), 239.

5. Ibid., 245.

6. Rod Heitzmann, personal communication,1999, re work being undertaken at the University of Calgary by Len Hills and his associates.

7. Waterton Park Management Plan. Review (1989), p. 58; and see Milne-Brumley, *The Narrows Site in Waterton Lakes National Park* (1971).

8. Reeves, "Early Holocene" (1975), 245.

9. Delane and Sharp, "The Blue Camas (*Camassia quamash*)" (1976), 79-80; Brown, Old Man's Garden (1970), pp. 43-46; and Milne-Brumley *The Narrows Site in Waterton Lakes National Park* (1971).

10. See Johnston, *Plants and the Blackfoot* (1987).

11. See Vickers, *Alberta Plains Prehistory* (1986), p. 54.

12. See Hurt, "The Altithermal and the Prehistory of the Northern Plains" (1966), 101-13; Wedel, "The Prehistoric Plains," in Jennings, ed., *Ancient North Americans* (1983), pp. 221-24.

13. See Buchner, *Cultural Responses to the Altithermal* (1980), pp. 204-8.

14. Reeves, "Head-Smashed-In: 5500 Years of Bison Jumping in the Alberta Plains" (1978), 151-74.

15. On this topic, see Daugherty, "The Intermontane Western Tradition" (1963), pp. 144-50.

16. Systematic work at stratified sites is still quite limited in the cordillera and plateau regions and attempts to formulate meaningful cultural sequences is still at an early stage. The prehistory of Waterton-Glacier country may be compared with findings at other regional sites. See Driver, *Holocene Man* (1978), Gryba, *Sibbald Creek* (1983), and Keeler, *An Upland Hunting Camp* (1973). Choquette, "A Proposed Cultural Chronology" (1985), and "Early Post-Glacial Habitation" (1996) and Fedje, "Banff Prehistory" (1988). These studies have made some preliminary suggestions towards cultural chronology in the Rockies and in the Columbia Trench.

17. Waterton Lakes National Park, *Management Plan Review* (1989), p. 51 f.

18. See Wormington and Forbis, *An Introduction to the Archeology of Alberta* (1965), pp. 194-5; Klimko, "New Perspectives on Avonlea" in Burley, ed., *Contributions to Plains Prehistory* (1985), pp. 64-85.

19. Milne-Brumley, *The Narrows Site: A Fishing Station-Campsite* (1971), p. 103; and Waterton Lakes National Park, *Management Plan Review* (1989), p. 59.

20. Vickers, *Alberta Plains Prehistory* (1986), pp. 101-2; Brink, *Dog Days in Southern Alberta* (1986). An attempt has been made to correlate the modern distribution of native languages with the dynamics of the retreat of the last glacial ice sheets. See Rogers, "Glacial Geography and Native North American Languages" (1985), pp. 130-37.

21. Wormington and Forbis (1965), pp. 198-99.

22. See Brink, *Dog Days in Southern Alberta* (1986), p. 59 f. and Vickers, *Alberta Plains Prehistory* (1986), p. 101 f.

23. Ewers, *The Horse in Blackfoot Indian Culture* (1955), p. 24.

24. See Milloy, *The Plains Cree* (1990), p. xv; Ewers, *The Blackfeet Raiders* (1958), p. 21 f.

25. See. Roe, *The Indian and the Horse* (1955), Ch. 5. Andrew C. Isenberg, *The Destruction of the Bison* (2000), p. 31 f.

26. Ewers, "The Influence of the Fur Trade" in *People and Pelts* (1972), p. 2.

27. Brink, *Dog Days in Southern Alberta* (1986); Dempsey, *Indians of Alberta* (1988); Schaeffer, "Le Blanc and La Gasse" (1966).

28. Schaeffer, "Plains Kutenai" (1982), 1-9; Brink, *Dog Days in Southern Alberta* (1986), pp. 28-34. Driver's maps of native culture areas in North America, printed in the 1960s, displayed a distinct blank in the zone around Waterton Lakes National Park with respect to

language and general affiliation of the Kootenay peoples. Driver, *The Indians of North America* (1961), Map 37. There is still no clear consensus on the ultimate affiliations of the Kootenay language. See Jorgensen, *Western Indians* (1980), pp. 56, 76; Whyte, *Indians in the Rockies* (1985), p. 25; and Goddard, ed. (1996), p. 81.

29. Teit, "Traditions and Information Regarding the Tona'xa" (1930), 627.

30. Reeves has argued for great time-depth for the ancestral Kootenay and Blackfoot in the Waterton-Glacier mountain region. See Reeves, *Glacier National Park* (1995-1998).

31. Hector's Journal, Sept. 15, 1858, in Spry, ed. *The Papers of the Palliser Expedition,* (1968), p. 327; Geographic Board of Canada, *Place Names of Alberta* (1928), p. 73; and Dempsey, *A History of Rocky Mountain House* (1973), pp. 11-13.

32. For the changing inter-tribal relationships of the Blackfoot, see Milloy, *The Plains Cree* (1990), pp. 83-96, and Smyth, "The Battle for the Peigan Trade" (1984), 2-17

33. Milloy, *The Plains Cree* (1990), pp. 104-5.

34. Cited in Milloy, *The Plains Cree* (1990), p. 105.

35. Ibid., pp. 116-18; Higinbotham, *When the West Was Young* (1978), pp. 232-35; Johnston, comp., *The Battle at Belly River* (1966); Dempsey, *Red Crow* (1980), p. 72.

Chapter Two
Intrusion of the European

1. Ewers, "The Influence of the Fur Trade," in *People and Pelts* (1972), pp. 3-4; Ray, *The Indians in the Fur Trade* (1974), pp. 59-61.

2. See Ray, *The Indians in the Fur Trade* (1974). This idea has been extended in Milloy, *The Plains Cree* (1990).

3. See Ray, *The Indians in the Fur Trade* (1974) and Weber, *The Taos Trappers* (n.d), pp. 21-31.

4. See Moodie and Kaye, "The Ac Ko Mo Ki Map" (1977), 5-15; and Beattie, "Indian Maps in the Hudson's Bay Company Archives" (1985-1986), 166-75.

5. See Schaeffer, "Le Blanc and La Gasse" (1966), and "Plains Kootenay" (1982), 1-9.

6. See Schaeffer, "Plains Kootenay" (1966).

7. Rich and Johnson, eds., *Peter Skene Ogden's Snake Country Journals* (1950).

8. Rich, *History of the Hudson's Bay Company*, Vol. III (1960), pp. 572-3.

9. Johnson, *Flathead and Kootenay* (1969), p. 187.

10. See Schultz, *Rising Wolf* (1919).

11. Rich, *History of the Hudson's Bay Company*, Vol. III, (1960), pp. 584-5.

12. For similar conclusions drawn more firmly with respect to the U.S. Glacier National Park area, see Schiere, *Glacier National Park* (1970).

13. Johnson, *Flathead and Kootenay* (1969). p. 187.

14. Ibid., pp. 187-8.

15. Harrison, *The History of the Hat* (1960); and Wilcox *The Mode in Furs* (1951).

16. See Hunter, *Glencoe and the Indians* (1996), p. 77 f.; Jackson, *Children of the Fur Trade* (1995), pp. 3-13; 45-52.

17. Smyth, "The Struggle for the Piegan Trade" (1984), 13 f; Sunder, *The Fur Trade on the Upper Missouri* (1965).

18. Dempsey, *Red Crow* (1980), pp. 2-5.
19. On De Smet, see Killoren, '*Come Black Robe*' (1994), p. 20. McGuinness, "Missionary Journey of Father De Smet" (1967), 12.
21. Cited in Johnson, *Flathead and Kootenay* (1969), pp. 62-3.
22. Kendrick and Inglis, *Enlightened Voyages* (1991), pp. 18-20; Chevigny, *Russian America* (1965), p. 223 f.; Ronda, *Astoria and Empire* (1990), p. 65 f.
23. J. Doty, *Report of a Survey* (1854) in Stevens, *Reports of the Explorations and Surveys* (1860).
24. See Jones, *To the Webster-Ashburton Treaty* (1977), p. 154 f; Deutsch, "The Evolution of the International Boundary" (1960), 63-79.
25. Spry, ed. *The Papers of the Palliser Expedition* (1968), pp. 547 f.; and see Haig, *In the Footsteps of Thomas Blakiston* (1982).
26. "Final Report of the British Commissioner" in *International Boundary Commission. Report.* (1937), p. 207.
27. Walker, ed. "The 1855 Blackfeet Treaty Council" (1982), 44-51; for the treaty, see Kappler, ed. *Indian Affairs, Laws and Treaties* (n.d.), pp. 736-40; Dempsey, *Amazing Death of Calf Shirt* (1994), 59-66.
28. Spence, *Montana: A History* (1978), Ch. 3.
29. Sharp, *Whoop-Up Country* (1960), p. 37.
30. Ibid., Ch. 3.
31. Jameson, *Ranchers, Cowboys and Characters* (1987), p. 7.
32. Rodney, *Kootenai Brown* (1969), p. 17.
33. Ibid., p. 39.
34. Ibid., pp. 35-6.
35. Ibid., p. 48.
36. Ibid., p. 52.
37. See MacDonald, "Kootenai Brown in the Red River Valley"(1995), 20-25.
38. Rodney, *Kootenai Brown* (1969), pp. 116-21.
39. Tait, "I Remember" GAA. Library. Typescript. p. 59.
40. Dempsey has suggested that many traders may have been moving through the south Alberta country after 1832. See Dempsey, ed. "Alexander Culbertson's Journey to Bow River" (1971), 8-29.
41. Cited in Dempsey, "Fred Kanouse: Calgary's First Businessman" (1957). See also, Kennedy, *A Whiskey Trade Frontier* (1991), pp. 70, 290.
42. Rodney, *Kootenai Brown* (1969), p. 125; Kelly *The Range Men* (1988), p. 159.
43. See Kennedy and Reeves, *An Inventory and Historical Description of Whiskey Posts* (1984); Kelly (1975), p. 47; Liddell, "Fort Warren or Kootinai Post" (1956). See also, Kennedy, *A Whiskey Trade Frontier* (1991), p. 290.
44. Berry, "Fort Whoop-up and the Whiskey Traders" (1969), 1-6.
45. Berry, *The Whoop-up Trail* (1995), p. 19.
46. Dempsey, *Red Crow* (1980), p. 78. The couple later separated, and each remarried. Details on the members of the Kanouse family may be found in GAA. M1021. Letter of Mrs. K.H. Kanouse to Bruce Ramsay.
47. Dempsey (1957).
48. Ibid., p. 125.

49. Kelly, *The Range Men* (1988) p. 57; *Calgary Herald*, Sept. 3, 1955; GAA, M1021. Kanouse Family Fonds. Excerpts from the Fort Macleod Gazette, 1882-1885.

50. Henry's lease was confirmed by Order in Council 722, April 11, 1882. Getty (1972), p. 16. Breen, *The Canadian Prairie West* (1983), pp. 43-5; "The South Fork Ranch" (1897); Kelly, *The Range Men* (1988), p. 83.

51. Hill, *From Home to Home* (1966), p. 330.

52. Rodney, *Kootenai Brown* (1969), Ch. 9, and Tolton, *The Rocky Mountain Rangers* (1994).

53. Rodney, *Kootenai Brown* (1969), p. 154.

54. Dominion Land Titles, Land Grant no. 2518. Dept. of the Interior. Dec. 15, 1885. Cited in Rodney, *Kootenai Brown* (1969), p. 153. This new land was in Twp. 9, Range 25 West of the 4th Parallel.

55. Ibid., p. 166.

56. This was a quarter in section 31, Range 1, and 29 West of the Fourth Meridian.

57. Rodney, *Kootenai Brown* (1969), p. 166.

58. On the Mormon entry into southern Alberta see Rosenvall, "The Transfer of Mormon Culture to Alberta," in Rosenvall and Evans, eds., *Essays on the Historical Geography of the Canadian West* (1987), pp. 122-44.

59. Rodney, *Kootenai Brown* (1969), pp. 171-6.

60. Ibid. p. 181.

Chapter Three
Ranchers, Resources and the First Waterton Park Reserve: 1895-1930

1. Breen, *The Canadian Prairie West* (1983), p. 16 f.

2. Jameson, *Ranchers, Cowboys and Characters* (1987), pp. 20-22.

3. Breen, *The Canadian Prairie West* (1983), pp. 78-9.

4. Ibid., p. 78.

5. Ibid., p. 81.

6. Ibid., pp. 70-74.

7. Ibid., pp. 34-5.

8. Rodney, *Kootenai Brown* (1969), pp. 172-3.

9. Cited in Lothian, *A History*, Vol. I (1976), p. 31.

10. *McLeod Gazette*, May 3, 1887, "Editorial"; May 24, 1887, "Mountaineer" and "Editorial."

11. Letter. F.W. Godsal to Wm. Pearce Sept. 12, 1893. Waterton Lakes National Park Library.

12. Lothian, *A History*, Vol. I (1976), p. 32.

13. P.C. 1621 May 30, 1895; and see Van Kirk, *The Development of National Park Policy* (1969), p.25.

14. Rodney, *Kootenai Brown* (1969), pp. 163-5.

15. Lothian, *A History*, Vol. I (1976), p. 45. On the ambiguous use of the term "superintendent" in these years, see R.A. Watt, "WLNP Fact Sheet. John George (Kootenai) Brown" (WLNP: Feb. 2000), p. 8. Waterton Lakes National Park Library.

16. Ibid., p. 46. In 1912 Brown was confirmed as Chief Forest Ranger, effectively the superintendent. On the ambiguous use of the term "superintendent" in these years, see R.A. Watt, "WLNP Fact Sheet. John George (Kootenai) Brown." (WLNP: Feb. 2000), p. 8. Waterton Lakes National Park Library.

17. R.H. Campbell, Superintendent of Forestry, to F.K. Vreeland, Camp-fire Club of America, New York. Cited in Lothian, *A History*, Vol. I (1976), p. 47.

18. Ise, *Our National Park Policy* (1961), Ch. 9.

19. Lothian, *A History*, Vol. II (1977). p. 15.

20. P.C. 1165. June 24, 1914.

21. Lothian, *A History*, Vol. III (1979), p. 42.

22. Lothian, *A History*, Vol. I (1976), p. 47.

23. See Spence, *Montana: A History* (1978), p. 39.

24. Abbott, "Montana: Political Enigma of the Northern Rockies," in Donnelly, ed. *Rocky Mountain Politics* (1940), p. 198.

25. See De Voto, ed. *The Journals of Lewis and Clark* (1953), p. 428 f.; Flandreau, *The Story of Marias Pass* (1925); Hidy, *The Great Northern Railway* (1988); and Coy and Del Grosso, *Montana's Marias Pass* (1996).

26. Several other tribes besides the Blackfeet, Piegan, and Blood, signed onto the 1855 Treaty, each receiving their own specific reservation lands, i.e., The Gros Ventre, Flathead, Upper Pend d'Oreille, Kootenay, and Nez Perce. See Ewers, *The Story of the Blackfeet* (1952), p. 37 f.

27. See DeSanto, "Foundation for a Park" (1995), p. 130.

28. See Ewers, *The Story of the Blackfeet* (1952), pp. 45-8.

29. See Diettert, *Grinnell's Glacier* (1992), pp. 61-71; 72-5; and De Santo, "Foundation for a Park" (1995), p. 130.

30. Diettert, *Grinnell's Glacier* (1992), p. 77.

31. See Hays, *Conservation and the Gospel of Efficiency* (1969), pp. 55-60; but see also Reiger's qualification of the Grinnell-Pinchot split in his *American Sportsmen and the Origins of Conservation* (1975), p. 50 f.

32. Ibid., pp. 87-95.

33. Wright, *Wildlife Research and Management* (1992), p. 9.

34. Buchholtz, "The Diary of Albert 'Death-on-the-trail' Reynolds"(1985), 49-50.

35. Ibid., Diary, Jan. 19,1913.

36. Cited in Rodney, *Kootenai Brown* (1969), p. 201.

37. See Dempsey, "One Hundred Years of Treaty Seven," in Getty and Smith, eds., *One Century Later* (1978), 20-30; on Native experience south of the border, see *Interior Salish and Eastern Washington Indians* (1974). On contemporary Native perceptions of the 1877 treaty, as related by oral tradition, see Treaty 7 Elders, *The True Spirit and Intent of Treaty 7* (1996).

38. The literature is large on these topics. See Utley, *Frontier Regulars* (1973); Carter, *Lost Harvests* (1990); Malone and Roeder, *Montana* (1976), p. 87 f.; Burlingame, *The Montana Frontier* (1980), p. 174 f. Pettipas, *Severing the Ties that Bind* (1993); and Snow, *These Mountains are our Sacred Places* (1977).

39. Cited in Snow, *These Mountains are our Sacred Places* (1977), p. 42.

40. For a review of this suggestion as applied to the Peigan Reserve, see Potyondi, *Where the Rivers Meet* (1992), p. 22 f.

41. See Dempsey, "The Story of the Blood Reserve" (1953), 27-36; and *Indian Tribes of Alberta* (1997), p. 22. Conditions were much different and less favourable to adaptation on the Stoney Reserve west of Calgary. See Snow, *These Mountains are our Sacred Places* (1977), p. 39 f.

42. See Mike Mountain Horse, *My People, The Bloods* (Calgary: Glenbow-Alberta Institute, Blood Tribal Council, 1979), Ch. 15, and Hugh Dempsey, *Charcoal's World* (Saskatoon: Western Producer Prairie Books, 1978).

43. See Taylor, *A History of National Parks Administration* (1988); Brown, "The Doctrine of Usefulness," in Nelson, ed. *Canadian Parks in Perspective* (1973), pp. 46-62.

44. Rodney, *Kootenai Brown* (1969) pp. 168-9.

45. GAA. File D 92 OJ38. Diary of Fred Forster.

46. GAA. M1432. *Patrick Oils Ltd. Prospectus.*; Lothian, *A History*, Vol. I (1976), p. 45.

47. Ernst S. Drader, Cutbank, Montana, to Mrs. G.R. Annand, Waterton. Nov. 11, 1963. Waterton Lakes National Park Library.

48. Lothian, *A History*, Vol. I (1976) p. 46.

49. Ibid.

50. DeSanto, "Drilling at Kintla Lake" (1985), 24-37.

51. DeSanto, "Foundation for a Park" (1995), 130-37; and Willis, "Stratigraphy and Structure" (1902), 305-52.

52. Ernst S. Drader to Mrs. G.R. Annand (1963). Waterton Lakes National Park. Library.

53. NA. RG 84 Vol. 2201. Townsite Development and Oil and Gas Development. W 29. John George Brown, Waterton, to A/Chief Super. Dom. Parks, Edmonton. June 8th, 1914.

54. Stutz, "The Gertrude and Waterton Mills" (1984), 19-23.

55. On the Hanson family, see *Prairie Grass to Mountain Pass* (1974), pp. 748-50.

56. Stutz, "The Gertrude and Waterton Mills" (1984), p. 22.

57. Getty, *The History of Waterton Lakes* (1972), pp. 46-9.

58. Ibid., p. 20.

59. Ibid.

60. On the gradual redefinition of land use in the Glacier country between 1885 and 1910, and on the early actions of the first superintendent, W.R. Logan, see Buchholtz, "W.R. Logan and Glacier National Park" (1969), 2-17.

61. Waterton Lakes National Park. *Resource Description and Analysis* (1984), p. 280.

62. Getty, *The History of Waterton Lakes* (1972), pp. 123-4.

63. Lothian, *A History*, Vol. II (1977), pp. 12-14.

64. Getty, *The History of Waterton Lakes* (1972), p. 124. The role of the forest reserves in the ranching cycle around Pincher Creek has been outlined in Brierly, "Climate and the Seasonal Cycle of Ranching" (1967-68), 38-44.

65. Ibid., p. 127.

66. Lothian, *A History*, Vol. II (1977), p. 35.

67. Buchholtz, "The Last Summer at Lake McDonald" (1976), 23-29.

68. Buchholtz, "W.R. Logan and Glacier National Park" (1969), 13.

69. See Sherfy, "The National Park Service and the First World War" (1978), 203-5.

70. Getty, *The History of Waterton Lakes* (1972), p. 125.

71. Ibid., p. 126.

72. Ibid., p. 200.
73. See Chapter One.
74. July, 26, 1861. Stanley, ed., *Mapping the Frontier* (1970), p. 157.
75. MacMillan, "Report on Proposed National Park" (1909).p. 6. Typescript. Waterton LakesNational Park Library. MacMillan was the Assistant Inspector of Forest Reserves. See also Getty, *The History of Waterton Lakes* (1972), p. 170.
76. Lothian, *A History*, Vol. IV (1981), pp. 19-20; Butler and Maw, *Fishing Canada's National Parks* (1985), p. 63.
77. Cited in Getty, *The History of Waterton Lakes* (1972), p. 171.
78. On Buchanan, see Steele, *Prairie Editor* (1960).
79. On Oland and Scott, see Djuff, *High on a Windy Hill* (1999), p. 36 f.
80. Getty, *The History of Waterton Lakes* (1972), pp. 176-7.
81. Ibid.
82. Lothian, *A History*, Vol. IV (1981), p. 20.
83. J.G. Brown to William McD Tait, in "I Remember" Ms. Waterton Lakes National Park Library.
84. See Potyondi, *Where the Rivers Meet* (1992), p. 125 f.
85. Eastcott, ed., *The Holroyd Journals* (1977), p. 20.
86. Waterton Lakes National Park Files. N-14. Hudson's Bay Company Land Transfer. 1925-1927. The property descriptions are as follows: 474 acres, NW 1/4 and S1/2 Sec. 26 Twp. 1, R 29 W of 4th meridian; 126 Acres, SW 1/4 Sec. 8 Twp. 2 R 29, W of 4th; 320 acres S 1/2 Sec 8 Twp. 2 R 30, W of 4th; 160 acres SE 1/4 Sec. 26 Twp 1 R 1, W of 5th. Memorandum. B. Scott, Dominion Lands Branch to J.B. Harkin, 1926. Cited in Seel, comp. *Waterton Lakes National Park* (1984), p. 343.
87. Gladstone, *History of Waterton* (1968). Waterton Lakes National Park Library.
88. On the Riggall family, see *Prairie Grass to Mountain Pass* (1974), pp. 808-13; Burton, *Bert Riggall: Mountain Guide Extraordinary* (1990), pp.11-12; Russell, *Memoirs of a Mountain Man* (1984), p. 117 f.
89. Waterton National Park. Realty Files.
90. *Lethbridge Daily Herald*. April 14, 1917. "If Waterton Lakes Park is to become Famous, Automobilists of Southern Alberta must make it so."
91. Carpenter, *Fifty Dollar Bride* (1988), p. 100; "Hardy Old Guide Now Superintendent of Waterton Lake Forest Reserve" *Lethbridge Herald*, Oct. 15, 1913; Palmer and Linebarger, *Sarah Luela Nielson* (1988. pp. 11, 24.Waterton Lakes National Park Library.
92. Rodney, *Kootenai Brown* (1969), p. 201.
93. GAA. M490. A.H. Harwood Papers and Correspondence. Folio 2. B.M. Annand. c. 1956.
94. Ibid.; and GAA. M3989. Arthur Henry Harwood in Interview with Gray Campbell, 1950, pp. 7-10; and *Lethbridge Herald*, July 24, 1948,"Waterton Park's Postmaster"; Rackette, "South's Last Round-Up" (1960).
95. "Irrigation in Demand" (1922), 1-2.
96. Getty, *The History of Waterton Lakes* (1972), p. 136 f.
97. NA. RG 84 Vol. 2206 ; Getty (1972), pp. 114-15.
98. Getty, *The History of Waterton Lakes* (1972), p. 140 f.
99. *Lethbridge Herald*, November 3, 1921; Getty, *The History of Waterton Lakes* (1972), pp. 142-3.

100. See Fraser, *Wheeler* (1987), p, 134.

101. Cited in Getty, *The History of Waterton Lakes* (1972), p. 140.

102. Waterton Lakes National Park. File N.21. H. Knight to Commissioner, March 9, 1922.

103. Getty, *The History of Waterton Lakes* (1972), p. 123. On the general politics of irrigation in this period see GAA. M3768 Canada. Department of the Interior. Water Resources Branch. Irrigation Registers, 1895-1960. 2 vol.; NA RG 84 Vol. 87 File W 41 Vol. 2 1921-22 Canada. Department of the Interior, Reclamation Service. Report on the Irrigation Problems in Southern Alberta; and NA. RG 84 Vol. 404 W41 Vol. 5 (1920-52). Canada. Dept. of Mines and Resources. Waterton Irrigation Scheme. 1939.

104. Ibid., p. 160.

105. Getty, *The History of Waterton Lakes* (1972), Ch. 4.

106. Janet Foster, *Working for Wildlife* (1978), pp. 157-8.

107. Getty, *The History of Waterton Lakes* (1972), p.163.

108. NA. RG 84 Vol. 75 U 300 no. 3. W.W. Cory, Memorandum. May 20, 1925.

109. Getty, *The History of Waterton Lakes,* (1972), p. 164 f.

110. Ibid., p. 164.

111. Cahalane, "The Evolution of Predator Control Policy" (1939), 229-37.

112. On American experience in these years, see Sellars, *Preserving Nature* (1997), pp. 72-5.

113. Lothian, *A History*, Vol. II (1977), p. 11.

114. See Martin, *Dominion Lands Policy* (1973), pp. 189-90; 204-26; Van Kirk, *The Development of National Park Policy* (1969).

115. See Mitchner, "The Bow River Scheme" (1984), p. 262. n. 9.

116. Taylor, *A History of National Parks Administration* (1988), Ch. 3.

117. Waterton Lakes National Park. History Files, E. Haug, Waterton, to Canon Middleton, Cardston. March 23, 1920; Forsberg, *Chief Mountain* (1964), p. 52.

118. Taylor and Buchik, *Waterton Townsite* (1991), p. 5.

119. Getty, *The History of Waterton Lakes* (1972), p. 169.

120. See Steele, *Prairie Editor* (1960).

121. Lothian, *A History*, Vol. III (1979), p. 43.

122. Getty, *The History of Waterton Lakes* (1972), pp. 168-9.

123. Taylor and Buchik, *Waterton Townsite* (1991), p. 11.

124. Ibid., p. 7.

125. On Cromarty, see Jacqueline Adell, "Upper Hot Springs Bathhouse, Banff National Park" Federal Heritage Building Review Office. Building Report 84-54 (Ottawa: National Historic Sites Branch, 1984).

126. Mills, *Waterton Townsite* (1999), p. 9.

127. Wood, *The Alberta Temple* (1989), pp. 104-5.

128. Ibid., pp. 54, 58.

129. Goble, *Waterton Park History* (1981). Waterton Lakes National Park Library.

130. See Djuff, *High on a Windy Hill* (1999), p. 38.

131. Ibid., pp. 31-2.

132. Ibid., p. 23 f.

133. McKercher, "The Prince of Wales Hotel" Typescript 1982. Waterton Lakes National Park

Library. On the career of Louis Hill and his role in Glacier National Park, see Sheire, *Glacier National Park.* (1970), p. 176 f. and Djuff, *High on a Windy Hill* (1999), pp. 12-13.

134. Djuff, *High on a Windy Hill* (1999), pp. 31-2; and Barnes, *Great Lodges of the Canadian Rockies* (1999), p. 65 f.

135. Djuff, *High on a Windy Hill* (1999), pp. 31-2, and Goble, *Waterton Park History* (1981).

136. Ibid.

137. See Morrison and Djuff, *M. V. International* (1993).

138. Mills, *Waterton Lakes National Park* (1998), p. 54.

139. Lothian, *A History*, Vol. III (1979), pp. 46-7.

140. Mills, *Waterton Lakes National Park* (1998), p. 54.

141. Ibid., p. 55; Getty, *The History of Waterton Lakes* (1972), pp. 146-8.

142. Wardle, "Highway Work in the National Parks" (1925), 4382-84.

Chapter Four
Waterton During the Years of Depression and War: 1930-1945

1. Morton with Copp, *Working People* (1980), p. 125.

2. Martin, *Dominion Lands Policy* (1973), p. 222.

3. See Steele, *Prairie Editor* (1961), p. 123 f.

4. For a review of the history of many Canada-United States boundary issues in the twentieth century, see Carroll, *Environmental Diplomacy* (1983).

5. See Hewitt, "Conservation of Birds and Mammals" in Commission of Conservation Canada.*Conservation of Fish, Birds and Game* (1916), pp. 141-3; and Dorsey, *The Dawn of Conservation Diplomacy* (1998).

6. *Encyclopedia Britannica*, 15th ed., Ready Reference. Vol. 10. 1986. p. 199.

7. See Forsberg, *Chief Mountain* (1964).

8. "Canon," *Waterton-Glacier International Peace Park* (1952), p. 6.

9. Scace, *Interpretive Background Materials* (1972). p. 4.2.

10. Ibid., p. 5.2.

11. Ibid.

12. Scace, *Interpretive Background Materials* (1972), 5.6.f.

13. Cited in Scace, Ibid.

14. Canadian Statutes. 23 G V Ch 55 May 26, 1932. P.C. 1386.

15. Scace, *Interpretive Background Materials* (1972), p. 5.1

16. Ibid.

17. Cited in Galbraith, *The Great Crash* (1979), p. 1.

18. Ibid., p. 70.

19. Wilbur, *The Bennett Administration* (1973), p. 222.

20. Ibid., p. 4.

21. See Palmer with Palmer, *Alberta: A New History* (1990), pp. 244-47, 249-50; Thompson with Seager, *Canada, 1922-1939* (1985), p. 224; Swankey, "Reflections of an Alberta Communist" (1979), pp. 7-8; Sebenik, "Points of Departure," in Knafla, ed., *Law and Justice in a New Land* (1986), pp. 313-32.

22. Gray, *Men Against the Desert* (1967), pp. 15-16.

23. Harkin, "Our Need for National Parks" (1918), 106-18.

24. See for example, Williams, *Waterton Lakes National Park*. (1929). Williams travelled widely in the parks and produced publications of this nature for all of the parks. The Waterton booklet was reprinted in 1982 by the Historic Trails Society of Alberta.

25. See Hewes, "America's Park Highways" (1932), 537-40; National Park Service. *Glacier National Park* (1936); and Houk, *Going-To-the-Sun* (1984).

26. Waiser, *Park Prisoners* (1995), Chapters 2 and 3; Rose, *Historic American Roads* (1976), p. 100; Brown, *Public Relief* (1940), p. 156 f.

27. Lothian, *A History*, Vol. II (1977), p. 17.

28. See Morton with Copp, *Working People* (1980) pp. 145-50; Waiser, *Park Prisoners* (1995); and Thompson and Seager, *Canada, 1922-1939* (1985), p. 267 f.

29. Banff National Park. Engineering Services Files. E.20-W. C.M. Walker to J.M. Wardle, "Inspection Relief Camps – Waterton Lakes Park," May 2, 1933; Waterton Lakes National Park. Files. H. Knight to J.M. Wardle, Sept. 7,1934.

30. Relief Program: Single Homeless Men. Winter, 1933-34.Waterton Lakes National Park Files.

31. J.M. Wardle Chief Engineer, Banff, to J. Harkin, Feb. 29, 1932. Report of Unemployment Relief Camp Conditions. Waterton Lakes National Park. Files.

32. Morton, *Working People* (1980), p. 147.

33. "Diary of a Relief Camp Worker," Canadian House of Commons. Debates 1935 IV, 4050. Cited in Thompson and Seager, *Canada, 1922-1939* (1985), p. 269.

34. Lothian, *A History*, Vol. II (1977), pp.17-18.

35. Gladstone, *History of Waterton*. (1965).

36. Ibid.

37. Goble, *Waterton Lakes History* (1981), p. 5.

38. Twenty Second Annual Report. Superintendent. Jan. 8, 1936, p. 2. Waterton Lakes National Park Files; Goble, *Waterton Park History* (1981), p. 5; and NA RG 84 Vol. 2210 Parks, Roads, Buildings.

39. Gladstone, *History* (1965).

40. Goble, *Waterton Lakes History* (1981).

41. Ibid., p. 5. Frank Goble has documented the physical nature of many of the relief camps in Waterton. See Fig. 55 and Frank Goble, *The Twenty-Cent Men* (n.d.) Manuscript. Waterton Lakes National Park Library.

42. Twenty Second Annual Report. Superintendent. Jan. 8, 1936. Waterton Lakes National Park Files.

43. Superintendent's Monthly Report. April, 1936.Waterton Lakes National Park. Files.

44. See Leuchtenburg, *Franklin D. Roosevelt and the New Deal* (1963), pp. 52-3.

45. See Ober, "The CCC Experience in Glacier National Park," (1976), 30-39.

46. Thompson and Seager, *Canada, 1922-1939* (1985), pp. 261-66.

47. Ibid., pp. 90-91; and see Hoar, ed., *Ronald Liversedge* (1973), p. 35 f.

48. Ober, "The CCC Experience in Glacier National Park" (1976), p. 32.

49. Ibid., pp. 32-7.

50. The education mandate was taken seriously by Washington. Impressive texts were produced for those enrolled in the programs. For an example of a textbook, see Kylie,*CCC Forestry* (1937).

51. Waiser, *Park Prisoners* (1995), pp. 106-7.
52. On the CCC program, see also Foresta, *America's National Parks and their Keepers* (1984), pp. 43-45; and Lee, *Family Tree of the National Park System* (1974), pp. 52-3.
53. Waiser, *Park Prisoners* (1995), p. 92.
54. Ibid., p. 126.
55. Banff National Park. File E. 20-W. J.M. Wardle to Herbert Knight, Feb. 20, 1933.
56. Banff National Park .File E.20-W. C.M. Walker to J.M. Wardle, May 2, 1933.
57. Report of Unemployment Relief Conditions. The Waterton Lakes National Park (B). Akamina Road Project, n.d. Waterton Lakes National Park Files.
58. Banff National Park. File E.20-W. Herbert Knight to J.M. Wardle, Jan. 20, 1933.
59. Banff National Park. File E.20. W J.M. Wardle to J.B. Harkin, March 18, 1933.
60. Banff National Park. File E.20-W. C.K. LeCapelain, to J.M. Wardle, Nov. 6, 1933.
61. Ibid.
62. Banff National Park. File E.20-W. J.M. Wardle, to J.B. Harkin, March 18, 1933.
63. See Waiser, *Park Prisoners* (1995), pp. 104-7.
64. Ibid., p. 127.
65. See Rea, *T.A. Crerar* (1997), pp. 172-3.
66. Lothian, *A History*, Vol. IV (1981), p. 75.
67. Ibid.
68. PAA. 69.354/97. Memo. P.J. Jennings, Superintendent, Banff. June 19,1937.
69. Ibid. Superintendent's Monthly Report. June, 1941. Item 11.
70. Ibid. File W. 50-1. Excerpt from Acting Controller's letter. Calgary, Sept.19, 1941.
71. Lothian, *A History*, Vol. IV (1981), p. 90.
72. See Gray *Men Against the Desert* (1967), pp. 15-16; Clarke, "Irrigation and the Settlement Frontier" (1993), p. 60; Jones, *Empire of Dust* (1987), pp. 220-21.
73. For a review of the circumstances surrounding early irrigation development in Southern Alberta, see Clarke, "Irrigation and the Settlement Frontier"(1993), 45-66.
74. Gray, *Men Against the Desert* (1967), p. xii.
75. Statutes of Canada, 25-26 George V. Chap. 23.
76. The literature on Mormon settlement, agriculture, and the relationship of both to irrigation, is extensive. An excellent review is provided by the historical geographer Meinig in his "The Mormon Culture Region" (1965), 191-220. See also den Otter, *Irrigation in Southern Alberta* (1975). On the early Mormon settlements, see Hicken, *Events Leading to the Settlement of the Communities of Cardston, Magrath, Stirling and Raymond*(1968), and Rosenvall, "The Transfer of Mormon Culture to Southern Alberta," in Rosenvall and Evans, eds., *Essays on the Historical Geography of the Canadian West* (1987), pp. 122-44.
77. Eastcott, comp., *The Holroyd Journals* (1977), p. 72.
78. See Superintendent's Reports. Supplementary Report. Jan 1, 1942, to March 31,1942. Waterton Lakes National Park Library.
79. Gray, *Men Against the Desert* (1967), p. 158.
80. Ibid.
81. See den Otter, *Irrigation in Southern Alberta* (1975).
82. See den Otter, *Civilizing the West* (1986), p. 207.
83. Clarke, "Irrigation and the Settlement Frontier" (1993), p. 58.

84. Palmer with Palmer, *Alberta: A New History* (1990), p. 121; Gross and Kramer, *Tapping the Bow* (1985), pp. 158-69; Clarke, "Irrigation and the Settlement Frontier" (1993), 45-66.

85. *PFRA* (1961), p. 41 f.

86. On Palmer, see Gray, *Men Against the Desert* (1967), pp. 74-82; 222-23. On the role of the research station, see Johnston, *To Serve Agriculture* (1977).

87. Long, "Prairie Irrigation" (1946), 152-59.

88. See Bloomfield and Fitzgerald, *Boundary Waters Problems* (1958), Docket no. 57, p. 177 f.

89. Ibid., p. 180; PFRA, (1961), pp. 41-45.

90. Dempsey, "The Story of the Blood Reserve" (1953), pp. 27-36.

91. Ibid., p. 27.

92. Canada. *Indian Treaties and Surrenders* (1891-1912), Vol. II (No. 163), pp. 56-59; Vol. III (No. 282), pp. 3-5; and see Dempsey, "The Story of the Blood Reserve" (1953), 27-36.

93. Ibid., p. 29.

94. Ibid.

95. Ibid., pp. 30-1; NA. RG 10. Canada. Department of Indian Affairs. John C. Nelson, DLS. Field Notes: Survey of Timber Limit "A." Blood Indian Reserve. Treaty No. 7. 1883.

96. Canada. Order in Council. P.C. 1151 , May 17, 1889.

97. Canada. *Treaties and Surrenders*, Vol. 3. (1912), No. 282. Sept. 2, 1889.

98. Canada. Order in Council. P.C. 1684 (1893).

99. Lothian, *A History*, Vol. IV (1981), p. 124.

100. Ibid.; and Getty (1972), p. 127.

101. NA. RG 84. Vol. 2165. W2 Part 2. Assist. Controller to Mr. Gibson. April 30, 1946.

102. NA. RG 84. Vol. 2165. Est. File. W.2 Part 2 Vol. 2; and Waterton Lakes National Park. File W-206-776. Blood Indian Timber Limit "A" to 1969. See also Alberta. Land Titles Office. Calgary. Plan of Survey of Blood Reserve Timber Limit "A." Filed under T649GT 1953.

103. Djuff, *High on a Windy Hill* (1999), p. 108.

104 Lothian, *A History*, Vol. III (1979), pp. 43, 48.

105. Waterton Lakes National Park. File 32-L3-12. Auto Bungalow Camp Plans. 1930's; and Lothian, *A History*, Vol. III (1979), p. 45.

106. *Lethbridge Herald*, March 6, 1933.

107. Mills, *Waterton Townsite* (1999), pp. 59-61.

108. *Lethbridge Herald*, Jan. 7, 1938.

109. Ibid. p. 12.

110. Ibid. p. 44.

111. Waterton Lakes National Park. File W.16-8. 1926 to Feb. 15, 1929.

112. Lothian, *A History*, Vol. III (1979), p. 44.

Chapter Five
The Literary and Artistic Response

1. See Hanna, *Stars Over Montana* (1988), p. 151 f.

2. Ibid. For a comprehensive listing of McClintock's works, see Dempsey and Moir, *A Blackfoot Bibliography* (1989).

3. See Hanna, *The Life and Times of James Willard Schultz* (1986); Dempsey, "Introduction" to Schultz, *My Life as an Indian* (1997), pp. vii-x.

4. See Leslie, *Moreton Frewen of England* (1966), pp. 42-87.

5. Merritt, *Baronets and Buffalo* (1985), p. 154.

6. *Prairie Grass to Mountain Pass*(1984), pp. 13-15; Potyondi, *Where the Rivers Meet* (1992), pp. 36-38.

7. On the birth of the stereotype, see Kelly, *The Rangemen* (1988), pp. 120-24.

8. See Dempsey, ed. *Claude Gardiner* (1988).

9. Thomas, "Privileged Settlers," in Dunae, ed. *Ranchers' Legacy* (1986), pp. 159-62.

10. Stegner and Etulain, *Conversations with Wallace Stegner* (1990), p. 123 f.

11. Russell, *Trails of a Wilderness Wanderer* (1971), pp. 121-56.

12. See Jackson, *With Lens and Brush* (1989), pp. 20-23; Stenzel, *James Madison Alden* (1975), pp. 133-7.

13. In Montana, the case of Rufus F. Zogbaum is instructive. See Taft, *Artists and Illustrators of the Old West* (1953), p. 183 f.

14. Nevitt, *A Winter at Fort Macleod* (1974).

15. A notable example is that of Tom Wilson (1859-1933), well known for his activities in the Banff area. See Whyte Museum of the Rockies, Archives. RG. M83. Wilson Family Papers.

16. See Brown, *Sketches From Life* (1981), and Fort Macleod, *Our Colourful Past* (1977), pp. 168-70; GAA. Library. Art Files. "Annora Brown."

17. Brown, *Old Man's Garden* (1954).

18. Taliaferro, *Charles Russell* (1996), pp. 329-35.

19. There has long been confusion about Russell's activities and whereabouts in this period. See Dempsey, "Tracking C.M. Russell in Canada" (1989), 2-15.

20. See Pettipas, *Severing the Ties that Bind* (1994); Carter, *Lost Harvests* (1990); Prucha, *The Indians in American Society* (1985), p. 55 f.

21. Cited in Prucha, *The Indians in American Society* (1985), p. 58.

22. Ibid., p. 23; and Prucha, ed., *Documents of United States Indian Policy* (1975), pp. 171-4.

23. See Garmhausen, *History of Indian Arts Education* (1988), pp. 30-34, 38.

24. Ibid., p. 41 f.

25. Sheridan, *Redskin Interlude* (1938), p. 56.

26. See Ewers, "Winold Reiss" (1971), pp. 44-55.

27. Sheridan, *Redskin Interlude* (1938), p. 294 f.

28. See Banks, "Jessie Donaldson Schultz" (1983), 18-35.

29. See Dempsey, *Tailfeathers, Indian Artist* (1970).

30. Sheridan, *Redskin Interlude* (1938), p. 169.

31. See Dempsey, *Tailfeathers, Indian Artist* (1970).

32. See Reeves, *Glacier National Park* (1995-1998).

Chapter Six
Changing Ideas of Wildlife, Parks, and Tourism: 1945-1975

1. See Haeckel, *Generelle Morphologie* (1866); and Bramwell, *Ecology in the Twentieth Century* (1989), pp. 39-41.

2. John Sheail, *Seventy -five Years in Ecology* (1987), p. 84.

3 Ibid., p. 91.

4. Leopold, *Wildlife Management* (1933).

5. See *A Sand County Almanac* (1949) and *The River of the Mother of God and other essays* (1991), particularly "The Ecological Conscience" (1947).

6. See Elton, *Animal Ecology* (1927); Hewitt, *The Conservation of the Wildlife in Canada* (1921); Rowan, *The Riddle of Migration* (1931).

7. See MacDonald, *Science and History at Elk Island* (1994).

8. NA. RG 84 Vol. 15. File K. 300 Wildlife Gen. 1920-40. Clarke's mature views may be noticed in C.H.D. Clarke, "A Philosophy of Conservation," in Dymond, ed., *Fish and Wildlife* (1964), pp. 189-98. Cowan's late views may be noticed in Cowan, "Man, Wildlife and Conservation in North America: Status and Change," in Geist and Cowan, eds., *Wildlife Conservation Policy* (1995), pp. 277-308.

9. Chas. J. Kraebel, Glacier National Park, to The Director, National Park Service, Washington, D.C. Jan. 6, 1927. Glacier National Park Records. Missoula. Univ. of Montana. Reel 1.

10. Ibid.

11. Aldo Leopold to Charles J. Kraebel, Jan. 18, 1927. Ibid. On Leopold, see Nash, *Wilderness and the American Mind* (1973), Ch. 11.

12. See Buchholtz, *Man in Glacier* (1976), p. 25.

13. Banfield. *The Wildlife of Waterton* (1947), p. 2.

14. Ibid.

15. Fisher, *Wolf Wars* (1995), p. 22.

16. Wright, *Fauna of the National Parks* (1933); NA. RG 84 Vol. 37. File U-300-10. Williamson to Anderson, July 23, 1938.

17. NA. RG 84 Vol. 37. File U-300-10. Fisher to Crerar, Dec. 31, 1938.

18. NA RG 84 Vol. 15. File. K-300. Wildlife General. Clarke to Lloyd. Dec. 4, 1942.

19. NA RG 84 Vol. 37. File U.300-9. Williamson's Report on Surplus Animals. July 27, 1937.

20. NA. RG 84 Vol. 2165. W2 Part 2.

21. Ibid., G.E. Watt to R.A. Gibson, Aug. 1, 1947.

22. Ibid. G.E.B. Sinclair to G.E. Watt, Aug. 23,1947.; Watt to Sinclair, Sept. 5,1947.

23. On the more distant history of elk in the park area, see C.J. Shattuck, The Elk of Waterton. Waterton Lakes National Park. File 67/7 A2.1 1966.

24. Ibid., R.A. Gibson to Watt, Sept. 18, 1947.

25. Hubert U. Green, *The Wolves of Banff National Park* (1951). Green enjoyed a journalistic career as well, writing under the name of Tony Lascelles. Cf. *Calgary Herald*, Feb. 4, 1939. Tony Lascelles, "Cougars of National Park have found a defender."

26. For a review of much of the important post-war literature of this kind, see Wright, *Wildlife Research and Management* (1992).

27. MacKenzie, *Fire Ecology* (1973).

28. Ibid., pp. 150-2.

29. Banfield, *The Wildlife of Waterton* (1947), p. 3.

30. MacKenzie, *Fire Ecology* (1973), p. 93.

31. Ibid.

32. Ibid., Table 17: 1945-1969, p. 153.

33. Ibid., p. 154.

34 Banfield, *The Wildlife of Waterton* (1947), p. 29.

35. Abattoir Building. Sept. 1947. Waterton Lakes National Park. File W65-45.

36. Ibid. The reference is to Prisoner of War Camp 130 at Kananaskis, used for prisoners of war during World War II.

37. Gladstone, "History" (1961); and see NA. RG 84 Vol. 482. E. 299. Vol. 9. Slaughter of Animals, 1961-64.

38. See Burns with Schintz, *Guardians of the Wild* (1999), pp. 8, 75.

39. See MacDonald, *Science and History at Elk Island* (1994), p. 42 f; B.I. Love, *Veterinarians* (1965), pp. 77-81.

40. Lothian, *A History*, Vol. IV (1981), pp. 90-2.

41. Camp, *Roots in the Rockies* (1993), pp. 139-40.

42. NA. RG 84 Vol. 2201. W 29. Vol. 1. Shell Oil to Deputy Minister of Northern Affairs and Natural Resources Dec. 11,1958; R.G Robertson, DM, to R.N. Gadbois, Dec. 31,1958.

43. NA. RG 84. Vol. 2201 W.29. S.A. Kanik, Report. Townsite Development and Oil and Gas Development: Oil and Gas Evaluation , Resources Division. 1963.

44. A formulation of this aspect of Waterton geology is to be found in Daly, *North American Cordillera* (1912), pp. 49-50.

45. NA. RG 84. Vol. 2201 W.29. Kanik, *Report* (1963).

46. Details of the commemoration may be reviewed in Waterton Lakes National Park. File 325 History and Sites.

47. NA. R.G. 84. Vol. 2166. W2A. 1954-61; Waterton National Park, File W-29. Administration of Petrol and Natural Gas Areas to 1968.

48. NA. RG. 84. Vol. 2165. W2 Part 2. Sept. 7, 1948.

49. Ibid., E .T. Kenney, Minister, to Hon. James A. MacKinnon, Dec. 20,1948.

50. NA. RG. 84 Vol. 2210. W 60-3 Vol. 2.

51.Ibid. Feb. 20, 1961.

52. Ibid. April 6, 1964 and following.

53. See M. Paquet, *Parks* (1990), pp. 173-4.

54. Herbert Knight. Superintendent's Report. Waterton National Park. April, 1937. Waterton Lakes National Park Files.

55. C. K. LeCapelain, 28th Annual Report. April 1,1941 to Dec. 31, 1942. Waterton Lakes National Park Files. Feb. 2, 1942.

56. Ibid.

57. Ibid.

58. Ibid.

59. Ibid.

60. Waterton Lakes National Park. File W-38. Feb. 23, 1938.

61. Mills, *Waterton Lakes* (1998), p. 54.

62. PAA. 69.354./93 W. 36-6 Cameron Lake Campground. Map.

63. NA. RG 84 . Vol. 2201 Townsite Development and Oil and Gas Development W. 29

64. Seel et al. (1984), p. 351.

65. The index to the *Canadian Alpine Journal* covering the years 1905-1987 contains no entries for Waterton or the main peaks in Waterton.

66. See the "Foreword" by Andy Russell in *Waterton and Northern Glacier Trails* (1984), p.7; and the general descriptions of Waterton geology in Baird, *Waterton Lakes National Park* (1971).

67. Stokes, *Round About the Rockies* (1923), p.76.

68. Palmer and Linebarger, *Sarah Luela Nielson* (1988), p. 16-18. Waterton Lakes National Park Library.

69. PAA. 69.218/179. W.83. H.A. de Veber to Controller, Ottawa, Dec. 17, 1946.

70. Personal Communication from Rob Watt, Waterton National Park Warden Service. Feb. 1993.

71. W. McD. Tait, "Kootenai Brown Tells Tales of Buffalo Hunting in Early Sixties," Vancouver Daily Province, March 8, 1924. Cited in Rodney, *Kootenai Brown* (1969), p. 61.

72. Waterton National Park. File 318 Museums. Dec. 1951-58. J.R.B. Coleman to J.A. Atkinson. 1954.

73. Lothian, *A History*, Vol. IV (1981), p. 140; and see Ise, *Our National Park Policy* (1961), pp. 199-202.

74. Lothian, *A History*, Vol. IV (1981), pp. 136-7.

75. Gladstone, *History* (1961).

76. Lothian, *A History*, Vol. IV (1981), pp. 140-44; and personal communication from Rob Watt, Waterton National Park Warden Service, Feb. 1993.

77. Ibid. p. 149.

78. See Gladstone, *History* (1968).

79. See Pomeroy, *In Search of the Golden West* (1990), pp. 125-31.

80. Ibid., p. 133.

81. Waterton Lakes National Park. File 32-L3-12. Auto Bungalow Camp Plans. And see Lothian, Vol. III (1979), p. 45.

82. Ibid. p. 46.

83. Ibid.

84. Ibid., p. 45.

85. Lothian, *A History*, Vol. I (1976)

86. Lothian, *A History*, Vol. III (1979), p. 48.

87. Lothian, *A History*, Vol. I (1976), p. 26.

88. Ibid., p. 24.

Chapter Seven
Towards Cooperative Relationships:
Waterton and its Neighbours, 1975-2000

1. Seel, *An annotated list of the avi-fauna of Waterton Lakes* (1969).
2. See Lewis, *Lively* (n.d.) Manuscript on file with the National Archives of Canada. NA. RG 109. Vol.1.
3. Soper, *The Mammals of Waterton Lakes National Park* (1973).
4. Kuijt, *A Flora of Waterton Lakes* (1982).
5. Lothian. *A History*, Vol. III (1979), p. 50.
6. Getty, *The History of Waterton Lakes* (1972).
7. See Yeo, "Making Banff a Year Round Park," in Corbet and Rasporich, eds., *Winter Sports in the West* (1990), pp. 87-98.
8. Lothian, *A History*, Vol. III (1979), pp. 47-9.
9. Ibid., p. 44.
10. NA. RG 84 Vol. 2210 W60-3; Waterton Lakes National Park. Resource Conservation. Annual Report. 1975, pp. 4-5; and Hill, *Late Spring Flooding* (1975); *Lethbridge Herald*, June 9, 1995.
11. Reinelt, "The Effect of Topography" (1967-68), 19-30.
12. "The Origin of the Seasons," in Boas, ed. *Kutenai Tales* (1918), pp. 179-83.
13. Merv Syroteuk, Briefing Notes. Flood. Waterton Lakes National Park. June. 1995. Waterton Lakes National Park. Superintendents Files; *Lethbridge Herald*, June 10, 1995. p. A3.
14. McMordie, "Ordinary Buildings in Extraordinary Places" (1988), 20-25.
15. Gowling and Gibb Architects. *An Architectural Motif* (1987).
16. Taylor and Buchik, *Waterton Townsite* (1991); Mills, *Waterton Lakes* (1998).
17. Wheaton, "Park Roads and Highway Standards" (1999), pp. 29-31.
18. See Mosquin, *The Idea of Cooperating Associations* (1978).
19. Parks Canada. Calgary. Central Registry Files. C. 4010-2. 1978-82. April 5, 1983.
20. See Mosquin, *The Idea of Cooperating Associations* (1978).
21. While grazing has not taken place in Waterton since 1947, the drought of 1977 placed severe pressure on the federal minister to issue grazing permits in Riding Mountain, Prince Albert and Waterton. Policy still allowed for such discretionary action by the minister, and only the complications of paperwork prevented the actual issue of such permits in 1977. See WLNP, Resource Conservation *Annual Report*, 1977.
22. NA. RG 84 Vol. 2167 W 15 Vol. 2. Land Admin. Outside Park. Chief of NPS to T. Pierce, Sept. 3, 1959.
23. NA. RG 84 Vol. 2167 W 15 Vol. 2 Land Admin. Outside Park. J.R.B. Coleman to Deputy Minister, Sept. 16, 1959.
24. On the objectives of UNESCO's Man and the Biosphere program and Canadian contributions to it, see Eidsvik, "Canada, Conservation and Protected Areas" in Dearden and Rollins, eds. *Parks and Protected Areas* (1993), p. 279 f.
25. Glacier National Park, *General Management Plan* (1999), p. 8.

26. Heywood, ed. *Global Biodiversity* (1995), p. 534.

27. See *Waterton Biosphere Reserve* (n.d.).

28. Waterton Lakes National Park. *Background Information* (1989), p. 269.

29. Minutes of the Waterton Biosphere Reserve Association. Parks Canada. Western Regional Office. Calgary. Central Records. 1981-1991.

30. Minutes of the Waterton Biosphere Reserve Assoc. March 2, 1982, op. cit.

31. Minutes of the Waterton Biosphere Reserve Assoc. 1981-1991, op. cit.

32. Boyer, "Waterton-Glacier International Peace Park" (1987), 803.

33. Sax and Keiter, "Glacier National Park and its Neighbours"(1987), 207-63.

34. Grumbine, *Ghost Bears* (1992), p. 157.

35. Sax and Keiter, "Glacier National Park and its Neighbours" (1987), 253-5.

36. See Munro and Willison, eds. *Linking Protected Areas* (1998).

37. See Glacier National Park, *General Management Plan* (1999), p. 8.

38. Cf. Valarius Geist and Niels Damgaard, "Game Farming needs Public Inquiry," *Calgary Herald*, July 18, 1991; *Calgary Herald*, "Editorial," July 20, 1991; Jeff Welke, "Health fears soar over Elk TB," *Calgary Herald*, July 20, 1991; *Calgary Herald*, "Editorial – Hands off Park Elk," July 27, 1991. The references are to passage of Province of Alberta Bill 31 (1991).

39. Van Tighem, "Waterton – Crown of the Continent" (1990), p. 28.

40. Robbins, "Wolves Across the Border"(1986), 6-14.

41. Ibid., p. 6.

42. Ibid., p. 10.

43. Mowat and Russell, *Estimating Population Size* (1998).

44. Seel, comp. *Waterton Lakes National Park* (1984), p. 352.

Bibliography

Primary Sources

In preparation of the text, the following records in the National Archives, Ottawa, were useful: Record Group 15. Department of Interior Records; RG 10. Department of Indian Affairs Records; RG 84. National Park Records; RG 109. Canadian Wildlife Service Records. In the Provincial Archives of Alberta (PAA), Edmonton, a group of former park records held by the National Archives in Ottawa are now retained in the following records series. Series 69.218. Series 69.354. Series 70.190. This provincial group is particularly rich in engineering records. The holdings of the Glenbow Archives, Calgary (GAA) is particularly valuable for southern Alberta studies. The following record holdings were consulted: M3937. Biography of the Dobbie Family, Pincher Creek. 1959; M1788 Blood Indian Agency. Correspondence, 1899-1944; M144 J. G. Brown, Reminiscences, 1865-1900. As told to W. McD. Tait; M3768. Canada. Department of the Interior. Water Resources Branch. Irrigation Registers, 1895-1960. 2 Vol.; D 92 OJ38. Diary of Fred Forster; M3989. Arthur Henry Harwood, in interview with Gray Campbell, c. 1950; M490. Arthur Henry Harwood Papers and Correspondence. 1876-1971; M517 f.93. J. D. Higinbotham, Correspondence,1875-1960; M3761. folio 116. William L. Jacobson, Compilation Project on History of Irrigation in Western Canada,

1814-1961. M612; M 1021; Kanouse Family. Fonds. M839. Canon S. H. Middleton, Papers; M956. William Pearce. Personal letters and histories of Alberta Oil, pre-1914 and the National Parks. 1892-1925. On Glacier National Park, Montana, microfilm copies of the Glacier Park Records held at the University of Montana Archives, Missoula (UM), were inspected at the Calgary Public Library. A variety of records held by Parks Canada at Waterton Lakes National Park and at Calgary were consulted. The main groupings are as follows: Waterton Lakes National Park: Central Files and Records. Administration Building; Historical Files. Warden Office, Library. Calgary Office: Central Records: Historical Files, Historical Services Division; Archaeological Records, Archaeological Services Division.

Secondary Sources

Adell, Jacqueline. "Upper Hot Springs Bathhouse, Banff National Park." Ottawa: National Historic Sites Branch, 1984.

Aikens, C. Melvin. *The Far West*. Edited by Jesse D. Jennings, *Ancient North Americans*. New York: W. H. Freeman, 1983.

Alberta. Land Titles Office. "Plan of Survey of Blood Reserve Timber Limit 'A'." Calgary, 1953.

"Alberta's Black Gold Rush." *Pincher Creek Echo*, May 27 1971.

Alden, W., and C. Hyndman. "The Geology of the Waterton-Glacier International Peace Park," 1972.

Aldington, Richard. *The Strange Life of Charles Waterton, 1782-1865*. London: Evans Bros., 1949.

Anderson, R. M. "Investigation into the Wildlife Conditions in the National Parks." Waterton Lakes National Park, 1938.

Anderson, Samuel. "The North American Boundary from Lake of the Woods to the Rocky Mountains." *Journal of the Royal Geographical Society* 46 (1876): 228-59.

Baird, D. M. *Waterton Lakes National Park: Lakes amid the mountains*. Misc. Report 10. Ottawa: Geological Survey of Canada. 1964.

Baker, Marcus. *Survey of the Northwestern Boundary of the United States, 1857-61*. Washington, D.C.: Government Printing Office, 1900.

Banfield, A.W.F. *The Mammals of Waterton Lakes National Park*. Ottawa: National Parks Branch, 1947.

———. "Management of Elk, Waterton Lakes National Park." Waterton Lake National Park, 1951.

Banks, Anne. "Jessie Donaldson Schultz and Blackfeet Crafts." *Montana: The Magazine of Western History* 33, no. 4 (1983): 18-35.

Barnes, Christine. *Great Lodges of the Canadian Rockies*. Beal: W.W. West, 1999.

Bauerman, H. "Report of the Geology of the Country Near the Forty-Ninth Parallel of North Latitude, West of the Rocky Mountains." Ottawa: Geological and Natural History Survey of Canada, 1884.

Beattie, Judith. "Indian Maps in the Hudson's Bay Company Archives: A Comparison of Five Area Maps Recorded by Peter Fidler, 1801-1802." *Archivaria* 21 (1985-86): 166-75.

Bernard, J. L., and G. W. Scotter. "Survey of Back Country Use in Waterton Lakes National Park." Ottawa: Canadian Wildlife Service, 1977.

Berry, Gerald L. "Fort Whoop-up and the Whiskey Traders, The Pioneer West, No. 1." *Alberta Historical Review* (1969): 1-6.

Blackburn, Julia. *Charles Waterton, Traveller and Conservationist*. London: Bodly Head, 1989.

Bloomfield, L. M., and G. F. Fitzgerald. *Boundary Waters Problems of Canada and the United States*. Toronto: Carswell, 1958.

Boas, Franz, ed. *Kutenai Tales*, Bureau of American Ethnology. Bull. No. 59. Washington, D.C.: Smithsonian Institution, 1918.

Bowers, M. C., ed. *Place Names in Glacier National Park*. Kalispell, 1960.

Boyer, David S. "Waterton-Glacier International Peace Park: A Pride of Two Nations." *National Geographic* 171, no. 6 (1987): 796-822.

Bramwell, Anna. *Ecology in the Twentieth Century: A History*. London: Yale University Press, 1989.

Breen, David H. *The Canadian Prairie West and the Ranching Frontier: 1874-1924*. Toronto: University of Toronto Press, 1983.

Brierly, J. S. "Climate and the Seasonal Cycle of Ranching, Pincher Creek, Alberta." *Alberta Geographer* 4 (1968): 38-44.

Brink, Jack. *Dog Days in Southern Alberta*. Edmonton: Alberta Culture, 1986.

British Columbia. *Kishinena-Akamina Co-ordinated Land Use Plan. A Guide to Development, Rehabilitation and Management*. Victoria, B.C.: Ministry of Environment, 1977.

Brown, Annora. *Old Man's Garden*. Sidney, B.C.: Gray's Publishing, 1970.

———. *Sketches from Life*. Edmonton: Hurtig, 1981.

Brown, Robert Craig. "The Doctrine of Usefulness: Natural Resources and National Park Policy in Canada, 1887-1914." In *Canadian Parks in Perspective*, edited by J. G. Nelson, 46-62. Montreal: Harvest House, 1973.

Buchanan, D. W. *A Complete Guide to Waterton Lakes National Park*. Lethbridge: Lethbridge Herald, 1928.

Buchholtz, C. W. "The Diary of Albert 'Death-on-the-Trail' Reynolds, Glacier National Park, 1912-1913." *Montana: The Magazine of Western History* 35, no. 1 (1985): 48-59.

———. "The Last Summer at Lake McDonald." *Montana: The Magazine of Western History* 26, no. 3 (1976): 23-29.

———. *Man in Glacier*. West Glacier, Mo.: Glacier Natural History Association, 1976.

———. "W. R. Logan and Glacier National Park." *Montana: The Magazine of Western History* 19, no. 3 (1969): 3-17.

Burley, David V., ed. *Contributions to Plains Prehistory: The 1984 Victoria Symposium*. Edmonton: Alberta Culture, 1985.

Burlingame, Merrill G. *The Montana Frontier*. Bozeman: Big Sky Books, Montana State University, 1980.

Burns, Robert J., and Michael J. Schintz. *"Guardians of the Wild: A History of the Warden Service of Canada's National Parks."* Ottawa/Calgary: Canadian Parks Service, 1999.

Burton, Doris. *Bert Riggall: Mountain Guide Extraordinary.* Hanna: Gorman and Gorman, 1990.

Butler, B. Robert. *The Old Cordilleran Culture in the Pacific Northwest.* Pocatello: Idaho State College Museum, 1961.

Butler, J. R., and Maw, R. R. *Fishing Canada's National Parks.* Edmonton: Lone Pine, 1985.

Byrne, M.B.V. *From the Buffalo to the Cross: A History of the Catholic Diocese of Calgary.* Calgary: Calgary Archives and Historical Publishers, 1973.

Cahalane, V. H. "The Evolution of Predator Control Policy in the National Parks." *Journal of Wildlife Management* 3, no. 3 (1939): 229-37.

Cameron, Duncan, ed. *Explorations in Canadian Economic History: Essays in Honour of Irene M. Spry.* Ottawa: University of Ottawa Press, 1985.

Camp, Frank. *Roots in the Rockies.* Ucluelet: Frank Camp Ventures, 1993.

Canada. *Indian Treaties and Surrenders from 1680 to 1902.* 3 vols. Ottawa: Brown Chamberlin, 1891-1912.

Canada. Department of Indian Affairs. "John C. Nelson, DLS. Field Notes: Survey of Timber Limit "A" Blood Indian Reserve. Treaty No. 7," 1883.

Canada. Department of Mines and Resources. "Waterton Irrigation Scheme," 1939.

Canada. Department of Resources and Development. "Statement of the National Park Service Regarding Proposals to Develop the Water Resources of Waterton," 1950.

Canada. Department of the Interior. "Regulations for the Administration of the Kootenay Lakes Forest Reserve," 1910.

Canada. Department of the Interior. Reclamation Service. "Report on the Irrigation Problems in Southern Alberta," 1921-22.

Canada. Governor in Council. "Memorandum 15th May, 1889 re Treaties, 4, 6, 7, and part of 2. P.O. 1161," 1889.

Canada. Governor in Council. "Formal Declaration of Waterton Lakes Forest Park." Privy Council of Canada, 1895.

Canon. *See* Middleton, S. H.

Carpenter, Jock. *Fifty Dollar Bride: Marie Rose Smith – A Chronicle of Metis Life in the Nineteenth Century.* Hanna: Gorman and Gorman, 1977.

Carter, E. *Alberta's Waterton Lakes National Park Formally Recognized as Biosphere Reserve.* n.p.: Man and the Biosphere Program, 1979.

Carter, Sarah. *Lost Harvests: Prairie Indian Reserve Farmers and Government Policy.* Montreal: McGill-Queen's University Press, 1990.

Catlin, George. *Letters and Notes on the North American Indians (1832).* North Dighton: J. G. Press, 1995.

Cautley, R. W., J. N. Wallace, and A. O. Wheeler. "Report of the Commission Appointed to Delimit the Boundary between the Provinces of British Columbia and Alberta. Part I: 1913-1916." Ottawa: Office of the Surveyor General, 1917.

Charles Waterton: 1782-1865. Traveller and Naturalist: An Exhibition Catalogue. Wakefield: Yorkshire Communications Group, 1982.

Chevigny, Hector. *Russian America: The Great Alaskan Adventure, 1741-1867.* Portland: Binford and Mort, 1965.

Chief Mountain. *See* Middleton, S. H.

Choquette, Wayne. "Early Post-Glacial Habitation of the Upper Columbia Region." In *Early Human Occupation in British Columbia*, edited by R. L. Carlson and L. D. Bona, 45-50. Vancouver: University of British Columbia Press, 1996.

Choquette, Wayne. "A Proposed Cultural Chronology for the Kootenai Region." *The Thunderbird: Archaeological News of the Northwest* 5, no. 4 (1985): 2-5; and 5, no. 5, 2-5.

Clarke, C.H.D. *The International Elk*. Ottawa: National Parks Bureau, 1940.

———. "A Philosophy of Conservation." In *Fish and Wildlife: A Memorial to W.J.K. Harkness*, edited by J. R. Dymond, 189-98. Toronto: Longmans, 1964.

Clarke, Ian. "Irrigation and the Settlement Frontier in Southern Alberta, 1878-1935." *Alberta: Studies in the Arts and Sciences* 3, no. 2 (1993): 43-58.

Corbet, E.A., and A.W. Rasporich. *Winter Sports in the West*. Calgary: Historical Society of Alberta, 1990.

Cosley, Joseph E. "The Meeting of Kootenai Brown." Unpublished manuscript. On file. Waterton Lakes National Park, n.d.

Coues, Elliott. "Field Notes on Birds Observed in Dakota and Montana Along the 49th Parallel during the Seasons of 1873 and 1974." *U.S. Geological and Geographical Survey of the Territories. Bulletin* (July 29, 1878).

Cousins, William J. *A History of the Crow's Nest Pass*. Lethbridge: Historic Trails Society of Alberta, 1981.

Cowan, Ian McTaggart. *Elk in Waterton Lakes Park*. Vancouver: University of British Columbia, 1945.

———. "Man, Wildlife and Conservation in North America: Status and Change." In *Wildlife Conservation Policy: A Reader*, edited by V. Geist and I. M. Cowan, 277-308. Calgary: Detselig, 1995.

Coy, John R., and Robert C. Del Grosso. *Montana's Marias Pass: Early Great Northern Mileposts*. Bonner's Ferry: Great Northern Pacific Publications, 1996.

Daly, R. A. *North American Cordillera: Forty Ninth Parallel*. Ottawa: Department of Mines, 1912.

Daughty, R. C. "The Intermontane Tradition." *American Antiquity* 28, no. 2 (1963): 144-58.

Davis, Donald. "Dependent Motorization: Canada and the Automobile." *Journal of Canadian Studies* 21, no. 3 (1986): 106-31.

Dawson, G. M. "Report on the Region in the Vicinity of the Bow and Belly Rivers." Montreal: Geological and Natural History Survey of Canada, 1884.

de Mille, George. *Oil in Canada West: The Early Years*. Calgary: Northwest Printing, 1969.

De Voto, Bernard, ed. *The Journals of Lewis and Clark*. Boston: Houghton Mifflin, 1953.

Dearden, Philip, and Rick Rollins. *Parks and Protected Area: Planning and Management*. Toronto: Oxford University Press, 1993.

DeCecco, E. *Waterton Townsite Improvement Survey*. Calgary: Department of Public Works, 1970.

Delafield, Joseph. *The Unfortified Boundary*. Edited by R. McElroy and T. Bigges. New York, 1943.

Delane, T. M., and W. H. Sharp. "The Blue Camas (*Camassia quamash*): A New Plant to Waterton Lakes National Park Canadian Field Naturalist." 90, no. 1 (1976): 79-80.

Dempsey, Hugh A. *The Amazing Death of Calf Shirt, and Other Blackfoot Stories*. Saskatoon: Fifth House, 1994.

———. *Charcoal's World*. Saskatoon: Western Producer Prairie Books, 1978.

———. *A History of Rocky Mountain House, Canadian Historic Sites. Occasional Papers in Archaeology and History.* Ottawa: Indian Affairs and Northern Development. National Historic Sites Service, 1973.

———. *Indian Tribes of Alberta.* Rev. ed. Calgary: Glenbow Museum, 1997.

———. *Indians of the Rocky Mountain Parks.* Calgary: Fifth House, 1998.

———. "Introduction." In *My Life as an Indian, by J. W. Schultz,* vii-x. Mineola: Dover Publications, 1997.

———. "One Hundred Years of Treaty Seven." In *One Century Later: Western Canadian Indian Reserves Since Treaty 7,* edited by Ian. A. Getty and Donald B. Smith, 20-30. Vancouver: University of British Columbia Press, 1978.

———. *Red Crow: Warrior Chief.* Saskatoon: Western Producer Prairie Books, 1980.

———. "The Story of the Blood Reserve, The Pioneer West, No. 2." *Alberta Historical Review* (1970): 1-6.

———. *Tailfeathers, Indian Artist.* Calgary: Glenbow-Alberta Institute, 1970.

———. "Tracking C. M. Russell in Canada, 1888-1889." *Montana: The Magazine of Western History* 39, no. 1 (1989): 2-15.

———, ed. Claude Gardiner, *Letters from an English Rancher.* Calgary: Glenbow-Alberta Institute, 1988.

———, ed. "Simpson's Essay on the Blackfoot, 1841." *Alberta History* 38, no. 1 (1990): 1-14.

Dempsey, Hugh A., and Lindsay Moir. *A Blackfoot Bibliography.* Metuchen and London: Scarecrow Press, 1989.

den Otter, A. A. *Civilizing the West: The Galts and the Development of Western Canada.* Edmonton: University of Alberta Press, 1982.

———. *Irrigation in Southern Alberta, 1882-1901, Occasional Paper No. 5.* Lethbridge: Historical Society of Alberta Whoop Up Country Chapter, 1975.

Denis, Leo G. *Waterpowers of Manitoba, Saskatchewan and Alberta.* Ottawa: Canada. Commission of Conservation, 1916.

DeSanto, Jerry. "Cooperation Helped Establish Canadian Boundary." *Hungry Horse News,* June 24 1987.

———. "Drilling at Kintla Lake: Montana's First Oil Well." *Montana: The Magazine of Western History* 35, no. 1 (1985): 24-37.

———. "Fifty Years in Glacier's Back Country: The Legendary Joe Cosley." *Montana: The Magazine of Western History* 30, no. 1 (1980): 12-27.

———. "Foundations for a Park: Explorer and Geologist Bailey Willis in the Area of Glacier National Park." *Forest and Conservation History* 39 (July 1995): 130-37.

———. "Uncle Jeff: Mysterious Character of the North Fork." *Montana: The Magazine of Western History* 32, no. 1 (1982): 14-23.

Deutsch, Herman J. "A Contemporary Report on the 49 Boundary Survey." *Pacific Northwest Quarterly* 53 (1962): 1-17.

———. "The Evolution of the International Boundary in the Inland Empire of the Pacific Northwest." *Pacific Northwest Quarterly* 51 (1960): 63-79.

Diehl-Taylor, Christiane. "Passengers, Profits and Prestige: The Glacier Park Hotel Company, 1914-1929." *Montana: The Magazine of Western History* 47, no. 2 (1997): 26-43.

Diettert, Gerald A. *Grinnell's Glacier: George Bird Grinnell and Glacier National Park.* Missoula: Mountain Press, 1992.

Djuff, Ray. *High on a Windy Hill: The Story of the Prince of Wales Hotel.* Calgary: Rocky Mountain Books, 1999.

Dorsey, Kurkaptrick. *The Dawn of Conservation Diplomacy: U.S.– Canadian Wildlife Protection Treaties in the Progressive Era.* Seattle: University of Washington Press, 1998.

Doty, James. "Report of a Survey from Fort Benton Near the Great Falls of the Missouri along the Eastern Base of the Rocky Mountains to Latitude 49°30' N." In *Reports of the Explorations and Surveys to Ascertain the Most Practicable and Economical Route for a Railroad from the Mississippi River to the Pacific Ocean,* edited by Isaac I. Stevens. Washington, D.C.: Thomas H. Ford, 1854.

————. "A Visit to Blackfoot Camps." *Alberta Historical Review* 14, no. 3 (1966): 17-29.

Dowling, D. B. *Review for Prospecting for Oil in the Great Plains, Geological Survey of Canada. Summary Report, Part B.* Ottawa: The King's Printer, 1920.

Downs, Art, ed. *Waterton National Park: Land of the Shining Mountains.* Surrey, B.C.: Heritage House, 1980.

Driver, Jonathan C. "Holocene Man and Environments in the Crowsnest Pass, Alberta." Ph.D., University of Calgary, 1978.

Dunlap, Thomas R. *Saving America's Wildlife.* Princeton: Princeton University Press, 1989.

Dusenberry, Verne. "An Appreciation of James Willard Schultz." *Montana: The Magazine of Western History* 10, no. 4 (1960): 22-23.

Dymond, J. R., ed. *Fish and Wildlife: A Memorial to W.J.K. Harkness.* Toronto: Longmans, 1964.

Eastcott, Doug, comp.,. "The Holroyd Journals: Chronicles of a Park Warden: 1919-1947." Waterton Lakes National Park, 1977.

Eidsvik, Harold K. "Canada, Conservation and Protected Areas." In *Parks and Protected Area: Planning and Management,* edited by Philip Dearden and Rick Rollins, 273-90. Toronto: Oxford University Press, 1993.

Elton, Charles C. *Animal Ecology.* London: Sidgwick and Jackson, 1927.

Ewers, John C. *The Blackfeet: Raiders on the Northwestern Plains.* Norman, Okla.: University of Oklahoma Press, 1958.

————. *The Horse in Blackfoot Indian Culture.* Washington, D.C.: Smithsonian Institution, 1955.

————. *The Influence of the Fur Trade Upon the Indians of the Northern Plains, People and Pelts: Papers of the Second North American Fur Trade Conference.* Winnipeg: Peguis, 1972.

————. "Iroquois Indians in the Far West." *Montana: The Magazine of Western History* 13, no. 2 (1963): 2-10.

————. "The Last Bison Drive of the Blackfoot Indians." *Journal of the Washington Academy of Science* 30, no. 11 (1949): 355-60.

————. *Plains Indian History and Culture: Essays on Continuity and Change.* Norman, Okla.: University of Oklahoma Press, 1997.

————. *The Story of the Blackfeet.* Indian Life and Customs; 6. Lawrence, Kan.: U.S. Department of the Interior. Bureau of Indian Affairs. Haskell Institute, 1952.

————. "Winold Reiss: His Portraits and Proteges." *Montana: The Magazine of Western History* 21, no. 3 (1971): 44-55.

Featherstonhaugh, A. *Narrative of the Operations of the British North American Boundary Commission, 1872-76.* Woolwich: A. W. and J. P. Jackson, 1876.

Fedje, Daryl. "Banff Prehistory: A Provisional Palaeocultural Sequence." Calgary: Archaeological Services. Parks Canada, 1988.

Fisher, Hank. *Wolf Wars.* Helena: Falcon Press, 1995.

Fisher, W. D. "Good Roads in the West." *Good Roads,* Jan. 1924, 9-10.

Fitzpatrick, Brian. "The Big Man's Frontier and Australian Farming." *Agricultural History* 21, Jan. (1947): 8-12.

Flandreau, Grace. *The Story of Marias Pass.* St. Paul: Great Northern Railway, 1925.

Flook, Donald R. *Appraisal of Elk Situation, Waterton Lakes National Park. Oct., 1955.* Edmonton: Canadian Wildlife Service, 1955.

———. *Some Biological Aspects of Grazing and the Problem of Grazing in the National Parks* (Lecture delivered at the Park Warden's School, Jasper National Park, May 4, 1966). Edmonton: Canadian Wildlife Service, 1966.

"Foreign Pioneers: A Short History of the Contribution of Foreigners to the Development of Hokkaido." Hokkaido Refectoral Government. Archives Section. General Affairs Department, 1968.

Foresta, Ronald A. *America's National Parks and their Keepers.* Washington: Resources for the Future, Inc., 1984.

Forsberg, Roberta J. *Chief Mountain: The Story of Canon Middleton.* Whittier, 1964.

Fort Mcleod History Book Committee. *Fort Macleod, Our Colourful Past: A History of the Town of Fort Macleod from 1874 to 1924.* Fort Macleod: FMHBC, 1977.

Foster, Janet. *Working for Wildlife: The Beginning of Preservation in Canada.* Toronto: University of Toronto, 1978.

Foster, R., and R. Brolly. *A Preliminary Heritage Impact Assessment in the Akamina-Kishinena and Flathead Areas of South Eastern British Columbia.* [Victoria, B.C.]: Archaeological Division. British Columbia Heritage Conservation, 1978.

Fraser, Esther. *Wheeler.* Banff: Summerthought, 1987.

Galbraith, John K. *The Great Crash, 1929.* New York: Avon, 1979.

Garmhausen, Winona. *History of Indian Arts Education in Santa Fe.* Santa Fe: Sunstone Press, 1988.

Geist, V., and I. M. Cowan, eds. *Wildlife Conservation Policy: A Reader.* Calgary: Detselig, 1995.

Getty, Ian A. L. "The History of Waterton Lakes National Park,1800-1937. Research Report." Ottawa: Canadian National Parks Branch, 1972.

———. "Oil City." *Canadian Collector* 1976, 35-7.

Getty, Ian. A. L., and Donald B. Smith, eds. *One Century Later: Western Canadian Indian Reserves Since Treaty 7.* Vancouver: University of British Columbia Press, 1978.

Glacier National Park. "General Management Plan." West Glacier: National Park Service, 1999.

"Glacier Park: Lost Names." *Montana: The Magazine of Western History* 10, no. 4 (1960): 9-21.

Gladstone, Leonard. "History of Waterton Lakes National Park." Waterton Lakes National Park, 1968.

Godsal, F. W. "Old Times." *Alberta Historical Review* 12, no. 4 (1964): 19-24.

Gowling and Gibb Architects. *An Architectural Motif and Guidelines for Waterton Lakes National Park.* Calgary: Environment Canada, Parks, 1987.

Grant, Madison. "The Beginnings of Glacier National Park." In *Hunting and Conservation: The Book of the Boone and Crockett Club*, edited by G. B. Grinnell and C. Sheldon, 446-70. New Haven: Yale University Press, 1925.

Gray, James H. *Men Against the Desert*. Saskatoon: Western Producer Prairie Books, 1967.

Green, Hubert U. *The Wolves of Banff National Park*. Ottawa: Department of Resources and Development. National Parks Branch, 1951.

Grinnell, George Bird. "The Crown of the Continent." *Century Magazine* September, 1901, 660-71.

Grumbine, R. Edward. *Ghost Bears: Exploring the Biodiversity Crisis*. Washington, D.C.: Island Press, 1992.

Gryba, Eugene M. *Sibbald Creek: 11,000 Years of Human Use of the Alberta Foothills, Archaeological Survey of Alberta, Occasional Paper No. 22*. Edmonton: Alberta Culture, 1983.

Haeckel, Ernst. *Generelle Morphologie der Organismen*. Berlin: G. Reimer, 1866.

Haig, Bruce. *In the Footsteps of Thomas Blakiston –1858*. Lethbridge: Historic Trails Society of Alberta, 1982.

———, ed. "The Gladstone Diary." Lethbridge: Historic Trails Society of Alberta, 1985.

Halterman, J. *Origin of Place Names in Waterton-Glacier International Peace Park*. n.p.: Red Eagle Ranch, 1982.

Hanna, Warren L. *The Life and Times of James Willard Schultz (Apikuni)*. Norman, Okla.: University of Oklahoma Press, 1986.

———. *Stars Over Montana: Men Who Made Glacier National Park History*. Helena: Glacier Park Natural History Association, 1988.

Harkin, J. B. "Our Need for National Parks." *Alpine Journal* 9 (1918): 106-18.

Harrison, J. E. "Evolution of a Landscape: The Quaternary Period in Waterton Lakes National Park." In *Geological Survey of Canada, Misc. Report 26*. Ottawa, 1976.

Harrison, Michael. *The History of the Hat*. n.p.: N.P.H. Jenkins, 1960.

Haskell, C.F.B. *On Reconnaissance for the Great Northern: Letters of C.F.B. Haskell*. Edited by D. C. Haskell. New York: New York Public Library, 1948.

Hays, Samuel P. *Conservation and the Gospel of Efficiency: The Progressive Conservation Movement, 1890-1920*. New York: Atheneum, 1969.

Hewes, L. I. "America's Park Highways." *Civil Engineering*, no. 2 Sept. (1932): 537-40.

Hewitt, C. Gordon. "Conservation of Birds and Mammals." In *Commission of Conservation Canada. Conservation of Fish, Birds and Game. Proceedings. Nov. 1-2, 1915*. Toronto: Methodist Book and Publishing House, 1916.

Heywood, V. H., ed. *Global Biodiversity Assessment*. Cambridge: Cambridge University Press. United Nations Environment Program, 1995.

Hicken, John R. "Events Leading to the Settlement of the Communities of Cardston, Magrath, Stirling and Raymond." M.A., Utah State University, 1968.

Hidy, Ralph, Murial Hidy, Roy Scott, and Don Hofsommer. *The Great Northern Railway: A History*. Boston: Harvard Business School, 1988.

Hill, Alexander S. *From Home to Home: 1881-1884*. New York: Argonaught Press, 1885.

Hill, M. C. *Late Spring Flooding at Waterton Park Townsite*. Calgary: University of Calgary, 1975.

Hoar, Victor, ed. *Ronald Liversedge, Recollections of the On-to-Ottawa Trek*. Toronto: McClelland & Stewart, 1973.

Hofstadter, Richard. *The Age of Reform*. New York: Vintage, 1955.

Holterman, Jack. *Place Names of Glacier/Waterton National Parks*. West Glacier, Mo.: Glacier Natural History Association, 1985.

Homgren, E. J. "Thomas Blakiston, Explorer." *Alberta History* 24, no. 1 (1976): 15-22.

Houk, Rose. *Going-to-the-Sun: The Story of the Highway Across Glacier National Park*. Englewood: Woodlands Press/Glacier Natural History Association, 1984.

Huddleston, F. M. *A History of the Settlement and Building Up of the Area in S. W. Alberta Bordering Waterton Park in the North from 1889*. Pincher Creek, c. 1969.

Hungry Wolf, Adolf. *Good Medicine in Glacier National Park, Good Medicine Books, No. 4*. Golden, B.C.: Good Medicine Books, 1971.

Hunter, James. *Glencoe and the Indians*. Edinburgh: Mainstream, 1996.

Hurt, Wesley R. "The Altithermal and the Prehistory of the Northern Plains." *Quaternaria* 8 (1966): 101-13.

Innis, Harold A. "Settlement and the Mining Frontier." In *Canadian Frontiers of Settlement*, edited by W. A. Macintosh and W.L.G. Joerg, 270-320. Toronto: MacMillan, 1936.

Interior Salish and Eastern Washington Indians. III. Commission Findings. New York: Garland, 1974.

International Boundary Commission. "Joint Report Upon the Survey and Demarcation of the Boundary Between the United States and Canada from the Gulf of Georgia to the Northwesternmost Point of the Lake of the Woods." Washington, D.C.: International Boundary Commission, 1937.

International Boundary Commission. "Report. Reestablishment of the Boundary Between the United States and Canada: Gulf of Georgia to Northwestern Most Point of Lake of the Woods." Ottawa: International Boundary Commission, 1937.

"Irrigation in Demand: Must Have Reservoirs." *Irrigation Review* 3, no. 6 (1922): 1-2.

Ise, J. *Our National Parks Policy: A Critical History*. Baltimore: Johns Hopkins University Press, 1961.

Isenberg, Andrew C. *The Destruction of the Bison*. Cambridge: Cambridge University Press, 2000.

Jackson, Christopher E. *With Lens and Brush: Images of Western Canadian Landscape, 1845-1890*. Calgary: Glenbow-Alberta Institute, 1989.

Jackson, John C. *Children of the Fur Trade: Forgotten Metis of the Pacific Northwest*. Missoula: Mountain Press, 1995.

Janz, B., and E. L. Teffry. *Southern Alberta's Paralyzing Snowstorms, April, 1967*. Ottawa: Meteorological Service of Canada. Department of Agriculture, 1968.

Jenkins, Alan C. *The Naturalists: Pioneers of Natural History*. London: H. Hamilton, 1978.

"Joe Cosley, The Trapper, Captured." *Hungry Horse News*, May 30 1975.

Johnson, Dorothy M. "Carefree Youth and Dudes in Glacier." *Montana: The Magazine of Western History* 25, no. 3 (1975): 48-59.

Johnson, Olga W. *Flathead and Kootenay, the Rivers, the Tribes and the Region's Traders*. Glendale: A. H. Clark, 1969.

Johnson, Patricia M. "Boundary Journal." *The Beaver* 286 (1955-56): 8-13.

Johnston, Alex. *Plants and the Blackfoot, Sir Alexander Galt Museum*, Occasional Paper No. 15. Lethbridge: Lethbridge Historical Society, 1987.

———. *To Serve Agriculture, 1906-1976: The Lethbridge Research Station, Research Branch. Canadian Department of Agriculture. Historical Series, No. 9*. Ottawa: Agriculture Canada, 1977.

————, ed. *The Battle at Belly River: Stories of the Last Great Indian Battle*. Lethbridge: Lethbridge Chapter of the Historical Society of Alberta, 1966.

Jones, Howard. *To the Webster-Ashburton Treaty: A Study in Anglo-American Relations, 1893-1843*. Chapel Hill: University of North Carolina Press, 1977.

Jorgensen, J. G. *Western Indians: Comparative Environments, Languages, and Cultures of 172 Western American Indian Tribes*. San Francisco: W. H. Freeman, 1980.

Kappler, James L., ed. *Indian Affairs, Laws and Treaties*, 58th Cong. 2nd Sess. Senate Doc. No. 319, II. Washington D.C.

Kehoe, Thomas F. *Stone Tipi Rings in North Central Montana and Adjacent Portion of Alberta, Their Historical, Ethnological and Archaeological Aspects*, Smithsonian Institution. Bureau of American Ethnology. Bull. 173. Washington, D.C.: Smithsonian Institution, 1960.

Kehoe, Thomas F., and Bruce A. McCorquodale. "The Avonlea Point, Horizon Marker for the Northwestern Plains." *Plains Anthropologist* 6, no. 13 (1961): 179-88.

Kelly, L. V. *The Range Men (1913)*. 75th anniversary ed. High River: Willow Publishing, 1988.

Kendrick, John, and Robin Inglis. *Enlightened Voyages: Malaspina and Galliano on the Northwest Coast, 1791-1792*. Vancouver: Vancouver Maritime Museum, 1991.

Kennedy, Margaret A. "Whiskey Trade Frontier on the Northwestern Plains." Ph.D., University of Calgary, 1991.

Kennedy, Margaret A., and Brian O. K. Reeves. "An Inventory and Historical Description of Whiskey Posts in Southern Alberta." Edmonton: Alberta Culture. Historic Sites Service, 1984.

Killoren, John J. *'Come Black Robe': De Smet and the Indian Tragedy*. Norman, Okla.: University of Oklahoma Press, 1994.

Klimko, Olga. "New Perspectives on Avonlea: A View from the Saskatchewan Forest." In *Contributions to Plains Prehistory*. Archaeological Survey of Alberta. Occasional Paper No. 26, edited by David V. Burley, 64-81. Edmonton: Alberta Culture, 1985.

Koepp, Donna P., ed. *Exploration and Mapping of the American West: Selected Essays, Map and Geography Round Table of the American Library Association*. Chicago: Speculum Orbis Press, 1986.

Kuchar, P. *Habitat Types of Waterton Lakes National Park*. Ottawa: Indian Affairs and Northern Development, 1973.

Kuijt, Job. *A Flora of Waterton Lakes National Park*. Edmonton: University of Alberta Press, 1982.

Kylie, H. R. *CCC Forestry*. Washington: U.S. Printing Office, 1937.

Lee, Ronald F. *Family Tree of the National Park System*. Philadelphia: Eastern National Park and Monument Assoc., 1974.

Lehr, J. C. "Mormon Settlement Morphology in Southern Alberta." *Alberta Geographer* 8 (1972): 6-13.

Leopold, Aldo. *The River of the Mother of God and Other Essays*. Edited by Susan L. Flader and J. Baird Callicott. Madison, Wis.: University of Wisconsin Press, 1991.

————. *A Sand County Almanac, and Sketches Here and There*. New York: Oxford University Press, 1949.

————. *Wildlife Management*. New York: C. Scribner's, 1933.

Leslie, Anita. *Moreton Frewen of England: A Victorian Adventurer*. London: Hutchinson, 1966.

Lewis, Harrison F. "Lively: A History of the Canadian Wildlife Service." Ottawa, n.d.

Liddell, Ken. "Fort Warren or Kootinai Post." *Calgary Herald* 1956.

Lohnes, D. "Towards a New Fire Policy." *Natural Resource Bulletin* (Spring 1981): 1-4.

Long, H. G. "Prairie Irrigation." *Canadian Geographical Journal* 33 (1946): 152-59.

Lothian, W. F. *History of Canada's National Parks.* 4 vols. Ottawa: Parks Canada. Indian and Northern Affairs, 1976-1981.

Love, B. I. *Veterinarians of the North-West Territories and Alberta.* Edmonton: Alberta Veterinary Medical Association, 1965.

MacDonald, Graham A. "Kootenai Brown in the Red River Valley." *Manitoba History* 30 (Autumn 1995): 20-25.

————. *Science and History at Elk Island: Conservation Work in a Canadian National Park, 1904-1994, Parks Canada. MRS. 525.* Calgary: Canadian Heritage, 1994.

MacGregor, J. G. *Peter Fidler: Canada's Forgotten Surveyor, 1769-1822.* Calgary: Fifth House, 1998.

MacKenzie, George A. "Fire Ecology of the Forests of Waterton Lakes National Park," University of Calgary, 1973.

MacMillan, H. R. "Report on Proposed National Park." Ottawa: Department of the Interior, 1909.

Malone, Michael P., and Richard B. Roeder. *Montana: A History of Two Centuries.* Seattle: University of Washington Press, 1976.

Maltby, J. R. *Charles Waterton (1782-1865): Curare and a Canadian National Park.* Calgary: Foothills Hospital, Department of Anaesthesia, n.d.

Martin, Chester. *Dominion Lands Policy.* Edited by Lewis H. Thomas. Toronto: McClelland & Stewart, 1973.

Mattison, Ray H. *The Army Post on the Northern Plains, 1865-1885.* Gering: Oregon Trail Museum Association, 1955.

McCabe, Richard, E. "Elk and Indians: Historical Values and Perspectives." In *Elk of North America: Ecology and Management*, edited by Jack Ward Thomas and Dale E. Toweill, 61-124. Harrisburg, Pa.: Stackpole Books, 1982.

McClung, Brian. *Belly River's Famous Joe Cosley.* Kalispell: Life Preservers, 1998.

McFee, Malcolm. *Modern Blackfeet: Montanans on a Reservation.* New York: Holt, Rinehart & Winston, 1972.

McGuinness, Fr. Robert. "Missionary Journey of Father De Smet." *Alberta Historical Review* 15, no. 2 (1967): 12-19.

McKercher, B.J.C. "The Prince of Wales Hotel. WLNP Alberta: Its Significance." Typescript, 1982.

McMordie, Michael. "Ordinary Buildings in Extraordinary Places." *Society for the Study of Architecture in Canada, Bulletin 1* (1988): 20-25.

Merritt, John. *Baronets and Buffalo: The British Sportsman in the American West, 1833-1881.* Missoula: Mountain Press, 1985.

Middleton, S. H. *Indian Chiefs: Ancient and Modern.* Lethbridge: Lethbridge Herald, 1951.

————. *Kootenai Brown.* Lethbridge: Lethbridge Herald, 1954.

————. "Legend and Folklore of the 'Inside Lakes'." *Canadian Cattleman* (August 1958): 6, 24-5.

————. *Waterton-Glacier International Peace Park:* n.p., 1952.

Millman, Thomas. *Impressions of the West in the Early Seventies from the Diary of the Assistant Surgeon of the British American Boundary Survey, 1872-75.* Toronto: Women's Canadian Historical Society of Toronto, 1927-28.

Milloy, John S. *The Plains Cree: Trade Diplomacy and War, 1790 to 1870.* Winnipeg: University of Manitoba Press, 1990.

Mills, Edward. "Waterton Lakes National Park. Built Heritage Resource Description and Analysis Outlying Facilities." Calgary: Canadian Heritage, Parks Canada, 1998.

———. "Waterton Townsite. Built Heritage Resource Description and Analysis." Calgary: Parks Canada, 1999.

Milne-Brumley, Laurie. "The Narrows Site: A Fishing Station-Campsite on the Eastern Flanks of the Rocky Mountains." In *Aboriginal Man and Environments in the Plateau of Northwest America*, edited by A.H. Stryd and R. A. Smith, 75-125. Calgary: The Student's Press, 1971.

———. "The Narrows Site in Waterton Lakes National Park, Alberta." M.A., University of Calgary, 1971.

Mitchner, A. "The Bow River Scheme: CPR's Irrigation Block." In *The CPR West: The Iron Road and the Making of a Nation*, edited by Hugh Dempsey, 259-73. Vancouver: Douglas and MacIntyre, 1984.

Moodie, D. W., and Barry Kaye. "The Ac Ko Mok Ki Map." *The Beaver*, Spring 1977, 5-15.

Morrison, Chris, and Ray Djuff. *M. V. International*. Waterton Park: Goathaunt Publishing, 1993.

Morton, Desmond, and Terry Copp. *Working People: An Illustrated History of Canadian Labour.* Ottawa: Deneau and Greenberg, 1980.

Mosquin, Theodore. *Alternative Institutional Structures and Legal Requirements for a National Parks Cooperating Association.* Ottawa: Department of Indian Affairs and Northern Development, 1978.

———. "The Idea of Cooperating Associations for Canada's National Parks." Aylmer, 1978.

Mountain Horse, Mike. *"My People the Bloods."* Calgary: Glenbow-Alberta Institute. Blood Tribal Council, 1979.

Mountain Horse, Mike, *My People the Bloods*. Introduction by Hugh Dempsey. Calgary: Glenbow Museum and Blood Tribal Council: 1989.

Mowat, Garth. "Estimating Population Size of Grizzly Bears Using Hair Capture and DNA Fingerprinting in Southwest Alberta. Final Report." Alberta Environmental Protection Natural Resources Service. Claresholm and Waterton Lakes National Park, 1998.

Munro, Neil W. P., and J. H. Martin Willison, eds. *Linking Protected Areas with Working Landscapes Conserving Biodiversity :* Proceedings of the Third International Conference on Science and Management of Protected Areas, 12-16 May 1997. Wolfville, N.S.: Science and Management of Protected Areas Association, 1998.

Munroe, Hugh. *Red Crow's Brother: Hugh Monroe's Story of his Second Year on the Plains.* Boston: Houghton Mifflin, 1927.

Murther, P. A. "Waterton Lakes National Park Management Plan." Planning Division, Parks Canada. WRO, 1978.

Nagy, J.A.S. "The Narrows Site in Waterton Lakes National Park." M.A., University of Calgary, 1974.

Nash, Roderick. *Wilderness and the American Mind*. Rev. ed. New Haven: Yale University Press, 1973.

Nelson, J. G., ed. *Canadian Parks in Perspective*. Montreal: Harvest House, 1973.

Nevitt, R. B. *A Winter at Fort Macleod*. Edited by Hugh Dempsey. Calgary: Glenbow-Alberta Institute/McClelland & Stewart West, 1974.

Nordenskiold, Erik. *The History of Biology: A Survey*. New York: Tudor, 1928.

Ober, Michael, J. "The CCC Experience in Glacier National Park." *Montana: The Magazine of Western History* 26, no. 1 (1976): 30-39.

Palliser, John. *Exploration: British North America. Further Papers, 1860*. New York: Greenwood, 1969.

———. *Exploration: British North America. Papers. June, 1859*. New York: Greenwood, 1969.

Palmer, Howard, and Tamara Palmer. *Alberta: A New History*. Edmonton: Hurtig, 1990.

Palmer, Mable J., and Joyce J. Linebarger. "Sarah Luela Nielson – 'Aunt Lu' – 4 Feb. 1885 – 26 Feb. 1965. Typescript, July, 1988. On File. Waterton Lakes National Park Library," 1988.

Paquet, Maggie. *Parks of British Columbia and the Yukon*. North Vancouver, B.C.: Maia Publishing, 1990.

Parsons, John E. *West on the 49th Parallel*. New York: William Morrow and Co., 1963.

Partoll, Albert J. "Fort Connah: A Frontier Trading Post, 1847-1871." *Pacific Northwest Quarterly* 30 (1939): 399-415.

Pearce, William. "History of the Establishment of the Chief Parks along the Main Line of the Canadian Pacific Railway: Waterton Lakes Park in Southern Alberta, and Jasper Park along the Canadian National Railway in the Neighbourhood of Yellowhead Pass in the Rocky Mountains" (Paper read to the Historical Society of Calgary, Dec. 16, 1924). Calgary: Glenbow-Alberta Archives, 1924.

Pettipas, Katherine. *Severing the Ties that Bind: Government Repression of Indigenous Ceremonies on the Prairies*. Winnipeg: University of Manitoba Press, 1993.

PFRA: The Story of Conservation on the Prairies, Department of Agriculture. Publication No. 1138. Ottawa: Queen's Printer, 1961.

Pincher Creek Historical Society. *Prairie Grass to Mountain Pass: History of the Pioneers of Pincher Creek and District*. Pincher Creek: Pincher Creek Historical Society, 1974.

Pomeroy, Earl. *In Search of the Golden West: The Tourist in Western America (1957)*. Lincoln, Neb.: University of Nebraska Press, 1990.

Potyondi, Barry. *Where the Rivers Meet: A History of the Upper Oldman River Basin to 1989*. Lethbridge: Alberta Public Works and Services. Southern Alberta Water Science Society, 1992.

Prairie Grass to Mountain Pass: History of the Pioneers of Pincher Creek and District . Pincher Creek: Pincher Creek Historical Society, 1974.

Price, Richard, ed. *The Spirit of the Alberta Indian Treaties*. Edmonton: Pica Pica Press, 1987.

Pringle, Heather. *Waterton Lakes National Park*. Vancouver: Douglas and MacIntyre, 1986.

"Proceedings of a Symposium Held to Commemorate the Bicentenary of Charles Waterton, Walton Hall, June, 5, 1982." *British Journal of Anaesthesia* 55, no. 3 (1983): 221-33.

Prucha, Francis P., ed. *Documents of United States Indian Policy*. 2nd ed. Lincoln, Neb.: University of Nebraska Press, 1975.

Prucha, Francis P. *The Indians in American Society*. Berkeley: University of California Press, 1985.

Quigg, J. M. "The Belly River: Prehistoric Population Dynamics in a North-western Plains Transition Zone." M.A., University of Calgary, 1973.

Raczka, P. M. *Winter Count: A History of the Blackfoot People*. Brocket, Alberta: Oldman River Cultural Centre, 1979.

Rawson, D. S. *Preliminary Biological Inventory of Waterton Lakes National Park*. Saskatoon: Department of Biology, University of Saskatchewan, 1936.

———. *Records and Recommendations for Fisheries Management in Waterton Lakes National Park*. Saskatoon: University of Saskatchewan, 1938.

Ray, Arthur J. *The Indians in the Fur Trade: Their Role as Hunters, Trappers and Middlemen in the Lands Southwest of Hudson Bay, 1660-1870*. Toronto: University of Toronto Press, 1974.

Reeves, B.O.K. "Archaeological Investigations in Pass Creek Valley, Waterton Lakes National Park. Preliminary Report," 1967.

———. "Archaeological Survey Reports, Waterton Lakes National Park." National Historic Sites Service, 1964-66.

———. "The Concept of an Altithermal Cultural Hiatus in Northern Plains Prehistory." *American Anthropologist* 75, no. 5 (1973): 1221-1253.

———. "The Coppermine Site, Waterton Lakes National Park," 1968.

———. *Culture Change in the Northern Plains, 1000 B.C. – A.D. 1000*, Archaeological Survey of Alberta, Occasional Paper No. 20. Edmonton: Alberta Culture, 1983.

———. "Early Holocene (ca. 8000 to 5500 B.C.). Prehistoric Land/Resource Utilization Patterns in Waterton Lakes National Park." *Arctic and Alpine Research* 7, no. 3 (1975): 237-248.

———. "Glacier National Park Archaeological Inventory and Assessment." Annual Field Season Reports, 1994-97. Leslie B. Davis, ed. Bozeman: U.S. National Park Service/Montana State University, 1995-98.

———. "Head Smashed-In: 5500 Years of Bison Jumping in the Alberta Plains, Part 2, Memoir." *Plains Anthropologist* 14, no. 23 (1978): 82.

———. "Notes on Site DgPl-42." Waterton Lakes National Park, 1968.

———. "Site Dg Pl-1." Waterton Lakes National Park, 1968.

———. "Site Dg Pl-10. A Winter Base Camp in Waterton Lakes National Park." Lifeways of Canada Ltd., 1980.

———. "Six Millenniums of Buffalo Kills." *Scientific American* 249, no. 4 (1983): 120-35.

Reiger, John F. *American Sportsmen and the Origins of Conservation*. New York: Winchester Press, 1975.

Reinlet, E. R. "The Effect of Topography on the Precipitation Regime of Waterton National Park." *The Albertan Geographer* 4 (1967-68): 19-30.

Rich, E. E. *Hudson's Bay Company*. 3 vols. Toronto: McClelland & Stewart, 1960.

Rich, E. E., and A. M. Johnson, eds. *Peter Skene Ogden's Snake Country Journals, 1824-25*. London: Hudson's Bay Record Society, 1950.

Robbins, Jim. "Wolves Across the Border." *Natural History* 95, no. 5 (1986): 6-14.

Robinson, Donald H. *Through the Years in Glacier National Park*. West Glacier, Mo.: Glacier Natural History Association, 1960.

Roe, Frank G. *The Indian and the Horse*. Norman, Okla.: University of Oklahoma Press, 1955.

Rogers, Richard A. "Glacial Geography and Native North American Languages." *Quaternary Research* 23 (1985): 130-37.

Ronda, James P. *Astoria and Empire*. Lincoln, Neb.: University of Nebraska Press, 1990.

———. *Lewis and Clark among the Indians*. Lincoln, Neb.: University of Nebraska Press, 1984.

Ross, Alexander. *Adventures of the First Settlers on the Oregon or Columbia River*. Edited by M. M. Quaife. New York: Citadel Press, 1969.

———. *The Fur Hunters of the Far West: A Narrative of Adventures in the Oregon and Rocky Mountains*, Peel bibliography on microfiche; No. 164. London: Smith Elder, 1855.

Rowan, William. *The Riddle of Migration*. Baltimore: Williams and Wilkins, 1931.

Ruggles, Richard I. *A Country So Interesting: The Hudson's Bay Company and Two Centuries of Mapping, 1670-1870*. Montreal: McGill-Queen's Press, 1991.

Russell, Andy. "Foreword." In *Waterton and Northern Glacier Trails for Hikers and Riders*, 7. Waterton Park: Waterton Natural History Association, 1984.

———. *Grizzly Country*. Vancouver: Douglas and MacIntyre, 1986.

———. *Memoirs of a Mountain Man*. Vancouver: Douglas and MacIntyre, 1986.

Sanders, Helen F. *Trails Through Western Woods*. London: Everett and Co., 1910.

Sanders, A. H., and R. A. Smith, eds. *Aboriginal Man and Environment in the Plateau of North West America*. Calgary: Archaeological Association of Calgary, 1971.

Sax, Joseph L., and Robert B. Keiter. "Glacier National Park and its Neighbours: A Study of Federal Interagency Relations." *Ecology Law Quarterly* (1987): 207-63.

Scace, Robert. "An Initial Bibliography of Waterton Lakes National Park, with Additional References to ... the International Peace Park." Calgary: National and Historic Parks Branch, 1972.

———. *Interpretive Background Materials for the Waterton-Glacier International Peace Park*. Ottawa: National Parks Branch, 1972.

Schaeffer, Claude E. *Bear Ceremonialism of the Kootenai Indians*, Studies in Plains Anthropology and History, No. 4. Browning, Mo.: U.S. Department of the Interior. Indian Arts and Crafts Board. Museum of the Plains Indian, 1966.

———. *Le Blanc and La Gasse: Predecessors of David Thompson in the Columbian Plateau*, Studies in Plains Anthropology and History, No. 3. Browning, Mo.: U.S. Department of the Interior. Indian Arts and Crafts Board. Museum of the Plains Indian, 1966.

———. "Plains Kutenai: An Ethnographic Review." *Alberta History* 30, no. 4 (1982): 1-9.

Scharff, Robert. *Glacier National Park and Waterton National Park*. New York: D. McKay, 1967.

Schultz, James Willard. *Blackfeet and Buffalo: Memories of Life Among the Indians*. Edited by Keith C. Seele. Norman, Okla.: University of Oklahoma Press, 1962.

———. *Rising Wolf, The White Blackfoot*. New York: Houghton Mifflin, 1919.

Schultz, Jessie D. "Beloved Storymaker of the Blackfeet – James Willard Schultz." *Montana: The Magazine of Western History* 10, no. 4 (1960): 2-18.

Scott, Anthony. "The State of Water Rights in Western Canada." In *Explorations in Canadian Economic History: Essays in Honour of Irene M. Spry*, edited by Duncan Cameron, 157-188. Ottawa: University of Ottawa Press, 1985.

Scotter, G. W. "Ecological Considerations of the Provisional Master Plan for Waterton Lakes National Park." Canadian Wildlife Service, 1969.

Sebenik, Peter M. "Points of Departure: Urban Relief in Alberta, 1930-1937." In *Law and Justice in a New Land: Essays in Western Canadian Legal History*, edited by Louis Knafla, 313-32. Calgary: Carswell, 1986.

Secoy, Frank R. *Changing Military Patterns of the Great Plains Indians (1953), Introduction by J. C. Ewers*. Lincoln, Neb.: University of Nebraska Press, 1992.

Seel, Kurt. "An Annotated List of the Avi-fauna of Waterton Lakes National Park." Waterton Lakes National Park, 1969.

———. "The Biogeography of Waterton Lakes National Park." Waterton Lakes National Park Library, 1972.

————. "Waterton Lakes National Park. Natural Resource Description and Analysis." Calgary: Parks Canada, 1984.

Sellars, Richard W. *Preserving Nature in the National Parks: A History*. New Haven: Yale University Press, 1997.

Shaw, Richard J., and Danny On. *Plants of Waterton-Glacier National Parks*. Missoula: Mountain Press, 1979.

Sheail, John. *Seventy-five Years In Ecology: The British Ecological Society*. Oxford: Blackwell, 1987.

Sheire, James W. "Glacier National Park. Historic Resource Study." U.S. Department of the Interior. National Park Service. Office of History and Historic Architecture. Eastern Service Centre, 1970.

Sheridan, Clare. *Redskin Interlude*. London: Nicholson and Watson, 1938.

Short, Mack. "Glacier National Park Archaeological Inventory and Assessment: 1994 Field Season. Final Report. Part II: Assessment," edited by Leslie B. Davis. Bozeman: U.S. National Park Service/Montana State University, 1996.

Smith, Donald B. *Long Lance: The True Story of an Imposter*. Lincoln, Neb.: University of Nebraska Press, 1982.

Smith, Marie-Rose. "Eighty Years on the Plains." *Canadian Cattleman* October, 1949.

Smyth, David. "Jacques Berger, Fur Trader." *The Beaver* 69, no. 3 (1989): 39-50.

————. "The Struggle for the Piegan Trade: The Saskatchewan Versus the Missouri." *Montana: The Magazine of Western History* 34, no. 2 (1984): 2-17.

Snow, Chief John. *These Mountains are Our Sacred Places: The Story of the Stoney People*. Toronto: Samuel Stevens, 1977.

Soper, J. D. "The Mammals of Waterton Lakes National Park." Canadian Wildlife Service, 1973.

"The South Fork Ranch." *Calgary Herald*, Aug. 26, 1897; reprinted in *Alberta Historical Review* 1974, 28-9.

Spence, Clark C. *Montana: A History*. Nashville: American Association for State and Local History, 1978.

Spencer, J. A. *Crystal Spring Indian Camp Site*. Rev. ed. Lethbridge: Archaeological Society of Alberta, 1996.

Spry, Irene, ed. *The Palliser Expedition: An Account of John Palliser's British North American Exploring Expedition, 1857-1860*. Toronto: MacMillan, 1963.

————, ed. *The Papers of the Palliser Expedition, 1857-1860*. Toronto: The Champlain Society, 1968.

Stanley, G.F.G., ed. *Mapping the Frontier: Charles Wilson's Diary of the Survey of the 49th Parallel, 1858-1862, While Secretary of the British Boundary Commission*. Toronto: MacMillan, 1970.

Steele, C. Frank. *Prairie Editor: The Life and Times of Buchanan of Lethbridge*. Toronto: Ryerson, 1961.

Stegner, Wallace, and Richard W. Etulain. *Conversations with Wallace Stegner: On Western History and Literature*. Rev. ed. Salt Lake City: University of Utah Press, 1990.

Stenzel, Frank. *James Madison Alden: Yankee Artist of the Pacific Coast, 1854-1860*. Fort Worth: Amon Carter Museum, 1975.

Stevens, Isaac I. *Reports of the Explorations and Surveys to Ascertain the Most Practicable and Economical Route for a Railroad from the Mississippi River to the Pacific Ocean*. Washington, D.C.: Thomas H. Ford, 1860.

Stokes, Charles W. *Round About the Rockies.* Toronto: Musson, 1923.

Stringer, P. W. "An Ecological Study of Grasslands at Low Elevations in Banff, Jasper and Waterton Lakes National Parks." Ph.D., University of Alberta, 1969.

Stryd, A. H., and R. A. Smith, eds. *Aboriginal Man and Environments in the Plateau of Northwest America.* Calgary: The Student's Press, 1971.

Sturko, A. N. "Ecology of the Rocky Mountain Big Horn Sheep." Waterton Lakes National Park. Warden Service, 1963.

Swankey, Ben. "Reflections of an Alberta Communist: The Hungry Thirties." *Alberta History* 27, no. 4 (1979): 1-12.

Taft, Robert. *Artists and Illustrators of the Old West, 1850-1900.* New York: Bonanza Books, 1953.

Tait, W. McD. "I Remember." *Recollections of Kootenai Brown.* Typescript. GAA. Library. Reproduced from the *Farm and Ranch Review* 15/16 (1919-20).

Taliaferro, John. *Charles Russell: The Life and Legend of America's Cowboy Artist.* Boston: Little Brown, 1996.

Taylor, C. J. "A History of National Parks Administration. Part I. The Harkin Era." Ottawa: Canadian Parks Service. Historical Research Division, 1988.

Taylor, C. J., and Pat Buchik. *Waterton Lakes National Park. Built Heritage Resource Analysis.* Calgary: Parks Canada, 1991.

Teit, James A. "Traditions and Information of the Tona'xa." *American Anthropologist* New Series 32 (1930): 625-32.

Thane, Eric. *The Majestic Land.* New York: Bobbs-Merrill, 1950.

Thomas, Jack Ward, and Dale E. Toweill, eds. *Elk of North America: Ecology and Management.* Harrisburg: Wildlife Management Institute with the U.S. Department of Agriculture, Forest Service; Stackpole Books, 1982.

Thomas, Lewis G. "Privileged Settlers." In *Ranchers' Legacy: Alberta Essays*, edited by Patrick A. Dunae, 159-62. Edmonton: University of Alberta Press, 1986.

"Thomas Blakiston." In *Dictionary of National Biography*, Vol. XXII. Supplement, 214-15. London: Oxford University Press.

"Thomas Blakiston, Obituary." *The Auk* 9, no. 1 (1892): 75.

Thomas Mayne Daly. Winnipeg: Historic Resources Branch, Manitoba Culture, Heritage and Recreation, 1985.

Thompson, John Herd, and Allen Seager. *Canada, 1922-1939: Decades of Discord.* Toronto: McClelland & Stewart, 1985.

Thomson, Don W. "A. P. Patrick, D.T.S., Discoverer of Oil in Alberta." *Canadian Geographical Journal* 79, no. 3 (1969): 100-4.

Tolmie, W. Fraser, and G. M. Dawson. *Comparative Vocabularies of the Indian Tribes of British Columbia, Geological and Natural History Survey of Canada.* Montreal: Dawson Bros., 1884.

Tolton, Gordon E. *The Rocky Mountain Rangers: Southern Alberta's Cowboy Cavalry in the North West Rebellion – 1885*, Lethbridge Historical Society. Occasional Paper No. 28. Lethbridge: Lethbridge Historical Society, 1994.

Treaty 7 Elders and Tribal Council, with Walter Hildebrandt, Sarah Carter, and Dorothy First Rider,. *The True Spirit and Original Intent of Treaty 7.* Montreal: McGill-Queen's Press, 1996.

Trottier, G. C. "Vegetation Change in Response to Protection from Grazing in the Fescue Grassland of Waterton Lakes National Park." Canadian Wildlife Service, 1977.

Turner, Nancy J. *Plant Technology of First Peoples in British Columbia*. Vancouver: University of British Columbia Press, 1998.

Turney-High, H. H. *Ethnography of the Kutenai*, Memoirs of the American Anthropological Association, No. 56. Menasha, Wisc.: American Anthropological Association, 1941.

Twinning, Major. "United States Northern Boundary Commission Report." Washington, D.C., 1873-1874.

Underwood McLellan and Associates. "Development Plan for Waterton Townsite," 1970.

United States. Congress. "A Bill for Establishment of the Waterton-Glacier International Peace Park." 72nd Congress. 1st Session, 1931.

———. Congress. "Waterton-Glacier International Peace Park. A Report by Mr. Leavitt from the Committee on Public Lands." Congress, 1st Session. House of Representatives, 1932.

———. Department of State. "Reports Upon the Survey of the Boundary Between the United States and the Possessions of Great Britain from the Lake of the Woods to the Summit of the Rocky Mountains." Washington, D.C., 1878.

———. Department of the Interior. *Glacier National Park – Montana*. Washington, D.C.: U.S. Department of the Interior. National Park Service. Government Printing Office, 1936.

Utley, Robert M. *Frontier Regulars: The United States Army and the Indian, 1866-1890*. London: MacMillan, 1973.

Van Kirk, Sylvia. "The Development of National Park Policy in Canada's Mountain National Parks: 1885 to 1930." M.A., University of Alberta, 1969.

Van Tighem, Kevin. "Waterton: Crown of the Continent." *Borealis* 2, no. 1 (1990): 24-33.

Vickers, Roderick J. *Alberta Plains Prehistory: A Review*, Archaeological Survey of Alberta. Occasional Paper No. 27. Edmonton: Alberta Culture, 1986.

Waiser, Bill. *Park Prisoners: The Untold Story of Western Canada's National Parks, 1915-1946*. Calgary: Fifth House, 1995.

Walter, David A. "The 1855 Blackfeet Treaty Council: A Memoir of Henry A. Kennerly." *Montana: The Magazine of Western History* 32, no. 1 (1982): 44-51.

Wardle, J. M. "Highway Work in the National Parks." *Engineering Journal* 8, no. 9 (1925): 382-84.

Wasem, C. R. *The History of Elk and Elk Management in Glacier National Park*. West Glacier, Mo.: U.S. National Park Service. Glacier National Park, 1963.

Waterton, Charles. *Essays on Natural History*. London: Longmans, Green, 1866.

———. *Letters of Charles Waterton*. Edited by R. A. Irwin. London: Rockliff, 1955.

———. *Wanderings in South America*. Edited by L. Harrison Mathews. London: Oxford University Press, 1973.

Waterton Biosphere Reserve. Claresholm: Parks Canada/Canadian Wildlife Service, n.d.

"Waterton Lakes National Park. Background Information: Management Plan Review." Calgary: Parks Canada, 1989.

Waterton Lakes National Park. *Waterton Townsite General Land Use Master Plan*, Planning Report No. 59. Calgary: Western Regional Office, 1967.

Weber, David J. *The Taos Trappers: The Fur Trade in the Far Southwest, 1540-1846*. Norman, Okla.: University of Oklahoma Press, 1971.

Wedel, Waldo R. "The Prehistoric Plains." In *Ancient North Americans*, edited by Jesse D. Jennings, 203-42. New York: W. H. Freeman, 1983.

Wheaton, Rodd L. "Park Roads and Highway Standards: Going to the Sun Road." *Cultural Resource Management* 6 (1992): 33-35.

White, W. Thomas. "The War of the Railroad Kings: Great Northern-Northern Pacific Rivalry in Montana, 1881-1896." In *Montana and the West: Essays in Honour of K. Ross Toole*, edited by R. C. Myhers and H. W. Fritz, 37-54. Boulder: Pruett, 1984.

Wilbur, Richard. *The Bennett Administration: 1930-1935*. Toronto: McClelland & Stewart, 1973.

Wilcox, Ruth Turner. *The Mode in Furs : The History of Furred Costume of the World from the Earliest Times to the Present*. New York: Scribner, 1951.

Williams, M. B. "Waterton Lakes National Park, Alberta Canada." Ottawa: Department of the Interior, c. 1926.

Willis, Bailey. "Stratigraphy and Structure, Lewis and Livingston Ranges, Montana." *Bulletin of the Geological Society of America* 13 (Nov. 15, 1902): 305-52.

Wilson, Charles, W. "Report on the Indian Tribes Inhabiting the Country in the Vicinity of the 49th Parallel of North Latitude" *Transactions of the Ethnological Society of London*. n.s. 4 (1866), 275-332

Wood, Ruth K. *The Tourist's Northwest*. New York: Dodd, Mead and Company, 1916.

Wood, V. A. *The Alberta Temple*. Calgary: Detselig, 1989.

The World's First Nature Reserve. Wakefield: Wakefield Naturalists' Society, 1989.

Wormington, H. M., and Richard G. Forbis. *An Introduction to the Archeology of Alberta, Canada*. Denver: Denver Museum of Natural History, 1965.

Wright, George M. *Fauna of the National Parks of the United States Contribution of Wildlife Survey, U.S. Department of the Interior. National Parks Service. Fauna Series No. 1*. Washington, D.C.: Government Printing Office, 1933.

Wright, R. Gerald. *Wildlife Research and Management in the National Parks* . Urbana: University of Illinois Press, 1992.

Yeo, W. B. "Making Banff a Year Round Park." In *Winter Sports in the West*, edited by E. A. Corbet and A. W. Rasporich, 87-98. Calgary: Historical Society of Alberta, 1990.

Index

203